Runaways

Runaways

How the
Sixties Counterculture
Shaped Today's
Practices and Policies

Karen M. Staller

Columbia University Press *New York*

Columbia University Press
Publishers Since 1893
New York   Chichester, West Sussex

Library of Congress Cataloging-in-Publication Data
Staller, Karen M.
Runaways : how the sixties counterculture shaped today's practices and policies /
Karen M. Staller.
p. cm.
Includes bibliographical references and index.
ISBN 0-231-12410-4 (cloth : alk. paper) — ISBN 0-231-12411-2 (pkb. : alk. paper)
1. Runaway teenagers—Services for—United States.   2. Runaway
teenagers—Government policy—United States.   3. Runaway teenagers—United
States—History.   4. United States—Social conditions—1960–1980.   5. Nineteen
sixties.   I. Title.

HV1431.S74 2006
362.74—dc22
2005033489
∞

Columbia University Press books are printed on permanent and durable acid-free paper.

Printed in the United States of America

c 10 9 8 7 6 5 4 3 2 1

I gratefully acknowledge permission to quote from the following works:

Burroughs, William S. Excerpts ("Dear Allen Jan. 30, 1949" and "Dear Jack March 15, 1949")
from *The Letters of William S. Burroughs, 1945–1959*, ed. Oliver Harris (New York: Viking,
1993). Copyright (c) 1993 by William S. Burroughs; introduction copyright (c) 1993 by Oliver
Harris. Used by permission of Viking Penguin, a division of Penguin Group (USA), Inc.

Coyote, Peter. Excerpts from *Sleeping Where I Fall* (Washington, D.C.: Counterpoint, 1998).
Copyright (c) 1998 by Perseus Books Group. Reprinted with permission.

Ginsberg, Allen. Excerpts ("With Neal") from *Allen Ginsberg: Journals Mid-Fifties, 1954–1958*,
ed. George Ball (New York: HarperCollins, 1995). Copyright (c) 1995 Allen Ginsberg;
introductory material copyright (c) Gordon Ball. Reprinted by permission of HarperCollins
Publishers, Inc.

Grogan, Emmett. Excerpts from *Ringolevio: A Life Played for Keeps* (Boston: Little, Brown,
1972). Copyright (c) by Eugene Leo Michael Emmett Grogan. Reprinted by permission of
Little, Brown and Company, Inc.

Huncke, Herbert. Excerpts from *The Herbert Huncke Reader*, ed. Benjamin G. Schafer (New
York: William Morrow, 1997). Reprinted with permission by Jerome Poynton, Executor,
Estate of Herbert Huncke.

New York Times. Various excerpts and headlines from *The New York Times*. Copyright (c)
various dates 1960–2005 The New York Times, Co. Reprinted with permission.

Redmond Rosanne Haggerty and Mark Redmond. Excerpts from "The Paradoxes of
Covenant House Mythmaking and Lifesaving," *Commonweal* (May 18, 1990). Copyright (c)
1990 Commonweal. Reprinted with permission.

Rubin, Jerry. Excerpts from *Do It!* (New York: Simon and Schuster, 1970). Reprinted with
permission.

To Clara, Wade, Margaret, Jimmy, Christine, and Jade

May you be blessed with a world where you can run free and with the individual and collective wisdom to use that freedom wisely

Contents

Contents

A new generation always awaits to undo the assumptions of the generation that came before.

—Richard Rodriquez

Acknowledgments

I think I started this book in fifth grade. We fifth graders, in upstate New York, were instructed to pick a state for study and produce a multichapter report. As I recall, most of my classmates made logically transparent choices in their selection by picking states where grandparents lived or they had vacationed. Not me—I picked California, a state clear across the country and to which I had absolutely no obvious connection. It took the ensuing decades and this book for me to realize that what drew my attention to California, in 1967, was the free spirits gathering there. My point is that if it takes several decades to complete a fifth-grade report, you are bound to have accumulated more debts than you can possibly adequately repay. Nonetheless, in the next few paragraphs I'm going to attempt the impossible.

First and foremost, my deepest thanks go to my parents, who have stood by me—and this project—since our inceptions. They have provided support of every conceivable variety. My father was willing to read through endless drafts, adding commas or asking poignant substantive questions (as well as inserting occasional commentary like, "those idiots," which I respectfully ignored), but also never failing to ask, "How are your finances? Are you doing OK?" My mom's support was even more ubiquitous. She has been willing to actively participate, offering concrete help, large and small, such as the sound advice to "think like Winnie-the-Pooh" on a day I was stuck naming things. (She herself is extraordinarily quick witted at naming things; I have my dog Digger to prove it.) She has readily absorbed my delight and dismay, as called for in the moment, but also kept pushing me toward a healthy balance between the two. Like the unforgettable Christmas that she and my sister Jane constructed handmade ornaments of notable counterculture personalities for my pathetic, unadorned tree. As I opened my tree-topping Timothy Leary angel, my mom—with deadpan delivery—worried she may have committed a faux pas by pasting him on "acid-free" paper. Humor is often at the heart of her offerings.

My siblings, their partners, and a crew of nieces and nephews have been in the cheering section all along, but my sister Jane—in addition to her artwork and counterculture research—has been one of my single biggest cheerleaders. Thank you, Janie, for all that enthusiasm. In this crowd I have to include Andy Short, a best friend for so long he is family. Andy was willing to do anything from a Lexis search for PINS cases to being abundantly generous with movie tickets and dinners out.

The rest of my thanks are to people who joined in the trip and inspired me along the way. My friends and colleagues at Covenant House, whose hard work, devotion, and dedication to the mission of saving children, were always on my mind. In particular I owe much to the Legal Department staff with whom I worked so closely—Kerry, Jay, Sharon, Rich, and Nancy. In addition, the young people with whom I had the privilege to work, and their life stories, are at the heart of my understanding of the street youth. Thanks as well to my law enforcement friends from the (New York) Port Authority, NYPD, and the FBI. Bernie (and staff), Joe, and Jim taught me much about thinking through the "street kid" problem from all sides.

As this writing project moved through its dissertation stage, there were classmates to thank like Marion Riedel, who was a source of encouragement when things looked bleak, and friends with whom I processed ideas so often I'm sure they are reflected in this work somewhere, particularly Mark Cameron, Margaret Domanski, Mark Holter, Kenneth Lauritzen, and Murray Nossel. I'm grateful to the faculty on my dissertation committee—including my chair, Sheila Kamerman, and Irv Garfinkel, Richard Nelson, Barbara Simon, and Barbara Tischler—who first encouraged me to turn this project into a book and, wisely, failed to mention how arduous a project that might be.

There are people who read and commented on drafts of various incarnations of this work including the Interdisciplinary and Interpretative Research and Writing Group at the University of Alabama (thanks Jerry, Sheri, Dan, Dexter, Amilcar, Natalie, Marysia, Catherine, et al.); Southern friends and colleagues, Debra Nelson-Gardell, Paul Stewart, and Joanne

Acknowledgments

Terrell; and from up north, Elana Buch and Frank Vandervort. I may not have done justice to all your insights and challenges, but I have benefited greatly from the struggle.

I am very grateful for the editorial efforts of Terri Torkko of the University of Michigan School of Social Work, and her willingness to get excited (and be critical) about this project. Leigh Gensler of the *New York Times* helped negotiate copyright rules that I found confusing. Jennifer Bowles has been willing to clean up little messes. Most recently, Roy Thomas of Columbia University Press has worked diligently (and with humor) to clean up even bigger messes, and Shelley Reinhardt has sympathetically endured my panic attacks while overseeing the final stages of this project.

Finally there are a few people who saved this project (and/or my mental health) at several crisis spots along the way. Without them I'm not sure it would have seen the light of day. At its beginning, Stuart Kirk turned over the study of his Malibu home and admonished me to "just write," but always rescued me at the end of the day with a glass of wine and the reward of Carol Ann's exquisite cuisine. (Thanks so much to you both.) At the other end of the project, when I found myself with one or two too many opinions clouding my vision, Bill Meezan laid out the conceptual pattern that was right before my eyes but I couldn't see. Last but certainly not least, Denise Burnette has done whatever was needed in the moment, moving mountains, clearing brush, or inevitably and invariably planting seeds. Thanks, Denise, for all the practical help and intellectual nourishment.

What seems most amazing as I think back over the years, and all these folks, is the extraordinary breadth and depth of their support, love, and encouragement. From brainstorming to house-sharing, from caretaking to inserting commas, from making me laugh or letting me cry; each and every gesture large and small has helped me along in this project in ways for which I am eternally in debt and enormously grateful.

Foreword

A Personal Journey to Some Research Questions

You don't know about me without you have read a book by the name of
The Adventures of Tom Sawyer, but that ain't no matter. That book was
made by Mr. Mark Twain, and he told the truth, mainly. There was
things which he stretched, but mainly he told the truth.

—Huckleberry Finn, as reported by Mr. Mark Twain,
who told the truth, mainly

Discovering Shelter

By my second year of law school the only thing I knew with any certainty
was that I wasn't cut out for work that required wearing a business suit
every day. In this restless state of professional indecision, I happened upon
a handwritten notice for "legal interns" posted on the law school's job bulletin board promising summer work at a shelter for runaway and homeless
youth in the Times Square area of Manhattan. I called immediately and
arranged an interview. Years ago, I recorded (albeit ungrammatically) those
first moments in the reception area before my appointment:

> I sank into the closest chair trying to quell my building nervous energy.
> As I glanced around the room, my eyes were instantly drawn to an easily
> recognizable pen and ink drawing by John Lennon. I stood up for closer
> inspection. It was a personal note signed by the singer that referenced a
> donation check and included a playful happy sketch of his whole family.
> As a devoted Beatles fan with a particular fondness for Lennon's wit, the
> little note spoke to me like an agency endorsement. I had the sudden sen-
> sation that I was in a place of some importance.

That place of importance was a crisis shelter for runaway youth, called Under 21/New York, but better known by its corporate name Covenant House. It provided short-term shelter to runaway and homeless street youth under the age of 21. In addition to emergency food, clothing, and lodging, Under 21 attempted to plug the innumerable institutional cracks through which its residents fell. Thus, the shelter was staffed by social workers, doctors, nurses, psychologists, lawyers, paralegals, and a host of other paid employees, and volunteers including members of the Faith Community.[1] Without exception, staff were united by the agency's mission to save street children, although there were inevitable squabbles over how best to achieve that goal.

I accepted the offer of a summer internship in 1984. After graduating from law school in 1985, I continued to volunteer at Covenant House while working in a legal services office in Queens. Finally, in 1988, I returned to head the shelter's legal department. It was, to say the least, a life-altering and unique learning experience. Like most of my colleagues, I started young and naïve. I left wiser, a bit bruised, and pondering some larger questions.

The House That Bruce Built

When I arrived, Covenant House was riding a crest of extraordinary public good will. Father Bruce Ritter, a Franciscan priest, founder and president of the agency, was its charismatic leader. His name was synonymous with the organization.

Covenant House's oft-repeated creation story recounted an evening in 1968 during which Father Ritter allowed six stray street youth to crash in his East Village apartment. Like any good creation myth there are various embellishing details, but what is indisputable fact is that Ritter spent the next twenty years building an international, highly touted—although not universally lauded—private youth care agency. He used the creation myth, and other stories gathered along the way, to catapult his work into the public limelight and to raise money to support the mission. By the late 1980s, the agency's annual operating budget was over $87 million a year and was "almost all raised from private donations."[2]

During this period, Covenant House ran programs in several major U.S. cities,[3] Canada, and Latin America.[4] It operated five facilities in New York

City alone, including a unit for younger boys, younger girls, young mothers with babies, a transitional living program called Rites of Passage, and what staffers referred to as "the Center." In this New York network the nightly census sometimes reached over three hundred youth.

The *New York Times* once noted that Covenant House's "near-legendary founder" Ritter had "won the hearts of Presidents, industrialists and ordinary contributors alike."[5] Winning the hearts and loyalty of "ordinary contributors" was central to Father Ritter's success; he was a fund-raising genius. The cornerstone of his effort was his compelling newsletters, which told tales of life and work among street youth. He asked for people's prayers and then (only in passing) for whatever donations they might send "his kids'" way to help out. By the 1980s, the mailing list had grown to include an estimated 800,000 individuals. Private donations, the agency's lifeblood, soared and sustained what is described as "Covenant House's meteoric growth in the 1980s[6] into one of the nation's largest, most conservative charities."[7] Between 1980 and 1985, Covenant House's annual budget more than tripled.[8] However, ex-Faith Community members Mark and Rosanne Redmond pointed out that while these newsletters won Ritter "an intensely loyal following, and convinced his supporters both of his expertise in dealing with troubled youth, and of the freshness and humility of his organization," it did so by convincing his donors "they were supporting a small, nontraditional charity that spent all its resources directly 'on the kids.'"[9] In fact, Covenant House had grown into a gigantic nonprofit child welfare agency.

Ritter was a player among power brokers. He received special treatment from his Franciscan order and was permitted to maintain an apartment on the shelter's premises rather than live in the friary among his Brothers. He won the heart and support of New York State governor Hugh Carey who, in 1979, practically hand-delivered the keys to property on 10th Avenue and 41st Street in which to operate the Center.[10] In an acrimonious and highly publicized duel in the fall of 1987, Ritter defeated powerful New York City mayor Ed Koch in a battle of public personalities over a piece of real estate known as the National Maritime Union Building. When Koch tried to offer alternative property in the form of an abandoned coffin factory to the then cancer-stricken priest, Ritter spat back that it was space he "wouldn't put a dead cat in."[11] The mayor, a scrappy street fighter in his own right, accused Ritter of "stealing," "dirty pool," "abuse of position," violating the "golden rule," and generally nonkosher play, but Koch ultimately acknowledged defeat. "I'm a pragmatist, and I know when you can win and when you can't win. I can't win it and I know I can't."[12]

Given Ritter's success at fund-raising and doing good, Covenant House gained visibility as a darling of the conservative cause. Republican presidents, who favored delegating social welfare responsibility to private charities, hosted and toasted Ritter. In January 1984, President Ronald Reagan cited Father Ritter in his State of the Union address as one of the nation's "heroes for the '80s" and praised the shelter for helping "abused and runaway children."[13] Ritter responded, in part, by supporting the president's agenda: "I really do agree with the President that the private sector must accept a greater responsibility for these social problems in this country."[14] In great photo-op fashion, First Lady Nancy Reagan paid a visit to Covenant House in June 1985[15] and former-president Reagan dropped by in November 1989. In between those events, in February 1987, the White House hosted Ritter after he received the Stone Foundation's "Endow a Dream" award.

Reagan's successor, George H. W. Bush, followed suit, citing Covenant House as one of his "thousand points of light" and visiting the Center in 1989. So familiar was Covenant House in public banter, that when President Bush referred to his scheduled visit as the "Covenant House thing" it wound up the subject of a *New York Times* editorial.[16] I was there for the Bush "thing," temporarily imprisoned—along with other staff members—in our offices, with strict orders not to fuss with the drawn Venetian blinds during the presidential visit lest the Secret Service sharp shooters who were posted on the rooftop across the street get antsy. Nonetheless, it was impossible not to take residual pride in all the attention. For me, it was like the John Lennon note: it was somehow indicative of the importance of our work.

Working in Myth Haven

Let me hasten to say that the rewards of working at Covenant House did not come primarily from outside attention. In fact, they came from the day-to-day dealings with the young people who sought help, or at least temporary relief, at the agency. The composite picture of youth marketed in Ritter's newsletters were only partially recognizable in the kids that flooded our offices. Most of these youth came and went so quickly that they are a blur in my mind's eye. However, there was a standard stock of kids so well known to the agency and all its departments that they continue to provide the topic of conversation when ex-staffers meet at reunions. In general, these kids were favorites because we came to know them best, usually because their situations were the most hopeless. Almost all of them were street-based, chronic runaways, hustlers, homeless youth, or undocumented aliens (who had little hope of gaining legal status). They were also kids who had been in and out of the juvenile justice system or the mental health system, and had left, or aged-out of, the foster care system. They had parted ways, voluntarily or involuntarily, with biological family years before. The staff at Covenant House were as much of a family as they had. I ran into one of them a decade after I had left Covenant House. He was curled up on a subway grate in upper Manhattan. We chatted about old times, I gave him five dollars for food, then he squinted upward at the sky behind me and asked if the sun ever talked to me. The next time I saw him he had black stitch marks on both wrists, tracing the jagged contours of two brutal-looking incisions. I never saw him again after that. He had been one of our favorite chronic kids, back in the days.

During my Covenant House years, it quickly became apparent that the public shorthand labels "runaway" or even "runaway and homeless" youth were too simplistic. They did not aptly describe a unified population of children who shared common characteristics, nor did "running away" describe a unifying behavior shared by the majority. They were every stripe but mostly black, Latino, and Caucasian. They were boys, girls, young adults, and teenage mothers with babies. Their ages ranged from 8 to 20. They came from wealthy as well as poor families. They were gay and straight, bisexual and transgendered. Many had been physically, sexually, and emotionally abused. Some were substance users and abusers and others abstained. They were from New York City's five boroughs but also from Kansas, California, Liberia, Guatemala, and Trinidad. In our real work, kids defied clear-cut categories, so we skipped labeling and simply worked with a lot of individual children in need. The variety, rather than the commonality, tested the intellectual prowess and professional skills of those who worked with them. Each day was filled with various cases and crises, and no two days were alike. It was, quite simply, the most challenging and rewarding work experience I have ever had.

The kids' legal offenses were mostly mundane, like theft of services for jumping a subway turnstile for lack of a token; however, some were serious. On one memorable day I received a client who was allegedly running from an arrest warrant for a double homicide in a distant state. New York State law, as interpreted and litigated by the Covenant House legal department, mandated strict confidentiality of our residents' identities, and staff routinely refused to confirm or deny the presence of individual youth in the program to law enforcement agents. Nonetheless, the New York Police Department (NYPD) somehow got wind that we were sheltering a fugitive and politely requested we hang on to him long enough for the appropriate interstate paperwork to be transmitted so they could take him into custody. In the tense hours that followed, I felt professionally obligated to inform my youthful client that his arrest was imminent, but urged him to surrender voluntarily rather than continue to run. Then I released him from my office so he could go eat lunch with all the other kids, across an open walkway, in another building. I was well aware that he could freely walk out the front door and disappear in the city streets, leaving me to answer to the police and possibly the press. To my surprise the young man returned to my office after lunch, and we negotiated his surrender. In the end, he expressed his displeasure with my counsel by sending me death threats from jail before being convicted of both homicides. My law enforcement friends encouraged me to file federal charges against him, but that just wasn't consistent with my work ethic. I unlisted my home telephone number instead.

Given the negative public relations potential of this case, I suppose I should not have been surprised that Father Ritter summoned me to his inner sanctum to account for my actions. Trembling, partly out of fear of having displeased him and partly because he kept his office temperature cooled to just above freezing (a tactic I interpret to this day—probably incorrectly—as an assertion of power), I appeared before him. In the most memorable personal exchange I would have with the man, he shook a finger at me and asked, "How *dare* you jeopardize our reputation?" In fairness to him, I think he was bit proud of me, as he was of any staff member willing to take personal risks on behalf of a youth and willing to confront law enforcement. Nonetheless, it is a question that I have longed to ask him. He died before I got the chance.

Scandal: A House Divided

Late Monday evening on December 11, 1989, I received an odd and somewhat cryptic phone call at home from Greg Loken, a personal friend and director of the agency's Institute of Youth Advocacy, an ex-Faith Community member, and a long-term member of Ritter's inner circle. In essence, Greg said I should expect to see some bad press the next morning but not to take it too seriously. He was right about the bad press, but wrong about not taking it too seriously.

The next morning, the *New York Post* ran a front-page story under the headline: "Times Square Priest Probed: Former Male Prostitute Cites 'Gifts.'" The story reported that the Manhattan District Attorney's office had opened an investigation into sexual misconduct and financial improprieties by Ritter based on allegations of a former male hustler.[17] The young man, using the alias Tim Warner (and later revealed to be Kevin Kite), had been introduced to staffers—at least staffers at my level and below—as Ritter's "nephew." He had worked down the hall from my office at Greg's institute for weeks. At the time, the allegations seemed so crazy that the *New York Times* didn't even report the investigation until December 14, when it did so in seven short paragraphs buried in its B section.[18]

Ritter himself remained unavailable for comment until December 15, when he stepped forward to deny the allegations and call them "nonsense."[19] Using tactics that would divide the loyalties of Covenant House staff, he set the full force of his public relations machinery into motion, using strategies designed to discredit Kite. For staff who believed in Ritter's innocence, the rhetoric was justified. For skeptics, particularly those of us whose covenant was with the kids first and Ritter second, the strategies seemed incongruent with our work.

Ritter characterized Kite as a "terrified, emotionally troubled" youth who had "regressed despite the Covenant House efforts to rehabilitate him," at the same time confessing that he had shared a hotel room with Kite on three occasions but admitting only to the *appearance* of impropriety.[20] By December 21, Covenant House's public relations department had located Kite's father, who was willing to call his son a "chronic liar," a thief with a "personality disorder" and accuse him of "hurting those who try to help him."[21] The agency hinted that the youth had deceived staffers by appropriating a false identity and using methods he reportedly had learned from the

Mafia, and it further reminded would-be Christmas benefactors that this hubbub was creating a "grave threat to the organization's support." Donations fell short that December by $3 million (of the expected $15 million), setting a trend-line for months to come.

This story, and these allegations, turned out to be the tip of the iceberg. The next nine months have been variously described in print as a " virtual siege,"[22] a "whirlwind,"[23] and a "meltdown,"[24] and the agency was described as "reeling"[25] and "shaken."[26] The public sexual misconduct allegations against Ritter multiplied;[27] allegations of financial improprieties expanded dramatically;[28] additional unseemly (if not illegal) behavior and practices came to light;[29] investigations—criminal,[30] civil, and church[31] of Ritter and Covenant House—were opened and closed.[32] Finally Ritter was directed by the Franciscan order to permanently leave the agency he had built; subsequently, leadership was so unstable that it changed hands three times in several months before a permanent replacement was named.[33] More than half the 17-member board of directors resigned, and donations plummeted, resulting in massive downsizing.[34]

By March 1990, Covenant House was so battered that its Board of Directors commissioned a series of investigations and appointed a prestigious oversight committee,[35] in order to clear the agency's beleaguered reputation. Perhaps the most important investigation (for general public consumption) was conducted by Kroll Associates under the direction of former New York City Police Commissioner Robert McGuire. The board asked McGuire to look into "every allegation—no matter how wild or outrageous—against anyone connected with the organization."[36]

When McGuire's four-month investigation was completed, the report found that the evidence that Father Ritter had engaged in sexual activities with young men who had sought shelter at Covenant House was "extensive" and credible; it criticized Covenant House's financial practices (although found no evidence of misappropriated funds), and it found that Covenant House's corporate board had failed in its responsibilities for overseeing the agency.[37] The report was careful to separate current work from past practices: "The investigators report that, wherever they went, they found dedicated, honest and good people doing difficult, often thankless work under extraordinarily trying conditions."[38]

As early as February 6, 1990, the *New York Times* observed that "the furor has taken a toll on the organization. Television news crews have repeatedly shown up at Covenant House buildings."[39] Media attention had been relentless. I was selfishly grateful for Donald and Ivana Trump's marital difficulties—it seemed to be the only story that periodically dislodged Covenant House from the front pages of the local tabloids. Yet it was not only the "furor" that took its "toll" on some of us, it was the mind-bending experience of watching and reading about a world you thought you knew as an insider as it morphed in and out of recognizable shape. The media was reinterpreting, reassessing, and repackaging it. To make matters worse, the Covenant House public relations department volleyed back with its own, only partially recognizable, spin. The effect was dizzying.

The inevitable result of all this commotion was that charitable contributions to the once-mighty agency plummeted. For months, stressed staff tried to reassure worried youth that Covenant House would continue to be there for them without knowing if that was true. In January contributions had purportedly fallen by 25 percent,[40] a disaster for an agency dependent on the Christmas-giving season for its ongoing existence. By June it announced it would lay off half of its 460-member New York staff and reduce its FY1991 budget by $10 million.[41] Agency management began to shut down or downsize unit after unit, program after program, department after department. For a crisis that had been created, brewed, and played itself out in the upper reaches of agency management and in the media, the real impact was finally localized. My job was on the line but eventually salvaged. However, half of my very beloved staff left.[42] Respected colleagues moved on, and the organization seemed to be crumbling on all fronts.

Eventually, however, with the intervention of Cardinal O'Connor, Sister Mary Rose McGeady, an experienced senior official with an impeccable record at Catholic Charities, was named Ritter's permanent successor.[43] She took the helm on September 1, 1990—only then did the listing agency begin to right itself. It had been nine months since the *New York Post* story first appeared. I left, exhausted, in January 1991.

Lingering Questions

Any good crisis provokes questions that reach beyond the bounded confines of the experience. I have carried my Covenant House questions with me in my life and work. Here are some:

Where do reality and myth intersect and diverge in public discussion of
"runaway" youth?

What is the role and power of the media in constructing and decon-
structing our world?

Where did the shelter movement come from?

What are the advantages and disadvantages of various funding streams
for social services? What are their implications for stability and
accountability?

What are the boundaries between public and private (sectarian and nonsectarian) responsibility for runaway youth?

What is the proper care and service structure for helping "runaway" children?

How do the interactions between key players, individual events, and
social movements influence problems, policy and programs?

What about the interactive roles of charisma, faith, and trust (public and
private)?[44]

These questions smoldered. They began to take new shape around three
major concepts: social problem construction, service design and delivery,
and policy responses. So the questions sharpened and became more focused
over time, until I had a set of research questions to explore.

How did the problem of "runaway" youth come to be constructed and
who influenced that construction?

As a form of service delivery for youth, where did the runaway shelter
movement come from and why do these shelters not fit neatly within
our existing policy frameworks for children?

What have been our public policy responses to "runaway" youth and what
values and goals do they embody?

I answer these questions on the following pages, where I consider the phenomena of "runaway" youth in the 1960s and '70s. This includes the emergence of running away as a publicly defined social problem, the rise of the
shelter movement, and examining our public policy responses to runaway
youth. Policy responses include state and federal legislation legitimizing
crisis shelter care like that provided at Covenant House. It is a research

process that necessarily ventures into the worlds of pop culture, media, demography, politics, court rooms, and Congress.

My public discussion about my personal experience at Covenant House ends here. However, according to the renowned historian Edward Hallett Carr, readers of historical forays are well advised to be as concerned with the historian who produces history as the narrative that is told because the historian is herself "the product of history."[45] Carr gives a bit of advice, which I feel compelled to pass along: "When you read a work of history, always listen out for the buzzing. If you can detect none, either you are tone deaf or your historian is a dull dog."[46]

I hate the thought of being a dull dog, so I invite you to listen for detectable buzzing as you read. I ask only that you accept my sincere contention that I have made an honest effort at integrity throughout my journey and at full disclosure at the beginning of yours.

Runaways

Testing Freedom
On the Road to a Runaway Problem

You can't run away forever,
but there's nothing wrong with getting a good head start . . .

—Meatloaf, *Bat Out of Hell*

Constructing a Social Problem:
Runaways as Premature Autonomy Seekers

In 1977 the circumstances of Veronica Brunson's life and death came to public attention, in part, through a front-page story in the *New York Times*. The headline was an attention-grabber: "Veronica's Short, Sad Life— Prostitution at 11, Death at 12." The facts seemed particularly horrendous. Among other things, this pint-sized, preteen waif had missed 121 out of 180 days of school, had been arrested a dozen times on prostitution-related charges in less than a year, and had run away from home so many times that her mother stopped reporting her missing to the police until compelled to do so by outside authorities. Six public and private agencies (including the juvenile court and social services providers) were "partly aware" of her troubles. Brunson fell (or was pushed) to her demise from the tenth-floor window of a sleazy Times Square hotel frequented by prostitutes. She lingered for four days, unconscious and unclaimed by family, in a hospitable bed before dying. The *New York Times* reported Brunson's case as illustrating the "problems and dangers confronting thousands of runaway girls and boys who turn to prostitution to survive alone on the streets of New York."[1]

In stark contrast, nearly two decades earlier, readers of the same daily newspaper may have been amused by the front-page story of the antics of a 13-year-old boy named Dean Siering.[2] Dean left his Long Island home early one morning in 1960 and made his way (by bike, train, and taxi) to the airport. There he told a United Air Lines representative a tall tale that involved a mother who had dropped him off at the curb and driven away, and a maiden aunt, "Miss Amelia Ralph," who was purportedly eagerly awaiting his arrival at Chicago's O'Hare Airport. He indicated that he was in a big hurry because he needed to get back to Chicago in time to attend school. When asked to produce a ticket, he said he had accidentally lost it, and cried for dramatic effect. None of this was true. Nonetheless, he had created a compelling story. After all, he had cast himself in the role of responsible schoolboy, and his fabrication included being supervised, more or less, by family members at either end of the trip. Dean's story managed to shift the burden of rectifying his problem onto an unwary airline agent. In a distant and much more innocent era, ticketless, unsupervised 13-year-old Dean Siering was permitted to board the plane alone and fly off to Chicago.

In Dean's mind Chicago was just a way station. His *real* plan was to continue on to California because, as he later told reporters, "it's a nice state." He had second thoughts after reaching Chicago. As airline officials frantically paged Miss Amelia Ralph, to no avail, Dean slipped out and boarded a train (as a stowaway) and headed back to New York State. He got as far as Buffalo before tiring of life on the run and essentially turned himself in. For safekeeping, two detectives temporarily deposited Dean in Erie County Detention until his mother could retrieve him; nonetheless, he confidently asserted to reporters that he "did not expect to be punished" for his behavior.

To the casual reader the cases of Dean and Veronica may appear unrelated because they differ so dramatically in basic facts and final outcomes, yet they do have three crucial characteristics in common. First, both children took matters into their own hands and left home without asking permission from their caretakers. Second, during their absence from home both made a series of decisions about their lives without the help or guidance of adults. Third, they did so at an age (below 13) when autonomous decision-making of this variety is generally frowned upon. In short, they asserted independence (to a greater or lesser degree) at an age that most of us would characterize as premature.

Of course their behavior also differed in several critical respects. Dean traveled a great distance; Veronica stayed close to home (at least geographically). Dean was gone a couple of days, Veronica for a long period of time. Dean appears to have been running toward an attraction of interest (California) while Veronica may have been avoiding school and family. As far as we know, Dean ran away once; Veronica left home so many times she was essentially homeless. Dean needed no help with basic needs (food, clothing, shelter) while Veronica turned to prostitution for "survival." Veronica's lifestyle was firmly entrenched with a "street" subculture; Dean's was not. Dean's story ended safely, Veronica's did not. Although both Dean and Veronica share the fact that they asserted premature independence, the strength of that assertion might be measured in various ways including distance traveled, time away, number of runaway episodes, reasons for leaving home, survival strategies employed while away, and level of family concern.

Runaway youth such as Dean and Veronica have both entertained and perplexed us for as long as children have laid claim to freedom without asking permission. For people in the business of labeling, characterizing, describing, helping, disciplining, and controlling such children—including parents, service providers, and policymakers—Dean's and Veronica's cases illustrate a basic nomenclature-related dilemma. Among other things, their situations involve deciding whether their behavior is similar enough to be called the same thing or, alternatively, so different that they warrant two distinct descriptive labels. If the latter is the case, another set of problems arises; where do we draw the line between the two such that we can distinguish one from the other, and based on what criteria (time, distance, parental rejection)?

In 1977 the *New York Times* referred to Veronica's case as typical, or illustrative, of "thousands of runaway boys and girls." In doing so, the journalist applied the label "runaway" to an entire population of youth who possessed characteristics shared with Veronica, foremost among them that they had turned to "prostitution" for "survival." In today's parlance, service providers, researchers, and legislators would more likely refer to Veronica as a "street youth,"[3] a "throwaway youth," or call her "homeless." On the other hand, today the label "runaway" would likely be used to describe Dean's flamboyant but short-lived, episode.[4] Interestingly, in 1960 during two days of reports on Dean, the *New York Times* never characterized his behavior as running away nor labeled him a "runaway."[5] At the risk of appearing prematurely to place too much evidentiary weight on the presence or absence of a word or two, the use of "runaway" in 1977—and its absence in 1960—reflects some basic social sensibilities typical of the discourse in their respective decades.

Over the last two hundred years or so, social scientists, reformers, jurists, legislators, and the like have experimented with many labels for these kinds of independent children. Around the turn of the nineteenth century, they were called *waifs, orphans, half-orphans, temporarily homeless, outcasts, maladjusted, destitute, indigent, wayward, wanderers, street Arabs, incorrigibles, street vendors, newsies, little laborers, morally depraved, fallen,* and *friendless.* In more recent decades, starting in the 1980s and 1990s, we have talked about them as *throwaways, castaways, shoveouts, homeless,* and *street kids.* However, in the 1970s, as the rhetorical dust settled in the aftermath of the hippies, yippies, freaks, and flower children of the 1960s, we temporarily endorsed, with renewed vigor, a new old label: *runaways.*

Why It Matters:
Linking Problems to Public Sympathies, Services, and Policy

It might seem that all this fretting over what label to attach to what domain of characteristics is merely an academic exercise. This is not the case when you consider that different public sympathies will be elicited based on the problem's presentation. For example, if 12-year-old Veronica had been a runaway boy who took to robbing tourists in order to "survive" on the streets of New York City, we might feel less compassionate. Yet both children may have been *driven* to their behavior as a way to support their premature autonomy. Charitable organizations seeking contributions from donors are more likely to be successful gaining support for their efforts to aid runaway children involved in "survival sex" than "survival thievery," so it is unlikely that you would see the latter featured in a fund-raising newsletter. Furthermore, the values of the historical moment matter. Had Veronica been born in a different decade, her involvement in prostitution might well have been framed as an exhibition of moral depravity rather than an act of "survival" and would have garnered less public sympathy.

As with any socially constructed problem, there is an ever-connective *pas de deux* between how we talk about it and how we respond to it. So the way the problem of "runaway" youth gets framed, the assumptions we make about the characteristics that it embraces, will be directly related to how we subsequently serve them, protect them, discipline them, or control them. It matters what we call "typical" of the problem. If we describe typical behavior as looking like Dean, we would design our services, outreach, or prevention activities accordingly (or not at all). Furthermore, if we developed services or interventions for "typified" runaways like Dean, but ended up delivering those services to children with characteristics more like Veronica, we should be concerned about mismatching problem and response.

The Range of Responses to Premature Autonomy Seekers

What are our options for responding to premature autonomy seekers? Keeping the label "runaway" static, just for the moment, it is instructive to consider the debut appearance of "runaways" in the 1919 *New York Times Index*[6] of articles. It reads:

RUNAWAY Girls, see Travelers Aid Society.

The next entry (in the genealogical quest) appears in 1921. It reads:

RUNAWAY Boys, Amer Consul at Liege seeks parents of boy named Mike.
RUNAWAY Girls, see Juvenile Delinquency.

The *Index* sends us to stories that involve three different possible *responses* to runaway boys and girls. Arguably, taken together, they illustrate the range of options that have historically been available to us. First, if we deem the "problem" to be a private family matter, we can simply send the child home, like Mike. In general, this response assumes that the child has a stable, functional, and willing family to receive him or her. Furthermore, it assumes that once returned, the child will stay put and not take flight again (and again), unlike Veronica.

Alternatively, the other two responses invoke and involve institutions outside the family: in the first case, the Travelers Aid Society, a private charity, and in the last the Juvenile Court, a public institution. To those in need, the Travelers Aid Society generally provided services and support, such as temporary lodging, clothing, food, and other transitional assistance for resourceless wanderers. In this context, "runaway girls" might have received charitable support that would facilitate their independence. The juvenile courts, on the other hand, were public institutions designed to train or treat youth in order to ensure their proper socialization and education. In general the goal was to shape children into model citizens. Although it is unclear from the *New York Times* how long Dean was held in juvenile detention in Buffalo while waiting for his family to arrive—or whether any further legal action was taken—securing him even temporarily would have been a matter of public authority. Veronica, on the other hand, had been involved with public authorities (family court, police, and criminal justice) as well as private charities (such as a runaway shelter and other services) apparently without success.

One final observation about these index entries is in order. "Runaway" was not gender neutral: boys and girls have their own categorical spaces. The gender-defined categories will disappear from *The New York Times Index* by the 1960s—in fact "runaway" will migrate in the *Index*, falling under the broader topic of "children" and lumped together under a subheading ("lost missing and runaway")—nonetheless the social and institutional practices of treating girls and boys differently will live on well past the 1960s.

In short, children who leave home briefly, return of their own volition, or can be returned home voluntarily pose no real problem for the public. However, children who leave for longer periods of time, travel longer distances, or leave repeatedly can present a problem for the public, posing a threat to themselves and perhaps to others. Interventions with those youth can occur in the private sector, the public sector, or both. Service responses can be framed in a way that supports independence and aids the transition from dependency to autonomy. Alternatively, the problem can be framed in a way that suggests they need control, correction, or reform rather than aid. Each of these responses to "runaway children"—charitable and public, aid and control—has roots in the Progressive Era.

Charitable Providers of Services in the Progressive Era

Lodging-Houses

Although several private charitable agencies were available to care for children in New York City during the late nineteenth century,[7] none turned its attention more vigorously to street youth than the Children's Aid Society (CAS). Although the CAS is perhaps better known for emigration parties (or "orphan trains")[8] and boarding out practices (a precursor to the foster care or child welfare system of today), its first organized foray into service delivery for New York City street youth was the Newsboys' Lodging-House.

At the turn of the nineteenth century, the commercial marketplace for the urban poor was in the city streets. Youthful peddlers were active wage earners and important contributors to family income. However, street peddling also provided vagrant and homeless youth with a means of earning income and supporting early independence. Children sold various goods, (including chewing gum, chocolate, candy, fruit, pocket watches, boot polish, etc.),[9] and street trading was generally open to any youth with enough initial capital to invest in stock (or to those who were industrious enough to go scavenging for sellable items).

Perhaps none of these child street peddlers is more legendary than the "newsies," the boys (and a few bold girls) who aggressively and competitively hawked newspapers on the streets of New York City. These young entrepreneurs, according to historian David Nasaw, learned important business skills while selling papers. They needed to assess market conditions carefully (including paper content, headlines, day of the week, weather conditions, etc.) because they were required to make a daily capital investment in their stock and to assume risk.[10] Children who bought too many papers had to "swallow the loss or stay out all night to sell them," and those who bought too few were in danger of losing regular customers.[11]

According to the First Annual Report of CAS (1854), these children were frequently homeless and independent street youth:

The great proportion of the news-boys live a homeless, vagabond life, sleeping, when the weather will allow, in the open air, and in winter, in the boxes and alleys about the printing-offices. They are entirely independent, living on their earnings, and forming a distinct class among themselves. Every thing trains them to shrewd, keen habits, but thus far very few good influences have been exerted upon them.[12]

Although the CAS was able to classify these newsboys as a "distinct class" and to characterize them as hardworking entrepreneurs, according to social reformers of the day these children were also wont to waste their money "in theaters and in gambling."[13] There was the additional fear that their immoral practices would eventually lead to a life of crime. However, because CAS found that they were "a class worth saving" and that they "would make useful, active men for our community,"[14] it developed a plan to "furnish rooms for these boys, supplied with wooden berths or bunks" in exchange for a small fee, six cents a night. The Newsboys' Lodging-House first opened its doors in 1854. It was located at the corner of Nassau and Fulton Streets in a space donated by the *New York Sun*, an important supporter of the CAS and its mission. Clearly, CAS had conceptualized the problem (the newsies as a "distinct class" of street youth) as one that held philanthropic appeal to the *New York Sun*, which was a direct beneficiary of the newsboys' labor.

In addition to providing shelter, CAS expected the boys to attend Sunday services, submit to instruction, and they were further encouraged to deposit some of their earnings in a savings account held in trust for them by the society. In short, the Newsboys' Lodging-House (later named the Brace Memorial Newsboys' Lodging-House in honor of Charles Loring Brace, one of the founders of CAS) provided for the basic needs of working, homeless street boys in exchange for submitting to some supervision, education, and moral guidance. Furthermore, it was a service structure that was pitched to the public as one that capitalized on the work ethic of street youth who could legally support themselves through their own industry. Thus it was an appealing and worthy cause, and CAS enjoyed public support.

The society worried about "the number of young girls who were falling into the hands of the police, or were wandering about, uncared for, in the streets,"[15] and in fact girls proved to be particularly nettlesome for CAS.[16] Unlike the hardworking boys, CAS characterized the girls in need of service as "of the lowest and most needy class" and faulted them for "their extraordinary power of deception, the bad habits they had acquired, their weakness under temptation and their foolish pride or prejudice against house-work."[17] Since the CAS was "pre-eminently a place of work, not of refuge," CAS found it "was necessary to prevent the Lodging-house from becoming a mere harbor for girls disinclined to work; yet girls could not be sent out every day on the street, or be suffered to go out, as boys are, to pick up their living as they might be able."[18] Thus CAS recognized that street-based peddling opportunities for girls—at least those that were moral and legal—were less plentiful, more dangerous, and less lucrative than for boys.

In spite of these problems, CAS opened its first lodging-house for girls in 1862. CAS describes its first female lodger as a "poor, forlorn, homeless little creature" who was quickly followed by "various wretched little objects" who were brought by the police or picked up at the station houses by CAS agents. Eventually, "small street singing-girls and cross-sweepers began also to come in, and, paying their three cents, to enjoy a light room, a bath and a good bed."[19] CAS focused on putting them to work learning domestic skills such as scrubbing, cleaning, cooking, ironing, or sewing. In addition, it also reported that some "little street-wanderers" would come to the lodging-house "only for a night" and receive "one night's washing and bathing"; these youth "occasionally returned, solely for this luxury."[20] So CAS was willing to provide transitional support, education, and vocational training. However, it was also willing to allow a young person to get one night's respite from life on the street.

Over the next eight decades, the CAS would open and close a half dozen or so lodging-houses, although its attention was increasingly occupied by other kinds of intervention (including industrial schools, its emigration efforts, boarding out, training farms, summer camps, day care and kindergartens, health services, and convalescent care). However, from its inception, the lodging-house model of service delivery was linked to religious education and vocational training, and sought to divert youth from criminal or immoral activities. It was a model introduced and supported by responsible and benevolent adults who designed it to help socialize and school children into citizenship by channeling their industrial inclinations into healthy occupations. Children could hone their street survival skills and parlay them into profit, or at least a livable wage, in part because street-based peddling provided viable employment options for independent youth.

By 1941 the only lodging-house still in business was the Brace Memorial Newsboys' Lodging-House, and it had shifted its focus considerably:

During depression years, our Brace Memorial Newsboys' House provided food, shelter, clothing, and medical attention to thousands of transient boys between sixteen and twenty-one who ended up in New York City jobless, homeless, and without friends or funds. In recent months, as local job opportunities increased all over the nation, the number of transient youth has declined. To make the most effective use of the House, we now provide temporary shelter for members of the armed forces on furlough and out-of-town lads newly enlisted and awaiting transfer.[21]

By the 1960s, the CAS lodging-houses had vanished altogether, as had most of the charitable organizations that provided transitional assistance for teenagers and young adults. Undoubtedly, many factors contributed to their demise, including the changing nature of the economy, child labor laws, and compulsory education (which conspired to leave few legitimate street-based employment opportunities available to support premature independence), and the changing nature of our understanding of childhood itself. Furthermore, an increasingly elaborate public system of child welfare and juvenile justice began to supplement and, arguably, overtake the role of private charities as primary caretakers of vagrant children.

Public Policy Response: Juvenile Courts of the Progressive Era

"Juvenile" or "children's" courts also have their roots in the Progressive Era. The first children's court was introduced in Chicago in 1899, and the idea quickly spread to other states and municipalities. By 1925 every state, with the exceptions of Maine and Wyoming, had some version of this specialized social and legal institution.[22] At the heart of the movement was the revolutionary notion that children were different from adults and that the state had a unique protective and custodial role in their upbringing.

The courts tended to be based on the understanding that "delinquent" children were also often "dependent, neglected, and destitute" children as well.[23] In this way, both poverty and lack of proper supervision were linked to the idea of "delinquency." Not surprisingly, during this period the children of recent immigrants received particularly intense scrutiny.

In addition, these specialized courts extended common-law practices that held that young children could not be held accountable or culpable for criminal behavior in the same manner as adults. Before the inception of juvenile courts, children "as young as seven years old could be tried in criminal court and, if convicted, sentenced to prison or death."[24] These children, convicted of adult crimes, were also routinely incarcerated with adults in jails and prisons. However, under common law, children below seven were considered unable to form *mens rea*[25] (the criminal intent)—an element necessary for finding a defendant guilty of a crime; therefore, children were deemed not culpable for their behavior. The juvenile courts of the Progressive Era extended that assumption to children who were older, usually up to 14, finding that these youth were not criminally culpable for their acts. Furthermore, separate institutional facilities, such as reform or training schools, were designed to treat youth rather than punish them. In short, these courts took an active role in the lives of children who were poor, those who were neglected by parents, those who committed acts that would be criminal if they had been adults, and those who were deemed to be acting in an undisciplined or unruly manner generally.

The rules applying to "runaway" children can be found among the regulations governing unruly, delinquent, destitute, wayward, and neglected children during the Progressive Era. In New York City, for example, authorities could turn either to the Wayward Minor Act or to the delinquency provisions of the Children's Court Acts in order to intervene with vagrant street youth.

The Wayward Minor Act,[26] originally enacted in 1923[27] and restricted to girls, was amended to include boys in 1925.[28] Although it purported to be gender-neutral, in application—as evident from case law and court statistics—it continued to target girls well into the 1960s. It covered young adults (ages 16–21) and specifically referred to "running away" in a section which applied to those "who without just cause and without the consent of parents, guardians or other custodians, deserts his or her home or place of abode, and is morally depraved or is in danger of becoming morally depraved."

However, in addition to this "running away" section, waywardness included a wide range of other often noncriminal but morally suspicious behavior, including drug and alcohol use; associating with dissolute persons, thieves, prostitutes, pimps, procurers, or disorderly persons; and frequenting houses of prostitution or ill-fame. The statute covered *morally depraved* individuals but also those who were *in danger of becoming morally depraved* ; so not only did it punish past behavior, it served as a prevention and intervention tool for youth who *might* become morally depraved sometime in the future. Finally, the moral jurisdictional base of the statute applied to those who endangered the morals or health of themselves *or others*. The Wayward Minor statute was most readily applied to sexually active young women, whose behavior was deemed both a threat to themselves and a public health risk. The sanctions for wayward behavior could range from probation to a sentence in jail, reform school, or training school, until the youth reached the age of 21.

Alternatively, public intervention with "runaway" youth could be managed through the delinquency provisions of the Children's Court Act.[29] In New York City, Children's Court Reports classified its "juvenile delinquency cases" into thirteen categories: assault, robbery, burglary, unlawful entry, stealing, disorderly conduct, peddling or begging, ungovernable or wayward, desertion of home, truancy, violation of railroad law, violation of corporate ordinances, and a miscellaneous category of unclassified allegations. This statute specifically mentioned "runaway" behavior by covering those who "without just cause and without the consent of his parent, guardian, or other custodian, deserts his home or place of abode."[30]

The definitions of delinquency associated with "running away" are sweeping when compared to today's standards and included violating any state law or city ordinance; being habitually truant; engaging in any occupation which was in violation of law; begging or soliciting alms or money in public places; associating with immoral or vicious persons; frequenting any place "the maintenance of which is in violation of law"; habitually using obscene or profane language; or deporting one's self as willfully to injure or endanger the morals or health of self or others.[31] Thus in this statute "running away" is situated alongside a whole host of noncriminal behavior (such as cursing or being habitually disobedient) as well as with criminal behavior (such as violating state law).[32] Like the Wayward Minor Act, intervention could be based upon concern for "the morals or health" of the child or others," and delinquent youth could be incarcerated for indeterminate amounts of time, up until adulthood.

These two statutes linked "leaving home without just cause" (running away) with a host of behaviors characterized for their moral and/or criminal nature. The State could exercise broad discretion and justified doing so in arguments about public morals, safety, and welfare of both youth and the community. Taken together, the State's reach over "runaway" youth and other minors was considerable from the 1920s into the 1960s.

Juvenile Courts of the 1960s: Reconceptualizing the Categories

All of this changed in the 1960s as state policymakers began to question the wisdom of lumping behavioral problems associated with childhood disobedience (such as running away) into the mix of other kinds of delinquencies committed by children (such as serious crimes). In the early 1960s, New York and California led a movement that began to reformulate the conceptual arrangement of classes of youth into three separate and distinct categories: abused and neglected youth, delinquent youth, and status offenders. The label "status offenses" was used because it was only the youth's "status" as a minor that justified state intervention for the behavior. These cases were also generically referred to as "in need of supervision" cases, based on the assumption that the youth were either ungovernable or lacked proper adult supervision. "Running away" (as well as truancy and other unruly behavior) fit squarely into this new category.

In 1962, New York State adopted this tripartite structure and applied it in a unified statewide system.[33] The status offense procedures were laid out in a section entitled "Persons in Need of Supervision" (PINS).[34] The original PINS statute applied to "a male less than sixteen years of age and a female less than eighteen" who was "incorrigible, ungovernable, or habitually disobedient" and beyond the lawful control of his or her parents. For the most part, the PINS statute separated unruly behavior from criminal acts. It deleted all references to "morality," covered habitual behavior (not potential future misconduct), and applied to girls and boys up to different ages. Given this new conceptual framework, courts in New York (and elsewhere) spent a couple of decades setting out the appropriate policies and procedures for dealing with youth in this new status offender category. The net result was that the public response to runaway youth was in considerable flux during the 1960s and 1970s.

Obviously, this turmoil over what to do with wandering youth had a direct impact on children engaged in the behavior during this period. For example, had Veronica Brunson wandered the streets in 1925, or 1945, or even 1965, there is a good chance she would have been labeled "wayward" and locked up, quite probably until her twenty-first birthday. However, by 1975 Veronica found herself under the jurisdiction of these relatively new PINS statutory provisions at a time when courts and judges were still trying to sort out the institutional rules. Every attempt would have been made to divert her from both the family court system and from being committed to a restrictive institution. In Veronica's case the diversion was successful; however, ensuring a safe alternative was not.

As state juvenile justice systems in the 1960s and 1970s wrestled with these status offenders, another service delivery model emerged on the public radar screen that had *runaway* youth specifically and uniquely in mind.

Runaway Youth Act of 1974

In 1974 the U.S. Congress enacted federal legislation entitled the *Runaway Youth Act* (see appendix 3). If ever there is an indicator that a socially constructed problem has reached public maturity, it may be when federal legislation is enacted in its name. With the 1974 version of the Runaway Youth Act, Congress recognized a stand-alone population of "runaway" children deserving of their own policy intervention. The significance is threefold. The label "runaway" is used to describe an entire population. Second, the legislation endorsed a specific kind of service approach to the problem that involved providing crisis shelters and counseling services. Third, the service was to be provided as an alternative to existing public child welfare and juvenile justice systems.

When Congress enacted this law in 1974, it did so in spite of a legislative finding that "the exact nature of the problem is not well defined because national statistics on the size and profile of the runaway youth population are not tabulated."[35] This raises a few immediately obvious questions—such as if we didn't know "the exact nature of the problem," to what were we responding? If we didn't know anything about the "size and profile of the runaway population," what was driving our characterization of the problem and our decisions about how to respond? Why did it seem such an acute problem in 1974? Why crisis shelters? Why place this service outside the traditional child welfare and juvenile justice systems? Why did we return to a model much like the lodging-houses of the nineteenth century at a time when independent entrepreneurship of street peddlers was no longer a sustainable lifestyle? In short, how did the relationships and development among problem construction, service response, and policy come to pass?

The answers to these questions have much to do with the coming of age of the Baby Boomers. Collectively, they were a noisy bunch of young Americans who were challenging authority and renegotiating their relationships with adults. Services and policies governing children, which had been designed to ensure the proper socialization of children since the Progressive Era, came under direct attack. The Baby Boomers had little interest in the care, protection, control, or supervision imposed upon them by adult authorities. They had ideas of their own about what this transition to independence should look like.

Autonomy-Seeking and Big New People

Between 1966 and the early 1970s, *New York Times* columnist, humorist, and social commentator Russell Baker devoted a fair amount of ink in his "Observer" columns to pondering the difference between his generation and the children his generation was raising. He captured a variation on the theme of youth with restless feet in one such column entitled, "The Nomadic Big New People":

> After awhile the children cease being children and become people. New people, as it were. One day, looking around the house, you notice that the children are all gone, and in their place are these new people. *Big* new people, very often. *Great* big new people. . . . In any case, one of the most common characteristics of these big new people is mobility. Something way back there in their diet—maybe the penicillin, maybe the permissiveness, maybe something we didn't even know we were feeding them—has made it impossible for many of them to be content unless they are in motion.[36]

He goes on to note that for his generation, "formed by the Depression and big war," for whom "hearth-and-home" was the "supreme virtue," the "eternal wandering" of this younger generation of new big people was extremely "baffling."[37] His asks the rhetorical question, "Where do they think they are going out on that endless road?"[38]

There are two independent points to be drawn here. The first involves the notion of "big new people" and the second has to do with their "nomadic" tendencies. Demographically, there were an awful lot of big new people between the early 1960s and mid-1970s. The Baby Boomers were coming of age, making the move from childhood to adulthood. However, it was also a

Table 1.1

Baby Boomer Ages Between 1959–1980

Teenage Years to Age of Majority

Age in Year / Birth Year	1959	1960	1961	1962	1963	1964	1965	1966	1967	1968	1969	1970	1971	1972	1973	1974	1975	1976	1977	1978	1979	1980
1946	13	14	15	16	17	18	19	20	21	22	23	24	25	26	27	28	29	30	31	32	33	34
1947	12	13	14	15	16	17	18	19	20	21	22	23	24	25	26	27	28	29	30	31	32	33
1948	11	12	13	14	15	16	17	18	19	20	21	22	23	24	25	26	27	28	29	30	31	32
1949	10	11	12	13	14	15	16	17	18	19	20	21	22	23	24	25	26	27	28	29	30	31
1950	9	10	11	12	13	14	15	16	17	18	19	20	21	22	23	24	25	26	27	28	29	30
1951	8	9	10	11	12	13	14	15	16	17	18	19	20	21	22	23	24	25	26	27	28	29
1952	7	8	9	10	11	12	13	14	15	16	17	18	19	20	21	22	23	24	25	26	27	28
1953	6	7	8	9	10	11	12	13	14	15	16	17	18	19	20	21	22	23	24	25	26	27
1954	5	6	7	8	9	10	11	12	13	14	15	16	17	18	19	20	21	22	23	24	25	26
1955	4	5	6	7	8	9	10	11	12	13	14	15	16	17	18	19	20	21	22	23	24	25
1956	3	4	5	6	7	8	9	10	11	12	13	14	15	16	17	18	19	20	21	22	23	24
1957	2	3	4	5	6	7	8	9	10	11	12	13	14	15	16	17	18	19	20	21	22	23
1958	1	2	3	4	5	6	7	8	9	10	11	12	13	14	15	16	17	18	19	20	21	22
1959		1	2	3	4	5	6	7	8	9	10	11	12	13	14	15	16	17	18	19	20	21
1960			1	2	3	4	5	6	7	8	9	10	11	12	13	14	15	16	17	18	19	20
1961				1	2	3	4	5	6	7	8	9	10	11	12	13	14	15	16	17	18	19
1962					1	2	3	4	5	6	7	8	9	10	11	12	13	14	15	16	17	18

Note: Highlighted area shows teenagers below the age of majority.

period in which our basic rules about what constituted "adulthood" were being challenged and legally altered. So not only were large numbers of big new people graduating into adulthood under the terms of an earlier social contract governing that transition, but a large number of "new big people" were being created through policy changes that were playing with the basic rules regarding the age of majority.

The second point has to do with their "nomadic" nature. If the Baby Boomers were making their transition to adulthood, we would expect them to be leaving home in large numbers under any circumstances. However, Baker was arguably commenting on bigger and broader cultural phenomena and what might be termed "the call of the road" in the 1960s and 1970s. The Boomers were not only actively exploring their world—out there hitchhiking and backpacking—but were calling upon their generational siblings to come join the expedition.

Not surprisingly, each of these three factors (the coming of age of the Baby Boomers, the changing rules of adulthood, and the call of the road) had a relatively direct impact on "runaway" youth during this period. First, if runaway youth are defined, in part, as premature autonomy seekers and we place these children in a historical context in which Baby Boomers are moving, en masse, from dependence to independence, and in a political context during which the basic rules of adulthood were being challenged and changed, it seems reasonable to assume that the notion of what constituted "premature" autonomy might surface in public discussion. Second, if we place those premature autonomy seekers in a cultural context in which there is a vibrant and enticing call of the road, it should not be surprising that children who were inclined to leave home anyway might be particularly intrigued by the invitation. Taken together, it seems reasonable to predict that public discussions about autonomy and freedom and about premature autonomy and premature freedom might come to the fore during this period.

Big New People and New Big People: Teenage Baby Boomers, 1959–1975

The year 1959 was a notable one for birthday parties for 13-year-olds, as the front edge of Baby Boomers[39] crossed the threshold into their teens (see table 1.1). Of course, that meant then that 1960 would be a notable year for birthday parties for both 13- *and* 14-year-olds, as Baby Boomers began to swell the ranks of teenagers. Depending on how you measure the end of the demographic blip, the last big cluster celebrated becoming 13 in 1975, just as the first group of celebrants was reaching the wise old age of 26. The points are fourfold. First, between 1965 and 1975 every teenage rank (13–19) was continuously saturated with Baby Boomers. Second, somewhere in the 1960s, arguably in 1967, these youngsters began to reach legal adulthood. Third, newly anointed adults were available in large-enough numbers to start giving advice on growing up to equally large numbers of younger teens. Fourth, there was a larger-than-average pool of younger teens available for premature autonomy-seeking. In short, there were a lot of people making the transition between dependence and independence during these years, but what distinguished premature autonomy from other sorts during this era of growing up?

Shifting Ground on the Basic Rules of Adulthood

In 1966, social observer Russell Baker captured (humorously, of course) a serious dilemma facing the nation regarding the rules of childhood and adulthood. He noted the irony that American youth between 18 and 20 were apparently "not up to the heavy adult responsibility of serious beer-guzzling" but that "a person of 16 is old enough to be put in command of two tons of metal capable of bouncing around corners at 40 miles an hour." Baker insisted we needed to "set up some rules," and the first rule "will have to state precisely the age at which youth stops and adulthood begins."[40] Given the escalating Vietnam War, Baker asked the amusingly framed but troubling question: "How can Congress make its beer law consistent with its draft law?"[41]

Certainly, Baker tapped into a dilemma that held special poignancy in the late 1960s. However, he raised a fundamental problem that continues to plague us today: the age of majority, which typically separates legal "infants" (presumed incompetent and suffering legal disabilities)[42] from adults (who are granted the full rights and responsibilities of citizenship), appears to be the kind of demarcation that would be useful. However, the age of majority also ends up establishing an upper age boundary at which we regulate all sorts of behaviors and activities of the minors below it, particularly those in the years closest to adulthood.

When we select different threshold ages to begin permitting beer-guzzling, or commandeering a sports car (or an Army tank), we wander into some conceptually problematic territory. Yet each state engages in such legislative rule-making for regulating its underaged citizens. Thus the right to marry without parental consent; to drive, drink alcohol, and smoke cigarettes; to purchase pornography; consent to sexual activity or medical treatment; commence a legal proceeding; and sign a contract (including for leases, loans, and employment) are all first permitted at different threshold ages, and each state makes different combinations of choices.

If all these regulations were correlated neatly with what we know about adolescent development, they might be justifiable. More often than not, however, they are paternalistic or moralistic in nature. Like the beer and draft quandary, our legal rules relating to childhood, adulthood, and the assorted rights and responsibilities thereof are nonsensical when examined for overall logical consistency. Today, for example, we will punish a store clerk for selling a 14-year-old a pack of cigarettes (based on the child's legal incapacity to decide whether or not to smoke and our paternalistic concerns for the child's well-being), but, at the same time, we are willing to hold the very same 14-year-old accountable in adult criminal court for committing a murder.

While most American youth, then and now, simply age through this morass of rules and regulations without taking any notice at all, these age-based regulations and prohibitions are problematic for runaway youth, particularly those who leave home for long periods of time. Runaway children challenge minority status directly and comprehensively, claiming the right to make their own autonomous decisions without having parents nearby to sign off on consent forms. This presents problems for adults who come in contact with them, including professional service providers (e.g., social workers, doctors, lawyers, etc.); nonprofessional helpers (e.g., relatives and friends); adults with commercial interests (e.g., landlords, employers, or shopkeepers); and state officials (e.g., police, child protective workers, or school personnel). In general, adults who do business with autonomous minors bear the criminal, financial, or professional risk of doing so if things go wrong along the way.

During the 1960s, the age of majority for the most part was set at 21, which meant the first Baby Boomers reached adulthood in 1967. Had all things remained static (which of course they didn't), the last of the Boomers would have reached adulthood in 1984. However, in 1971, in the midst of all this coming of age, Congress ratified the Twenty-sixth Amendment to the U.S. Constitution, lowering the voting age from 21 to 18.[43]

At the time, the change in voting age affected forty-five states. More to the point, however, the Twenty-sixth Amendment amounted to the imposition of a new nationally recognized and lower age of majority. Immediately after its ratification, states began to lower their legal age of majority to 18. In a study conducted by the Department of Health, Education, and Welfare in 1974–75, researchers concluded that, "whatever the reason, the movement to lower the age of majority below 21 is definitely on among the states."[44] The researchers offer several possible explanations for the trend, but an obvious one was that it became increasingly difficult to justify a state age of majority that was higher than the one set for voting for president.

In 1972, just a year after ratification of the Twenty-sixth Amendment, two heavily populated states, New York and California, lowered the state-recognized age of majority from 21 to 18. On March 4, 1972, the day California's law took effect, the *New York Times* painted the picture: "about 1.1 million young people reached adulthood at midnight" in California. That created—to borrow from Mr. Baker again—a lot of new big people all at once. According to the *New York Times,* these new adults were granted "virtually all the privileges of their parents except the right to drink"[45] (so much for resolving Mr. Baker's beer and draft quandary). These rights included the right to "serve on juries, become policemen, sign contracts, obtain credit, conduct driver education classes, and record cattle brands."[46] This phenomenon was replicated, state by state, across the country.

"Premature" Adulthood and Problems for Policymakers

During this period, the age at which we recognized complete autonomy plummeted from 21 to 18, but lowering the age of majority created secondary philosophical, ideological, and logistical problems for state lawmakers: what to do about regulating the behavior of minors? The lower age of majority meant a forced compression of the transitional years to adulthood. The ages at which we regulated "premature" autonomy necessarily dropped precipitously to well below 18.[47] So where we once might have permitted 18- to 21-year-olds to engage in some quasi-adult activities, that age range is now more likely to be 16 to 18, or even lower.

Of course both changes—lowering the age of majority and tinkering with the ages of transitional activities—occurred at a time when maximum numbers of American youth were affected by the alterations. For most of them, all this boundary-shifting had little direct impact. However, for run-away youth—minors who were prematurely testing their liberty—there were some very real consequences, as there were for those state authorities who wished to govern or supervise their behavior.

Nomadic Big People: The Call of the Road

It wasn't just the shifting boundaries of adulthood that was putting pres-sure on social and legal institutions, it was the volume of the collective voices of the Baby Boomers, the substance of their ideas, and the activities in which they were engaged. They were, as Mr. Baker noted, a nomadic group. Not only were they taking to the road, American youth were desig-nating their own spiritual leaders, heroes, and spokespersons. They were initiating their own conversations. They were staking out their own geo-graphic territories and building their own communities.

During the 1960s there was a renewed romance with the road. Arguably, the publication of Jack Kerouac's *On the Road* in 1957 helped incite a new generation's romance and passion for movement. In 1964, inspired by Ker-ouac, Ken Kesey and his Merry Pranksters sputtered their way from West Coast to East Coast and back again in a refurbished school bus painted in psychedelic colors and bearing the destination sign FURTHER. In 1965, Bob Dylan sang: *how does it feel, to be on your own, with no direction home, just like a rolling stone?* In 1966 or so, the Grateful Dead began collecting a loyal entourage of migrant "deadheads." In 1968, Simon and Garfunkel sang of boarding a Greyhound in Pittsburgh and going in search of America, and in 1969 Peter Fonda climbed on a Harley and began a tragic cross-country trek, movie audiences in tow, in *Easy Rider*. Pop culture was recording, reporting, and selling American youth on the move.

In addition to all the wandering, many of these youth were challenging and arguably even rewriting some cherished American values held by their parents' generation. They protested what they found unconscionable. They abandoned materialism and reveled in communalism. They found work in scavenging rather than the meaningful employment of their parents. They temporarily replaced the traditional nuclear family with tribal communities. They defined freedom with adolescent innocence as "doing your own thing." They turned exploration inward, with the aid of hallucinogenic drugs, seeking new levels of consciousness while publicly advocating the insights gained while "tripping." In this marketplace of youthful ideas, the messages were about exploration, experimentation, freedom, defiance, and independence from the shackles of blind loyalty and boring conformity in areas sexual, intellectual, social, cultural, economic, and spiritual.

Furthermore, these youth were staking out their own geographic territories and building their own communities. One was the East Village in New York City (situated just a bit farther east than that of the older and more established Bohemians of Greenwich Village). There were various other youth meccas scattered across the United States, but none other reached the legendary status of an area marked by an intersection of two cross streets—Haight and Ashbury—in San Francisco. If Dean Siering had amused reporters in 1960 by saying that he wanted to visit California because it was "a nice state," a half-decade later California was far more than just "a nice state" for wandering youth; Haight-Ashbury was *the* place to be. Youth had gathered in the area to build an alternative community based on their own views of freedom and according to their own social, economic, and political rules. A clarion call to and from youth was extended nationwide in 1967, inviting free spirits to come join the party, for a celebration dubbed the "Summer of Love." Reporters from the mainstream press, such as the *New York Times*, were less than charmed by the long-haired, scruffy, undisciplined, irreverent youth gathering in the Haight (as well as other counterculture territories across the country). Nonetheless, the youth themselves were engaged in an independent and important cultural critique.

Youth Constructions

In 1968, East Villager and youth movement spokesman Abbie Hoffman (a self-appointed hippie, Digger, yippie, youth activist, and general agitator, as well as defendant among the Chicago Seven) wrote a passage that reads like an instruction manual for those studying the 1960s counterculture:

First, it is important to distinguish between hippies and Diggers. Both are myths. . . . Hippies, however, are a myth created by media and as such they are forced to play certain media-oriented roles. They are media-manipulated. Diggers too are myth, but a grass-roots myth created from within.[48]

Putting aside the difference between hippies and Diggers—just for the moment—Hoffman's observations are useful for two reasons. First, all counterculture groups are *not* alike and, second, the source of the "myth" matters. In short, the social construction of counterculture groups is subject to as much turbulence as that of "runaway" youth. Furthermore, we can expect different versions of the construction, depending on who is doing the talking.

The Digger movement, born in the Haight-Ashbury district of San Francisco during the mid-1960s, is central to a youthful discussion on autonomy, power, freedom, and "dropping out" (albeit mostly temporarily). Although Diggers were physically and historically situated in the midst of the gathering hippies, Diggers themselves claimed greater kinship with their Beat elders (such as Kerouac and others) than with the other youth movements around them. Arguably, however, the essence of Beatness, from which the Diggers draw, owed its own mythical origins to yet another source: it was derived largely from the real-life experience of a handful of individuals who started their own "Beat" existence as runaway teenagers. Messages about that street-based, vagrant, survivalist lifestyle and its accompanying worldview were appropriated by the Ivy League–educated, middle-class Beat writers who disseminated it—through poetry and literature—to wider audiences, including a next generation of coming-of-age Baby Boomers. This movement of ideas about renouncing privilege, being outside the mainstream, being "on the road," and living on the fringe influenced the behavior, life philosophies, and worldviews of a generation of Baby Boomers, the Diggers among them.

A Reading Roadmap

With the demographic scales tipped in favor of adolescence in the 1960s and 1970s, youthful legions exerted pressure on existing rules around independence, freedom, and growing up in general. This era marks a period of significant reformulation of our views and responses to youth. Ideas and rhetoric of the day—on freedom, self-determination, civil rights, gender equity—wove their way into our youth-policy frameworks. While Baby Boomers negotiated their positions with individual institutions (universities, courts, Congress), as a collective force they were rewriting the underlying assumptions that had historically characterized the relationship between adults and youth. As a result, youth gained real institutional power relative to their parents and to the state and left a profoundly altered landscape of rights and responsibilities in their wake. The legacy of this renegotiated power structure has a direct impact on our relationship with youth, and with youth policy, today. One of the best places to examine this renegotiated relationship is in the evolving discussions on "runaway" (premature autonomy-seeking) youth.

I contend that the interplay between runaway discourse, runaway service development, and policy was particularly lively and volatile in the 1960s and 1970s. I revisit these decades in order to examine the "running away problem" formulation, to look at the services that were developed, and to consider the policies that emerged and took shape. Using as evidence a series of individual case studies of particular relevance, and primary texts of the period (including court cases, media reports, literature, poetry, song lyrics, counterculture broadsides, autobiographies, and legislative testimony), I consider the various influential public discussions and their intersections during the 1960s and 1970s.

In part I of this book, I examine how the problem of "runaway youth" was constructed from two decidedly different perspectives—first in the mainstream press (as evident in the *New York Times*) and, second, from the counterculture perspective (as evident in the life histories and positionality of Beat "muses"). Arguably, the latter developed a romantic vision of "Beatness" that embraced a nomadic, survivalist, and street-inspired lifestyle, and the mainstream press came to accept these characteristics as illustrative of the generic problem and population of "runaway" youth.

In part II, I examine how Diggers adopted and adapted the counterculture discourse of their Beat elders and used it as a blueprint for enacting, or performing, an alternative lifestyle. By borrowing a conceptualization of "Beatness," the Diggers briefly built a community, social structure, and alternative lifestyle that was premised on their own values and ideas about autonomy, power, and being "free." Grassroots community organizers and service providers borrowed this Digger model to develop alternative services for runaway youth (such as crisis shelters and hotlines) which were outside the mainstream authoritative responses of the existing public child welfare and juvenile justice systems and which challenged the basic premises upon which these traditional services were governed. These alternative providers bridged the gap between counterculture and mainstream on behalf of "runaway" autonomy-seeking youth.

Part III examines policy and institutional structures that dealt with "runaway" children—first, by looking at the uncomfortably unfolding and institutionalization of the PINS statute in New York State, and its inability to successfully accommodate "runaway" youth whose characteristics are primarily of the street-based variety; second, by examining federal legislators' decision to enact the Runaway Youth Act in 1974, thus endorsing the alternative service structure and providing legitimacy to the shelter model, which had its roots in the counterculture.

Taken together, these three sections on social problem construction, service delivery development, and policy responses take a micro, mezzo, and macro look at the dynamic, interactive, and evolutionary nature of forces (personal, social, political, cultural, and institutional) that are at play in the movement of ideas about social problems, programs, and policy. It is not a work that can be told in simple chronological order, in part because each of these storylines (media, counterculture, grassroots organizer, service provider, judicial, legislative) has its own longitudinal historical rhythm. Yet taken together, the voices collectively inform the narrative of the "runaway" problem during this period.

While this endeavor—focusing on "runaway" youth during these turbulent decades—may seem narrow in focus, it really is illustrative of much broader and more significant discussions. Engraved on the Korean War memorial in Washington, D.C., are the words, *freedom is not free.* Clearly, this is the case when we fight wars in the name of freedom; however, freedom is not free in the context of civil rights and civil liberties either. Consider Veronica Brunson once again. Had we incarcerated her (denied her freedom and limited her civil rights), she might have lived past the age of 12. On the other hand, had we done so, the inevitable consequence would be to curtail the liberty of other children unnecessarily. So the price of freedom—when discussing "runaway" children in the abstract—can be measured in the lives and liberties of individual children. It raises a fundamental and very American question: freedom for whom and at what cost?

Constructing Runaway Youth

Media Myth Spinning
From Runaway Adventurers to Street Survivors
(1960–1978)*

> Someone told me it's all happening at the zoo,
> I do believe it, I do believe it's true.
>
> —Simon and Garfunkel (1967)

In 1977, Veronica Brunson served as a poster child for runaway youth. However, she was a far cry from the public's prototypical runaway of the previous decade. The rhetoric of runaway children underwent dramatic transformation in the mid-1960s. In particular, discussions of innocent and harmless adventures were subsumed by a more hostile discussion on hippies and other older dropouts (along with dangerous activities associated with them). Furthermore, the behavior of younger Baby Boomers was intermingled with descriptions about independence-seeking behavior of older Baby Boomers. The net result was that running away emerged as a public problem involving an ostensibly large population of youth who were vulnerable to exploitation and victimization. Once conceptualized and framed as a public problem, running away became ripe for policy responses.

The dramatic evolution in public discussion is evident in the mainstream press. While certain events are important (such as the "Summer of Love" in 1967, the murder of Linda Fitzpatrick in October 1967, and in Texas the Dean Allen Corll serial killings of 1973), events alone are not as informative as a close examination of how the construction of runaway

*A version of this material was previously published in the *Journal of Communication* 53.2 (June 2003): 330–46.

stories changed over time. The public gaze shifted from children who engaged in short and possibly harmless runaway adventures to those who were at extreme risk. Evidence of the shift can be found in headlines, photographs and artwork, literary references, the choice and use of sources, as well as in the selection of language in media story construction. The *New York Times*'s coverage between 1960 and the mid-1970s serves as evidence for this case study of the evolution of media discourse.[1]

Safe Adventuring

In the early 1960s, basic news reporting on runaways rested on a very simple and reassuring portrait of the runaway child and the child's family. Running away was characterized as safe, harmless, and even predictable behavior. Children did not flee bad homes but, rather, were lured into adventure by identifiable attractions such as fairs, carnivals and beaches or by compelling romantic ideas like "going West." Springtime offered an annual opportunity to report on the seasonal impulse to run away as is evident in the opening paragraphs from one article in June 1961 and illustrated in another from March 1964:

> This is the peak season for fashion shows, fresh strawberries and frightened runaways.
>
> The "reluctant travelers," as Eda J. Le Shan, a psychologist, has so aptly labeled them, are smitten with wanderlust—or bitten with defiance—and strike out on their own during this month more than any other. There are myriad reasons. One of the compelling ones is simply a primitive response to spring. (June 1961)[2]

> Spring is the season when Iowa's cornfields seem never ending and Manhattan's bright towers beckon most insistently to boys and girls from the hinterlands.
>
> Spring is the season, too, when New York seems closed in for youngsters living here and the roads leading to the South and West call them. (March 1964)[3]

In the first, the possible importance of an expert's label ("reluctant travelers") is immediately overshadowed. The journalist seized on the notion of "travelers" and writes of them being "smitten with wanderlust" or "bitten with defiance," while subsequently ignoring the troublesome part of the psychiatrist's label ("reluctant"). This selective use of sources is typical. References to "peak season," "fresh strawberries," and "fashion shows" were underscored by situating this article on the "Family, Food, and Furnishings" page between a Fourth of July recipe for grilled spareribs and a photograph of women's spring fashion. The message was clear: running away is a normal, even pleasant, seasonal ritual of primary concern to mothers. In the second piece, springtime running is attributed to a call and beckoning. The romantic images of the bright lights of New York City or merely going to the South or West provided sufficient explanation and justification for the behavior.

In addition to the predictable, seasonal nature of running away, episodes were characterized as short in duration, only two or three days (which, admittedly, seems long by today's standards but at the time was accepted as about the appropriate length of time for an adventure), and these always ended with the safe return of the child to anxious families and happy homes. During the early 1960s, stories are not reported when children were still missing from home, but were told after the child's safe return; thus, the harmless nature of the behavior was emphasized while the dangers or uncertainties were minimized.

Long adventures were thwarted for one of two reasons. Either the child was forced home by lack of a basic survival plan and inadequate resources such as food, shelter, or money or, alternatively, the child was intercepted by a kindly adult authority figure, most often a police officer (or an employee of the railroad, airline, or other transit service). In fact, police sources were quoted as confidently reporting near-perfect return rates of runaways to their homes.[4]

Evidence of these story features is captured in illustrations from a *New York Times Magazine* story entitled "Why They Run Away from Home" (1964).[5] One boy is shown returning home (lugging an overstuffed bag) and peeking into the kitchen—his absence apparently so brief it has gone unnoticed—where his mother tends to food on the stove, with dinner's aromas surely wafting through the air. The second illustration depicts a tearful luggage-toting boy and a police officer who paternalistically drapes his arm around the child while making a call from a street pay phone (and presumably talking to the child's parent). These visual renditions summarized the principles underlying the situation: runaways were easy to detect, easy to intercept, and quickly and safely returned home. Although luggage may seem like a humorous addition to these illustrations, the public was ready to believe that children would quickly be returned home because adults, particularly police officers, could easily identify them by their appearance. Runaways were often described as confused, tearful, dirty, disheveled, or otherwise easy to spot. For example, in 1964 New York City hosted the World's Fair in Queens, which provided a predictable attraction for runaways. The *New York Times* ran a story under the headline, "To the Runaways, the Fair Is a Lure: Unkempt, Without Rest, They Will Be Drawn to City."[6]

Using words such as "lure" and "drawn" in the headline emphasized the irresistible nature of the fair as an attraction for runaways; however, the description of children being "unkempt" and "without rest" suggest they will be readily identifiable, and the first two paragraphs of the article elaborated on this visual imagery:

> They are unkempt, unbathed and sleepy. They wander aimlessly, have a furtive air and speak in accents not native to New York City.
> They are runaways.

A natural consequence of constructing a story that assumes both the predictable nature of the behavior and the easy identification of runaway children is that runaway episodes are quickly thwarted. So another, equally predictable consequence in this article construction is that it continues to elaborate on the preparation of detectives and police officers from the Missing Persons Unit, as they ready themselves for the "early arrival" of the "young visitors" for the World's Fair.[7]

Front-Page Boys and Their Adventures: Dean and Dominic

Given the prediction that runaways would venture to the World's Fair and the confident response of the police department, it is perhaps not surprising that 12-year-old Dominic Tucci's little escapade made front-page news.[8] Dominic managed to spend nine days living on the World's Fair grounds while cleverly avoiding adult detection. His behavior was described as "living off the land" and an "experiment in rugged individualism."[9] He ate hamburgers at the Brass Rail except on Friday when he ate chow mein because—as a Catholic who attended parochial school—he was trained to avoid meat on Fridays. (Apparently there was a limit to the level of authority he was willing to defy.) He obtained money for his food by scavenging change out of public fountains. He spent nights sleeping in the exhibit halls, including those for the Gas Pavilion, Continental Insurance, Coca-Cola, and the Johnson's Wax Theater. He washed in public bathrooms (although we are told he didn't brush his teeth) and cleverly avoided adult capture even when he was stopped and questioned by police officers. A fair employee who recognized him from a missing-person poster and observed how dirty he was finally spotted Dominic. In the end, Dominic was reunited with his family. He was described as heading back to the family station wagon, which was filled with his cheering siblings. Dominic's photograph appeared—a smiling lad squeezed between two beaming parents—above a photo caption declaring, "end of adventure at fair."[10]

Dominic's story is constructed as that of an adventurer. What made it worthy of front-page treatment was his ability to avoid adult detection and to survive for so long on his own, thus making it atypical of the normally shorter 2-to-3-day episodes of other children. On the other hand, he survived in a highly unique environment where food, money, shelter, and even security were readily available. Dominic ironically reported not being afraid during his time on the fairgrounds because "the place is crawling with cops."[11] (Presumably these were the very same cops who were looking for him.) So Dominic never strayed far from protective adults. From a public perspective, nothing presented seemed particularly dangerous about his behavior or his situation.

The stories of individual runaway children like Dominic are not placed on the front page of the *New York Times* very often, so it is noteworthy when they do appear. The only other such story from the early 1960s was that of Dean Siering, the Long Island boy who talked his way onto a Chicago-bound plane (see chapter 1). He was also portrayed as a boy adventurer. Of course, Dean's accomplishment was not in the duration of his journey (which lasted only a few days) but rather in its distance[12] since he managed to travel from Long Island to Chicago and back to New York using just his wit and $25 from savings. Dean was described as having "insatiable wanderlust," "bravado," a "high spirit of adventure," and a "fertile imagination," as well as experiencing an "odyssey" and being a "youthful traveler."[13] The article was accompanied by two maps that traced his cross-country route and appeared alongside his photograph, highlighting both the explorer and his exploration on the front page of the *New York Times*.

Dean's and Dominic's stories are about harmless adventures. Signs of family trouble existed but were minimized in both sets of stories. For example, readers learn that Dean was "very emotionally upset" by his parents' divorce, but this comment, made by his caretaker-grandmother, is buried in a follow-up article and is minimized by placing it before a neighbor's assessment that Dean merely had a "high spirit of adventure."[14] Dominic had school problems, had had three previous runaway "escapades" (this being the longest), and his parents hadn't bothered to report his disappearance to authorities. Dominic's recidivism, the increasing duration of his runaway excursions, his struggle in school, and his parents' delay in reporting his disappearance were subsumed by the adventurer story frame. In later decades these kinds of facts will be used to illustrate more endangered children and to paint a portrait of a more troubled family life. In the early 1960s, however, the end result was that both boys did what little adventurers are supposed to do: they had some fun and then returned home safely.

First Fission, 1966: Missing Girls

The first fission in this safe runaway portrait occurred in 1966. Two articles appeared, one in August written by Bernard Weinraub,[15] and the second in December, by Stephen A. O. Golden.[16] They are remarkable in comparison. Both journalists relied on the same central fact—that for the first time the number of missing-person complaints filed on behalf of *girls* outnumbered those filed on behalf of *boys*—but the journalists constructed profoundly different stories using this key piece of information.

Weinraub equated *complaints filed* with *actual runaways* and concluded that there were more girls running away from home than boys. He then reverted to generic runaway information,[17] such as a police officer reiterating classic themes (i.e., that children leave home because of a "spirit of adventure," particularly around "Easter time" when they run off to "Fort Lauderdale"),[18] and using police officer informants he assured the public of the quick and safe return of runaway youth.

Golden, on the other hand, focused on the fact that girls were being reported *missing* in greater numbers.[19] In his telling, Golden broke every existing public convention in constructing a runaway article. He opened with two vignettes featuring girls who had been missing a long time. One, a 15-year-old, had left home 55 days earlier and had had trouble both at home and school. Her mother described her as "sad, sort of dejected."[20] The second involved a 15-year-old Puerto Rican girl[21] who had been gone 58 days and whose mother had delayed reporting her missing for the first two weeks. Golden used traditional informants differently. Earlier, in Weinraub's story, police officers had been treated with deference while mental health experts were discounted. Golden reversed the emphasis. He solicited, and then reported, a confession from the police that they were only "guessing" about their explanations for the increasing problem. Golden's mental health expert, a psychiatrist, characterized the runaway as a troubled, unhappy child with personality problems and a low frustration tolerance whose "bond of love and loyalty to his family isn't strong enough."[22] Rather than undermining this opinion, Golden buttressed it with the first mention of runaway recidivism and with the opinion of other "authorities" that recidivists often have "legitimate gripe[s]" or may be "mentally or emotionally disturbed."

Finally, Golden uses two underage runaway sources who were interviewed while *missing* from home. One is a 15-year-old girl who moved into her boyfriend's Greenwich Village apartment after her mother refused to permit her to date him. The other was a 17-year-old long-haired boy who left home three months earlier to "get away from it all—school, parents, people in general." The youth admitted having smoked marijuana and reportedly lived with "a homosexual who gave him money."

The Golden article is a first on a number of counts. It is the first to shift the emphasis to missing children (rather than those safely returned home), to concentrate on children who have been gone for months, to discuss children of color, to discount police officer experts, to mention runaway recidivism, to hint that runaways may come from troubled homes, to bolster the words of warning from a mental health professional, to use child sources who reported from the street while they were still missing from home, and to talk about the "Village image," including long hair, use of marijuana and LSD, and rampant sexuality.

It is this last set of firsts which puts Golden on the trail of a story that will dominate coverage on children and youth over the next thirteen months.

Golden's work will include observations on the counterculture in both the East Village in New York City and Haight-Ashbury in San Francisco. He, along with others, will attempt to understand and characterize what is happening by labeling the youth participating in the scene with terms such as *hippies, plastic hippies, summertime hippies, borderline hippies, old-line hippies, younger hippies, pure hippies, second-generation beatniks, older hippies, weekend hippies, aspiring young hippies, Diggers, flower children, teeny-boppers, love children,* and *yippies.* Runaways will continue to be traceable—sometimes explicitly, sometimes implicitly—through the web of public discourse on this new phenomenon of "dropping out." However, during this crisis period, the simple and safe portrait of runaway little boy adventurers of the early 1960s will be lost forever.

The Establishment's Hippies

Hippie coverage in the Establishment press was dramatic but short-lived. In the *New York Times,* stories began appearing in 1966, reached a climax in 1967, and faded completely from discussion by 1973. From the start, articles about hippies were located alongside those on domestic social issues, unlike the benign runaway articles which had routinely been relegated to the pages of the "Family, Food, and Furnishings" section. Thus, hippies were immediately conceptualized as a public nuisance, whereas running away was mostly initially characterized as a private family matter. The public discussion of runaway behavior moved from private matter to social problem status between 1966 and the early 1970s. The pivotal year, however, appears to be 1967, perhaps because of the media attention given to Haight-Ashbury's Summer of Love.

To understand the impact of the collision between runaway and hippie discourses, it is useful to understand the independent construction of hippies by the Establishment press. Journalists provided definitions of hippies which appeared to cluster around five major categories: cultural lineage, rejection of traditional society, family substitution, drugs and promiscuity, and a carefree lifestyle (box 2.1). Taken together, these painted a picture of hippies as older teens (or young adults) from middle-class families, who had voluntarily gathered in a community and were living independently of biological families. They were either "rejecting" or "seeking liberation from" traditional social values and institutions, including family and work. They

Box 2.1
Hippie Population Definitions
New York Times (1967)

CULTURAL LINEAGE

- Hippies are "the descendant's of the beats, usually older teens . . . more involved with drugs, usually living away from home and perhaps working at odd jobs" (Sale and Applebaum, 5/28/1967);[a]
- "There are two philosophical trends in hippiedom . . . the old-line hippies [and] . . . younger hippies" (M. Arnold, 5/5/1967: *see* note 23).

REJECTION OF TRADITIONAL SOCIETY

- Hippies are "a cult of young people seeking liberation from contemporary society through the use of drugs, withdrawal from the economy and a search for what hippies call individual identity" (S. A. O. Golden, 8/19/1967: *see* note 23);
- A hippie is "a person who has dropped out of society because he has made a conscious decision that the Establishment is untenable and unflexible and will not accept his radical ideas" (S. A. O. Golden, 8/20/1967: *see* note 34);
- Hippies are "generally young people who have rejected middle-class standards and mores in favor of what they consider a freer, more spontaneous life. They live in areas such as the East Village and the Haight-Ashbury district of San Francisco" (Fox, 5/31/1967);[b]
- Hippies are "hipped on the value of the individual and the disvalue of the state" (Bingham, 9/24/1967);[c]
- Hippies "consider themselves dropouts from society" (E. Perlmutter, 10/9/1967: *see* note 37).

FAMILY SUBSTITUTIONS

- Hippies reject "the biological family form and live in communes, or extended families with each family a tribe" (S. A. O. Golden, 8/22/1967);[d]
- Hippies "discarded all ties with a biological family and extended families are their only ties" (S. A. O. Golden, 8/7/1967: *see* note 23);
- Hippies "want to be open, honest, loving and free. They . . . prefer to go back to the 'natural life,' like 'Adam and Eve'" (H. S. Thompson, 5/14/1967: *see* note 23).

DRUGS AND PROMISCUITY

- Hippies "like LSD, marijuana, nude parties, sex, drawing on walls and sidewalks, not paying their rent, making noise, and rock 'n' roll music" (Arnold, 5/5/1967: *see* note 23);
- Hippie society is totally drug-oriented (M. Arnold, 10/15/1967);[e]
- Hippies "smoke grass, or marijuana; take LSD trips together, and sleep on mattresses on littered floors" (S. A. O. Golden 5/5/1967);
- "Marijuana and LSD are an integral part of the hippie scene" (S. A. O. Golden, 8/19/1967: *see* note 23).

(Box 2.1 cont. next page)

(Box 2.1 cont.)

CAREFREE, SELF-CENTERED LIFESTYLE

- "A hippy is somebody who 'knows' what's really happening, and who adjusts or grooves with it" (H. S. Thompson, 5/14/1967: *see* note 23);
- Hippies "are unstructured, flower-carrying, bearded, nonaggressive, turned-on and as one admirer put it, 'always having interesting sex'" (Zion, 6/4/1967);[f]
- Hippies "wish to live by whim, by spontaneity, by the non-rules of Now" (Bingham, 9/24/1967);
- Hippies "do not bother to turn the leaves of the calendar, or look at their watches (if they own any), or read or listen to the news" (Bingham, 9/24/1967);
- Hippies "advocate 'love' as a way of life" (E. Perlmutter, 10/9/1967: *see* note 37).

[a]J. Kirk Sale and Ben Applebaum (1967, May 28), "Report from Teeny-Boppersville," *New York Times*, 77.

[b]Sylvan Fox (1967, May 31), "9 Hurt, 38 Arrested as Hippies Clash with Police," *New York Times*, 1.

[c]June Bingham (1967, Sept. 24), "The Intelligent Square's Guide to Hippieland," *New York Times Magazine*, 73.

[d]S. A. Golden (1967, Aug. 22), "What Is a Hippie? A Hippie Tells: And in So Doing He Indicts Society and the School System," *New York Times*, 36.

[e]Martin Arnold (1967, Oct. 15), "The East Village Today: Hippies Far from Happy as Slum Problems Grow," *New York Times*, 77.

[f]Sidney E. Zion (1967, June 4), "Policeman's Lot / Is Not a Happy One," *New York Times*, E3.

were searching for "identity" or "spontaneity" or "natural life." They were the cultural descendants of the Beats, beatniks, and older-generation counter-culturists. Drugs (including but not limited to psychedelic drugs such as LSD) and sexual experimentation played an instrumental role in the community. Their lifestyle (as portrayed by the nonhip Establishment press) was whimsical, delinquent, and irresponsible.

Hippies were isolated and marginalized. They were primarily associated with identifiable geographic areas such as New York City's East Village and San Francisco's Haight-Ashbury or other similar urban counterculture territories. By featuring the colorful carnival-like atmosphere of hippiedom, the media helped advertise these possible places for pilgrimage. Tourism flourished and provided fodder for a number of hippie-related stories during 1967.[23] In San Francisco, the Gray Line tour bus company began running daily commercial tours called the "Hippie Hop," which was described as "an immediate hit with tourists who thought the Haight-Ashbury was a human zoo."[24] (Hippies sometimes responded by focusing *their* binoculars on the passing tour bus inmates.) Significantly, this "human zoo" served as an attraction, much like the World's Fair had earlier, in subsequent runaway story constructions. Thus, in public discourse, counterculture areas such as Haight-Ashbury and the East Village became identified as a new draw, a new magnet—alluring destination points for runaway children.

In addition to their separate geographic communities and territories, hippies were clearly recognizable by the length of their hair and the way they dressed. Journalists delighted in describing hippie attire[25] and often did so objectively.[26] However, unconventional hippie appearance also served as a proxy for an array of other deviant behaviors and questionable social values. For example, immediately after asserting that "all pure hippies" have "long dirty hair," one journalist wrote: "And though many of them work—a number of them are postmen—and have cars, they do not like to pay their bills, so often the water is shut off in their pads, making it difficult for them to wash."[27] This passage rests on some extraordinary leaps in logic—from "long dirty hair" to a defective work ethic, irresponsible behavior in paying bills, and deficiencies in personal hygiene. However, this is not atypical of reporting by the "straight" press.

In the spring of 1967, in anticipation of the media-touted Summer of Love to take place in Haight-Ashbury, the New York Times published a story reporting that the city feared "a mass migration" of "would-be hippies" and that the resident hippies predicted "100,000 teenagers will flock here this summer to become hippies."[28] In a four-part series on the Haight, Golden subdivided the hippie population into "regular" and "summer-time" (or "part-time") hippies. He noted that the tension between "hippie regulars" and "part-timers" or "summer hippies" had resulted in a "social crisis of sorts." In the spring of 1967, these stories of summer-time, part-time, or would-be hippies substituted for the annual seasonal runaway story. Instead of fairs and beaches, runaway children (now labeled as a subset of older, more established hippies) were characterized as being attracted to the messages, activities, and culture of hippie communities.

This created a predictable problem for those constructing stories on runaway youth. Children who were once deemed easily recognizable by appearance now blended in with the disheveled, hairy hippie crowd. Police were no longer effective agents of social control. Once-harmless destinations (like the World's Fair) were replaced by dangerous, drug-infested, and morally suspect environments of the counterculture. Resources (such as "crash pad" shelters and free food, provided by the community) under-mined the notion that children would be driven home quickly from lack of resources. In short, the bedrock assumptions that upheld runaway story construction in the early 1960s eroded in 1967, requiring new conceptual-izations and formulations of prototypical runaways.

For example, in the fall of 1967, the disappearance of the 16-year-old daughter of a prominent New York State GOP leader instigated reports on massive search efforts for her in New York City's East Village. The episode and its coverage are interesting for at least three reasons. First, it triggered extensive police involvement. Two photographs of officers—one of patrol-men in Tompkins Square Park and the other of detectives questioning a man in front of a hippie business—provided a visual message that consid-erable police power, at two department levels, had been deployed to infil-trate the hippie neighborhood without much success. Readers were told that "dozens of detectives searched the East Village during the day, and all night," but the girl had not been found.[29]

Second, the story was reported five times over a two-week period, includ-ing on three consecutive days while the girl was still missing.[30] Within these three stories was information about other runaway girls (most of them still missing), suggesting this was all part of a much more widespread problem of straying girls. Third, hippie elders were not helping authorities in spite of the unwanted police and media attention the girl's disappearance was drawing to the community. They were not responding to the rewards offered for their cooperation. Said one, "A cop was in here and told us, 'There'll probably be a lot of bread [money] if you find her and if you don't want bread, you'll get any favor you want.'"[31] Said another, "I wouldn't turn her in. I'm not a bounty hunter."[32] Yet a third said, if he spotted her, he would advise her to call her mother. Even this hippie source was unwilling to cooperate directly with parents or police but rather would provide coun-sel to the runaway herself. Finally, another suggested he would "tell her to dye her hair."[33] Of course, doing so would permit her to blend further into the scene and avoid detection. Taken together, these factors undermined two of the ways runaways had been controlled (at least rhetorically) earlier in the decade: first through easy identification, and second because of coop-erative adults acting in supervisory roles.

Police pointed to both the lack of cooperation of the older hippies (e.g., "there's a code among kids to tell police nothing. It takes digging, and our men have to work hard to get kids to trust them and tell them about their friends") and the ease with which runaways blended into the counterculture scene. One police informant to the *New York Times* said, "pictures aren't much help. By the time they get here they may have grown their hair anyway. The pictures are usually six to eight months old."[34]

In a Sunday *New York Times Magazine* feature story on deteriorating conditions in Haight-Ashbury, the lead photograph occupies a full page-and-a-half spread and offers a panoramic view of a bulletin board in the San Francisco police station showing "pictures of runaway youngsters."[35] By a rough count there are easily at least one hundred photos, haphazardly posted one on top of the other. The *Times* spread makes its point. Photos of individual missing children were lost in the multitude and soon relegated to an untended corner of the police station.

From Linda to the Runaway Flower Child (October 1967)

Once again, the front-page of the *New York Times* serves as an excellent spot to observe the transformation of public concern toward runaways. It occurs, in microcosm, in the brilliant work of journalist J. Anthony Lukas. For four consecutive days in October 1967, the Lukas byline appeared on the front page of the *New York Times* in a series of stories that slowly melded older hippie discourse with the problem of younger runaways.[36]

On October 8, 1967, Linda Rae Fitzpatrick, the 18-year-old daughter of an affluent Connecticut family, and her hippie boyfriend—a colorful figure in the local counterculture community in his own right—were found brutally murdered in the basement of a decrepit tenement building in the East Village. The incident was first reported by Emanuel Perlmutter in a story with a headline that read, "Girl, Youth Slain in 'Village' Cellar: Handyman Finds Bodies—Girl Was from Wealthy Family in Greenwich."[37] The opening paragraph summarized the scene: "A teen-aged girl from a wealthy Connecticut family and a tattooed 21-year-old hippie were found beaten to death yesterday in the basement of a slum tenement in the East Village."[38] The important facts were there: wealthy family, teenage girl, adult hippie (tattooed no less), brutal death, East Village.

A week later, Lukas wrote a feature story on Linda, tracing the downward spiral leading to her grim death. The story was remarkable in all respects, and the article won Lukas a Pulitzer Prize. Its brilliance is not only in its detailed factual content but also in its ingenious design and meticulous construction.

It ran under the headline, "The Two Worlds of Linda Fitzpatrick." Lukas fully exploited the media-constructed notion that hippies belonged to an altogether different world from the one inhabited by the *New York Times*'s regular readers. He used the notion of Linda's two worlds, one in a wealthy Connecticut community and the other in the hippie territory of the East Village, to construct the entire story. The story alternated between the two worlds, using a visual trick of printing the East Village segments of the narrative in italics while the Connecticut segments were printed in roman type. The reader was always aware of which world he or she was in while reading.

Furthermore, Lukas only used informants rooted firmly in one world or the other. Any source that might have been able to explain the links between Linda's two worlds (such as a police officer or mental health professional) was noticeably absent. Instead, Lukas himself acted as a conduit between the two constructed worlds, conveying information back and forth between them. For example, in one segment Lukas described Linda's two bedrooms. To get to one, he climbed "dark and narrow" stairs "reek[ing] of marijuana" in a hotel for transients, only to observe a "sway-backed double bed," "peeling gray dresser, with the upper left drawer missing," "red plastic flowers . . . hung from an overhead light fixture," and communal bathroom. In contrast, in Connecticut he described climbing the "thickly carpeted stairway" to an "airy bedroom" with its "white, canopied bed," rock 'n' roll records, and a shelf holding "a ceramic collie and a glass Bambi." The contrasts become more and more chilling as the reader moves with Lukas along Linda's tragic path and through his article.

In the process of telling this story, Lukas revealed how oblivious Linda's parents were to their daughter's situation, and he generalized the story to "the thousands of youths who are leaving middle-class homes throughout the country." Essentially, he introduced the worst of hippie society to middle-class homes and certainly tapped into the fears of millions of American parents whose Baby Boomer children were beginning to strike out on their own.

Linda was not a runaway per se, although in 1967 her age still placed her below the legal age of majority in New York State. Over the next three days, however, the issue morphed under Lukas's pen. He followed up the Fitzpatrick exposé with three more articles, first calling into question the police's interest in her case, then linking police inadequacy with the runaway problem in general, and, finally, illustrating it in compelling detail in a parallel story about a 14-year-old runaway girl named Pamela Koeppel.

In the second of four articles, Lukas raised questions about the police's commitment to the Fitzpatrick case. A spokesperson defends the Police Department by pointing out that an arrest had already been made and that further "details about her life in the Village and statements by her friends and acquaintances" were "more or less irrelevant." The police were further quoted as saying that the department was "not interested in the girl's sociological background, what kind of life she had been leading or whom she knew" and that their job was to go after "the bare essentials" needed to make arrests. "We don't care," remarked a deputy inspector, "whether she was a speed freak or whether she knew warlocks." Given some historic distance, the police department offered a fair defense—its job was done; however, the words "we don't care" hung heavy in the context of the Lukas stories.

On the third day of front-page stories, Lukas linked police inadequacy dealing with runaways to the Fitzpatrick murder. A police officer "conceded" that "there was a 'hard-core' of runaways who were never found," but insisted the number was small and that the police were "working hard on the problem of young runaways in the Village" and were "returning many to their homes." This is similar to what police officers had said all along. However, unlike most earlier runaway articles, Lukas focused on the small segment of the population who remained missing permanently, rather than on the majority who were returned home.

Furthermore, he used hippie sources to confirm that runaways were "even less willing than most hippies" to talk to the police and that "they blended easily into the scene." While these hippie informants agreed that "the youthful naiveté of some newcomers" had made them "easy marks" for those who wanted to exploit them, they expressed doubt that the police were "equipped to deal with runaways" and suggested that "hippie institutions" such as local underground newspapers and the Diggers were more likely to gain the confidence of runaways and talk them into returning home.

Finally, Lukas's fourth front-page article ran under the headline "The Case of a Runaway Flower Child." Lukas narrated this "case" study from the perspective of the child's father, an interesting choice since the child in question, Pamela Koeppel, had returned home safely by the time the story went to press. Historically, the fact that runaways had returned home was comforting, and the child provided information for the account about his or her own adventure. Here, Pamela's voice was silenced and Lukas wrote that, from the moment of Pamela's departure, "her movements were unclear," as though access to her information was unavailable to him. It is a story of a father's race against an imaginary clock to save his daughter from the imminent danger that had confronted Linda Fitzpatrick in the East Village. Pamela's father had enlisted the help of friends, family, and police in his search, and he "called the *New York Times* in hopes that publicity would not only help find her, but also warn other parents of the difficulty in finding runaway girls." Thus, Lukas suggests that this case was representative of a large constituency of frantic parents concerned about missing daughters. He meticulously details four days of search efforts, which included trying to engage the police, scouring the Village and East Village several times, tracing Pamela's phone calls, and finally discovering the hotel phone number of a boy Pamela had been "seeing secretly," which led to brief police surveillance. It was at this point, according to Lukas, that Pamela, "apparently convinced that her flight was now useless," called her mother and returned home. Traveling alone, she took a train home.

Of note, the actual core facts of the story include that Pamela first ran to a friend's house, she phoned home three times, and she returned home on her own volition within four days. Lukas characterized the phone calls as being tantalizing to her parents, not reassuring. He discounted any resourcefulness or common sense that Pamela may have exhibited by finding safe shelter close to home. Finally, he wrote that her return home was inevitable because she had been caught. Earlier in the decade, these core behaviors (running to a friend's house, repeated phone calls home, returning home on her own) would have been characterized as harmless (and far from being newsworthy enough for the front page). It is ominous in this historic moment because this 14-year-old runaway "flower child" was in the vicinity (ideologically and physically) of Linda Fitzpatrick's dangerous world.

In addition to taking the parental perspective, the details of the search are interesting for four reasons. First, intensity and futility were underscored. Pamela's father emphasized how hopeless it was to search among the gathered crowds of young people in the East Village. Second, the police were only minimally helpful. Pamela's father was reported as saying that "the cops were so bored by the whole thing and when I got out to Washington Square, I realized why. There were more than a thousand people out there.... I realized we were facing a massive search." Third, finding Pamela was attributed to chance ("changed luck" and "blind luck"). Finally, Lukas described locating her on the "edge" of the Village and quoted her father as saying, "If she'd been really down in the heart of hippieland it would have been good-bye."

In short, Pamela was teetering on the brink of the counterculture abyss, but was saved by chance. In choosing to tell the story of a safely found runaway from the viewpoint of a frantic parent, Lukas shifted public perspective and ratcheted up public anxiety in a case that would probably not have received attention earlier in the decade. The narrative perspective changed from child to parent, story timing changed from successfully resolved runaway episodes to featuring missing children, and parents were cast in an active rather than passive role in conducting exhaustive searches for children.

In this four-day series, Lukas cultivated the notions of police inadequacy and crystallized the new rules of constructing the runaway problem. He cross-pollinated the problems of older, voluntary social dropouts with those of younger runaways. He focused on girls. There was a new emphasis on the dangers of running away, and an erosion in the traditional methods of social control through easy identification and benevolent police intervention.

Not surprisingly, in this rhetorical atmosphere and under these social conditions a generic runaway article toward the end of the year ran under the headline, "Homicides Swell 'Missing' Reports: Parents of Runaways Fear Children Are in East Village."[39] The headline reads like a *Cliff's Notes* version of all the concerns of the moment. It links homicides, missing persons, runaways, the East Village, and it takes the parental perspective.

The concern for missing children is confirmed by experts of all sorts. In another article, Rabbi Samuel Schrage, the assistant director of the NYC Youth Board, is quoted as saying, "There are thousands of parents all over the country who haven't heard from their kids for months" and glumly observes, "once gone, it's easier to find a pedigree dog in this country than a runaway kid."[40] It is the perpetual mobility that "makes it virtually impossible to find a youngster who is moving from place to place."[41] Furthermore, he argued that "the ghetto runaway had always been with us, today's runaway was increasingly a middle-class concern."[42] Thus the problem of street youth had moved up the social ladder, another factor in engendering public concern and media attention.

In 1967, of course, there were two demographic realities at play. First, by this time Baby Boomers had saturated all teenage years and, second, the initial group of Boomers was entering adulthood. At the same time, running away, which had once been characterized primarily as an intrafamily problem, was beginning to be labeled as an "acute" and "national" problem. The image of long-term and long-distance runaway youth replaced that of short-term local runaways. Perhaps this was to be expected, given that large numbers of young adults were beginning to leave their family home permanently. Nonetheless, several different phenomena were blended in public discussion.

Post-Hippie Discourse (1967–1972)

In the aftermath of the hippie phenomenon, runaway youth were characterized as a uniform population with common features that included the notion that they were street-based, vulnerable to exploitation, and subject to victimization. In particular, during the mid-1970s, runaways were increasingly linked to sexual exploitation. Children who were once described as returning home because of lack of resources were now assumed to be living on the street, on their own, and thus driven to survival sex or petty theft in order to meet their basic needs. Teenage girls engaged in prostitution, once described as a threat to the general welfare of the community earlier in the decade, were now characterized as victims of their circumstances. Thus, there is a transformation from the notion of these street-based behaviors as being immoral and deviant to interpreting them as acts necessary for survival. Social conditions, rather than individual moral failings, explained the behavior.

During the 1970s, two influential events—one a mass murder in Texas and another about an alleged "Minnesota Pipeline" (which was said to be supplying runaway Midwestern teenagers to New York City's sex trade industry)—came to epitomize the dangers of running away and were linked to sexual victimization. In mid-August 1973, Americans were shaken by the unearthing of the badly decomposed bodies of dozens of teenage boys outside Houston, Texas. The final body count reached twenty-seven, making it the largest serial murder in American history at that time.[43] Most of the murdered boys were runaways and had been reported missing by parents. Like the Linda Fitzpatrick murder in 1967, "Houston" would serve as a shorthand reminder in the press and in political circles for months to come of the dangers that could befall runaway children.

The Minnesota Pipeline was largely a New York City–based story. In the mid-1970s an area along midtown Manhattan's Eighth Avenue came to be known as the "Minnesota Strip." According to police officers, changes in Minnesota law that made the punishment of second offenses harsher had allegedly resulted in a mass migration of prostitutes to "New York's more hospitable climate."[44] The Minnesota Pipeline gained independent life as a news story. The mass migration of prostitutes was linked to underaged prostitution in general, and runaway girls specifically. Between November and December 1977, Selwyn Raab and Nathaniel Sheppard wrote eight stories addressing the "pipeline" controversy.[45] The stories on the pipeline were part of broader coverage on the efforts of Mayor Abraham "Abe" Beame and then mayor-elect Ed Koch's plan to root out the sex industry from midtown Manhattan.[46] Vulnerable runaway girls, victimized by exploitative pimps, proved to be useful currency in the political debate. Veronica Brunson's story was situated in the midst of this ongoing discussion.[47]

The pipeline was characterized as an organized network supplying runaway teenage girls for New York City's sex trade. As the pipeline story unfolded over two months in late 1977, it included the fact that two Minneapolis police officers were visiting the city on a rescue mission. They claimed they had come to locate and retrieve runaway girls and return them home safely.[48] With the press in tow, the officers arrived and searched Times Square but failed to locate a single Minnesota teenager. The officers responded by accusing the New York Police Department (NYPD) of sabotaging their efforts.[49] In the end, there seemed to be scant evidence for the existence of an organized pipeline. Nonetheless, it made interesting reading for a couple of months.

During this period, runaways were characterized as being seduced by "promises of love and affection" by pimps, and then "entrapped into prostitution" and taken to New York.[50] In a story that examined the first leg of their alleged journey from home to Minneapolis before coming to New York, the story's headline made the links explicit: "Teen-Age Runaways

Turn to Prostitution as Rebellion: Expectations of Adventure and Affection Lures Thousands of Midwestern Girls to Minneapolis."[51] Runaway girls were described as "longing for adventure and craving for the affections of men" and that sharing an "overwhelming sense of loneliness and boredom had made them easy prey for the smooth-talking pimps who wooed them with protestations of love and promises of fun and big money."[52] Interestingly, girls' "adventuring" behavior during this period is linked to stereotypic, gender-appropriate justifications such as looking for love, affection, and romance. Earlier in the decade, boys like Dean and Dominic were permitted to engage in adventures with no further explanation than they had a desire to explore.

Front-Page Prostituting Girls: Karen and Veronica (1972–1977)

Like the two front-page stories about adventuring boys in the early 1960s, the front-page stories of Karen Baxter[53] and Veronica Brunson[54] provide a 1970s bracket on the runaway issue. Both girls were characterized as coming from troubled homes and having serious problems in school. They were running *away* from home rather than being lured toward an attraction. Karen was described as coming from a family where her parents separated "on and off for 11 years"; her father was unemployed and her mother was a welfare recipient.[55] Her family lived "a kind of nomadic life-style" within a housing project apartment where six children had no "steady places to sleep."[56] Family fights and disputes with neighbors were reportedly common. Karen's "repeated truancy" from school finally led to court involvement, which triggered her decision to run away.[57] Similarly, Veronica came from a "fatherless" home, had a mother who could not control her, and had an extensive record of truancy.

In both cases, police officers had arrested the girls on prostitution charges and released them to the street before their deaths. The girls were described as looking older than their years, not carrying identification, and misleading officers as to their age and identity. In essence, police were excused from their once-central role in spotting and controlling runaways.

Both girls were murdered in the context of prostitution, Karen by a john and Veronica probably by her pimp. Veronica, who was pushed or fell out of a tenth-floor window, died after four days alone in a hospital because police couldn't locate her mother. A detective in Karen's case is reported as saying, "These kids, 15 and 16 years old, come here, don't know what they're getting themselves into and get exploited by pimps."[58] Veronica was described as a "familiar figure on the 'Minnesota strip.'"[59]

Both situations were typified and generalized. Karen was reported to be "one of a million juveniles who run away from home each year and one of thousands who come to New York City" who were "unable or unwilling to get legitimate jobs" and thus "turn to prostitution"; because they are "young, vulnerable, inexperienced," they become "easy prey."[60] She was described by one detective as being "representative of a whole slew of kids of her generation."[61] A homicide detective was unsympathetically quoted as saying, "There are a lot of them in the city. . . . The only difference is that this one is dead."[62] Raab wrote of Veronica Brunson: "[She] illustrate[s] the problems and dangers confronting thousands of runaway girls and boys who turn to prostitution to survive alone in the streets of New York."[63] In short, teenage prostitutes, at risk of exploitation and death at the hands of pimps and johns, became the typified runaway for public consumption. Said Officer Warren McGinniss of the police department's Youth Aid Division and a "specialist in runaways," Veronica's case was a "classic example of how a kid can float through the entire system without getting any help."[64]

Conclusion

As evident in the *New York Times*, there was a dramatic shift in the construction of runaway stories and thus in runaway discourse between 1960 and the late 1970s. In the early part of the 1960s, runaway adventures were characterized as safe, harmless, and predictable. Intervention by police (or other adults) was quick, in part, because runaways were so easy to identify by their dress or demeanor. If children weren't quickly caught by adults, they were forced back home by lack of resources (such as food or shelter). Children came from relatively happy homes or, at the very least, ones to which they could return. They did not go very far away or, if they did, they went to predictable places at predictable times of year (making intervention easier). Dean and Dominic made front-page news because they were atypical runaways (Dean because of the distance he traveled, and Dominic because of the length of time he avoided detection).

In the mid-to-late 1960s (with a crisis year in 1967), runaway discourse commingled with that on hippies. During this period, the story frame of the safe adventurer imploded as it mixed with discussions about wandering long-haired youth of the counterculture and its underground. Adventures were no longer safe. Children were drawn to counterculture areas (rather than to fairs and carnivals). Children could be gone for long periods of time, and they were not easy to identify because they blended into the counterculture scene. Adult hippies were uncooperative, and police no longer were effective agents of social control. In short, runaway children could vanish in the underground counterculture abyss and disappear forever. The earlier 1960s story frame of safe runaway adventures could not survive these new rhetorical and social conditions.

As public discussion on hippies receded, a newly constituted "typical" runaway emerged. This one represented an entire population of similarly situated children. This typical runaway was street-based, left home for long periods of time, and was in danger of exploitation and victimization. These runaways came from unhappy homes to which they were unwilling to return. So rather than being forced home by lack of resources (as in the early 1960s), these runaways were driven to "survival sex." Police were no longer able to thwart runaway episodes nor could they protect children. In fact, runaway youth were mostly on their own. Karen and Veronica were illustrative of this typical runaway. Given this newly constituted conceptualization, runaway youth emerged as a socially constructed public problem. Once framed in this way, it was a public problem that begged for the attention of the service provider and the policymaker alike. It received both.

Spinning Myths from Runaway Lives
A Hip Beat Version of Dropping Out

> One wonders what a modern version of "The Adventures of Huckle-
> berry Finn" would be like, or even if it would be permitted reading in
> our Nation's high schools.
>
> —Sen. Birch Bayh, Runaway Youth Act Hearings (1972)[1]

> With the coming of Dean Moriarty began the part of my life you could
> call my life on the road. Before that I'd often dreamed of going West to
> see the country, always vaguely planning and never taking off.
>
> —Jack Kerouac, *On the Road*[2]

Given the demographic dominance of teenagers and young adults during
the 1960s, it should not be surprising that American youth were holding
conversations among themselves about leaving home.[3] The discussions
included their own interpretative versions of running away, expressing
autonomy, and freeing themselves from authoritative supervision and control. Youth were anointing their own representatives, speakers, and spiritual leaders. The Establishment press, such as the *New York Times*, understood these messages only in part.

Various Views of Standing on a Street Corner: Beat, Digger, Straight

Among other things, the Diggers of Haight-Ashbury were interested in creating a new, or altered, *frame of reference*. They believed that if you convinced
enough people to participate in rethinking their own entrenched values and
ways of life, and to act on a new vision, a replacement society, a utopia perhaps, would emerge. It was this endorsement of an outsider perspective

that greased the wheel of freedom to act in accordance with one's own ideas, inspirations, and desires and to ignore or challenge the existing cultural, legal, and social norms and mores of American society. Digger historian Michael Doyle referred to this vantage point as an "itinerant outlaw posture."[4] Although Doyle refers to it as a "posture" (which it certainly was because it was primarily an assumed role), at its heart the "itinerant outlaw" is about a roaming, street-survivalist mentality that is the very essence of being Beat.

Obviously, the romance with flaunting cultural and social rules was not universally shared. From the straight world's perspective of responsible adults, this "itinerant outlaw posture" appeared to be a hybridization of bad behavior, delinquent acts, and social deviance. On the list of suspicious activities was sexual promiscuity, drug use, hanging out idly on the street for no apparent reason, kinship with outcasts and outlaws, dressing strangely and acting bizarrely, as well as engaging in activities and explorations of questionable meaning.

It should not be surprising, given these two decidedly different perspectives on youth behavior and values, that the hip world and the straight world would have some difficulty communicating with each other. In early 1967, at the onset of the hippie phenomenon, a *New York Times* journalist struggled to distinguish between New York's Greenwich Villagers and San Francisco's Haight-Ashbury "hippies" for its readers. From the start, the comparison was misplaced because the Haight hippies were much more akin to the young people collecting in New York City's East Village rather than to the older and more established bohemian inhabitants to the west in Greenwich Village. Nonetheless, the journalist writes: "Villagers are for things: non-involvement in Vietnam and Negro civil rights. Hippies are for nothing. 'Why can't I stand on a street corner and wait for nobody? Why can't everyone?'"[5] Apparently unbeknownst to this journalist, his source was paraphrasing a line from Beat poet Gregory Corso's poem, *Power*, written for Allen Ginsberg in 1956. The line actually reads:

Standing on a street corner waiting for no one is Power[6]

The article's "hippie" informant is, in all probability, a Digger and the line—which is used by the journalist as evidence that Haight-Ashbury hippies are "for nothing"—may be the closest thing Diggers had to an organizational philosophy.

Digger associates Emmett Grogan, Peter Coyote, and Jerry Rubin each referred to this line of poetry's importance to the movement. Each interpretation has its own distinct spin, but together they are telling. Grogan reported that Diggers "wanted to maintain their anonymity in the hope of achieving the kind of autonomy Gregory Corso talks about in his poem, *Power*."[7] Coyote is the most thoughtful in explaining the link to Digger philosophy:

> A big key was Gregory Corso's poem, *Power*, where he said: "Power is standing on a street corner doing nothing." Because what we were about was autonomy, finding what authentic, autonomous impulses were. And then being responsive to them, and not making excuses, not waiting for the revolution.[8]

While the *New York Times* equated "doing nothing" as being "for nothing," Coyote correctly interprets the poem as Corso's attempt to unravel true sources of power from false ones. For Corso, the deliberate and conscious act of waiting on a public street corner for no one was an act of personal autonomy. Unregulated, unfettered personal autonomy *was* power. For West Coast Diggers Grogan and Coyote, anonymity, coupled with autonomous action, provided the mechanism to transform the world, or at least challenge the status quo. It was the inspiration for a social revolution that was to be conducted through street theater (see chapter 4).

Although the West Coast Diggers might not willingly embrace Rubin as an authentic Digger, or what Grogan called "died-in-the-wool [sic] originals,"[9] Rubin and his colleague-in-action Abbie Hoffman nonetheless briefly associated themselves with the movement. They specialized in more notorious confrontational politics than those of the original San Francisco Diggers, who favored individual anonymity and engaging the general public as life players. So when Rubin used the Corso poem, it has its own East Coast Digger spin. He wrote:

> Watching the world from a street corner is loitering. Hitchhiking is a crime. It's against the law to panhandle, to rap to a crowd in the streets,

to give out free food in the streets, to stop traffic. . . . And when all else
fails, they establish a curfew, a Nazi law designed to prevent us from getting together.[10]

For Grogan and Coyote, autonomous action (including standing on a street
corner waiting for no one) was a source of power that came from doing
things because you believed they should be done, from taking control, from
taking action. For Rubin, issues of power were characterized as confronta-
tions with authority over socially constructed rules, particularly those regulating behavior that impinged on youths' autonomy. Rubin cites curfews,
loitering, and hitchhiking regulations as a direct assault on youths' freedom
of movement and assembly.

Taken together, these two interpretations of power reflect different facets
of growing up and claiming independence from adults. One involved
autonomy rooted in personal action and responsibility (and, as a consequence, being responsible for shaping one's own world); the other involved
being free from regulation or constraint imposed by authoritative rules (or
the values upon which the regulations rested). It is not surprising that these
various definitions of power and autonomy were being discussed in the
mid-1960s with particular rigor, given the fact that these Baby Boomer
spokesmen were making their developmental transitions past the regulated
and controlled days of their youth and into autonomous adulthood (see
table 3.1).

Interestingly, Corso, the Beat responsible for fathering these philosophical Digger musings, wrestled with his own relationship with being Beat
and his surrounding society in another poem entitled *Variations on a Generation*, which reads in part:

—I don't understand. I don't want to be in the society at all, I want to be
   outside it.—
—Face it, man, you're beat.—
—I am not! It's not even a conscious desire on my part, it's just the way I
   am, I am what I am.—
—Man, you're so beat you don't know.[11]

Corso implicitly distinguished Beatness as the way one is ("I am what I
am") from Beatness by choice ("conscious desire"). Corso himself wrote

Table 3.1

Individual	Year of Birth	Ages by Year										Year of Death
		1955	1956	1957	1958	1959	1960	1961	1962	1963	1964	
William Burroughs	1914	41	42	43	44	45	46	47	48	49	50	1997
Neal Cassady	1926	29	30	31	32	33	34	35	36	37	38	1968
Gregory Corso	1930	24	25	26	27	28	29	31	32	33	34	2001
Peter Coyote	1942	13	14	15	16	17	18	19	20	21	22	
Bob Dylan	1941	14	15	16	17	18	19	20	21	22	23	
Jerry Garcia	1942	13	14	15	16	17	18	19	20	21	22	1995
Allen Ginsberg	1926	29	30	31	32	33	34	35	36	37	38	1997
Emmett Grogan	1944	11	12	13	14	15	16	17	18	19	20	1978
Abbie Hoffman	1936	19	20	21	22	23	24	25	26	27	28	1989
Herbert Huncke	1915	40	41	42	43	44	45	46	47	48	49	1996
Jack Kerouac	1922	32	34	35	36	37	38	39	40	41	42	1969
Ken Kesey	1935	20	21	22	23	24	25	26	27	28	29	2001
Jerry Rubin	1938	17	18	19	20	21	22	23	24	25	26	1994

Ages of Influential Youth Authorities, Birth Year, Death Year, and Ages Between First Publication of *On the Road* (1957) and Reprints (Beginning in 1959)

about Beatness from firsthand experience. His personal background included being abandoned as an infant by his 18-year-old mother. Corso spent most of his early years moving from foster home to foster home. As an adolescent, he was arrested for minor offenses and incarcerated in adult facilities (not an uncommon experience at the time). He had limited formal education and was socialized to the street in his early teens.[12] Beginning as a teenager, he lived a quasi-homeless existence and learned to survive on the streets by himself. In short, his background reflected one typical of a street-acculturated runaway and homeless youth.

Corso's background is significant because he was Beat, because it was "what I am." Most of the rest of the prominent Beat writers were beat by "conscious desire." The writers were willing and able students; they were gifted writers and poets; but their primary inspiration came from those around them who were Beat by personal heritage. They were schooled into a Beat worldview through the tutoring of those who knew it firsthand. This tension between true Beat insiders and those temporarily appropriating the Beat lifestyle continued into the next generation, and youth discourse reflected both an insider and outsider perspective. However, what may seem like an abstract discussion had real consequences for authentic runaway youth of the next generation.

Separating "Died-in-the-Wool Originals" from Beat-by-Desire

The founding fathers of the Beat movement (Jack Kerouac, Allen Ginsberg, and William Burroughs) met in the mid-1940s when Kerouac and Ginsberg were attending Columbia University and Burroughs, a Harvard graduate, was living in New York. The group was joined early on by Herbert Huncke, a Times Square junkie who supplied drugs and colorful tales to the aspiring writers. In 1946, Neal Cassady joined the group, becoming one of Kerouac's primary muses, his travel companion, and, briefly, Ginsberg's lover. Joined by John Clellon Holmes, Carl Solomon, and finally, in 1950, by Gregory Corso, this group of men constituted the original nucleus of the Beat movement.[13]

Huncke and Cassady, while only minor writers, were nonetheless integral and inspirational figures for the Beats and have been described as "muses and Virgilian guides."[14] Ginsberg confessed to eventually seeing Huncke and Cassady as "metaphors."[15] Yet these "metaphors" that defined "beat" were extracted from real life and lived experiences. Both Huncke and Cassady were children of the streets—genuine runaways—whose childhood experiences and subsequent life trajectories informed and permeated the very notions of Beat.

As part of a foreword to an anthology of Huncke's writings, William Burroughs wrote that

> Huncke had adventures and misadventures that were not available to middle-class, comparatively wealthy college people like Kerouac and me. . . . Huncke had extraordinary experiences that were quite genuine. He isn't a type you find anymore.[16]

Burroughs was wrong about Huncke being a "type" you can't "find anymore." They are still out there: runaway, quasi-homeless and homeless children from troubled families, growing up on their own and learning to negotiate the streets in order to survive. What distinguished Huncke from today's runaway street child was his association with an eager and talented group of Ivy League–educated writers.

In the hands of the Beat writers, Huncke and Cassady were "transformed into literary icons"[17] and their lived experiences into myth. In the process of their literary canonization, features of hard-core, street-acculturated runaway existence were absorbed and promoted.[18] The next generation of Baby Boomer consumers would be inspired by these ideas. Yet the metaphors that were extracted from Huncke's and Cassady's lives were familiar life experiences for any "died-in-the-wool" authentic runaway youth.

From Runaway Existence to Beat Metaphor

Herbert Huncke's Vantage Point

Herbert Huncke is credited with introducing the term *beat* to Jack Kerouac, who used it in an interview with John Clellon Holmes, who used it in his book *Go*,[19] and which ultimately led the *New York Times* to request that Holmes write an article for the magazine section which was entitled, "This Is the Beat Generation."[20] The label stuck.[21]

Both Ginsberg and Kerouac offered an interpretation of Huncke's use of the word *beat*. According to Ginsberg, Huncke's "original street usage" included being "exhausted, at the bottom of the world, looking up or out, sleepless, wide-eyed, perceptive, rejected by society, on your own, street-wise."[22] According to Kerouac, "The word 'beat' originally meant poor, down and out, deadbeat, on the bum, sad, sleeping in subways," although it was extended to "include people who do not sleep in subways, but have a certain new gesture, or attitude."[23] From the college-educated, middle-class perspective, it was a new and fascinating vantage point from which to explore the world, and it offered a position from which to challenge the values and norms of American society. It was an interesting, but mostly voluntary, flirtation with rootlessness, homelessness, and poverty.

Huncke received full credit for his role in both naming the movement and inspiring its writers in his *New York Times* obituary. Its headline called him "the Hipster Who Defined 'Beat,'" and his photograph's caption reads "inspiration for Beat writers." The text says he "enthralled and inspired a galaxy of acclaimed writers," who were described as "an aspiring, Columbia-centered literary crowd" who were "soon learning at Mr. Huncke's feet."[24]

In addition to Huncke's influence, the *New York Times* elaborated on Huncke's character, calling him a "charismatic street hustler, petty thief and perennial drug addict" and noting he would steal "virtually anything he could get his hands on throughout his life and never once apologizing for a moment of it."[25] Huncke himself aptly named his autobiography *Guilty of Everything*.[26] He characterized himself as "a wastrel, a thief, a bum, a chisler—a petty small time character not even good in amounting to anything." "All this," the *New York Times* obituary summarized, "for a teen-age runaway who said he was using drugs as early as 12" and "selling sex by the time he was 16."[27]

Huncke, a high school dropout, lived the classic life of a runaway until he met his Beat friends and benefactors.[28] According to Huncke, "As soon as I was old enough to manage even a little bit, I ran away."[29] He first fled his Chicago home at the age of 12, and "never told anybody I was running away. I had picked up a road map at a filling station, and had decided to say I was going to the next big city" (229). He wrote of his adventure: "It was just fantastic. I felt so free and light; all my shackles were suddenly dropped" (228).

En route to New York City, his trip ultimately ended in Geneva, New York. Huncke reported: "I neglected myself pretty badly. My hair got long . . . it was unkempt. My shirt had gotten dirty and rumpled, and I guess I must have looked strange, standing there on the highway thumbing a ride" (229). He wrote, "Eventually somebody in town had seen me and reported me to the police. These towns, they know everybody. It was obvious that I certainly didn't belong in Geneva. All of a sudden, zoom, here comes the motorcycle cop alongside me" (230). The cop took him to the local jail and, after sufficiently humiliating the young Huncke, got him to confess he was from Chicago. The next morning his father arrived to pick him up.

Whether poetic license or not, Huncke's tattered appearance (and perhaps demeanor) marked him as a runaway for the vigilant eye of adult authorities in a small town and put an end to his freedom. His adventure was frustrated according to the rules of social control of runaways in his day, and he landed in a local jail until his father retrieved him. It was the kind of ending expected of a runway adventure during the 1940s and 1950s.

Like most runaways, Huncke had a family life that was less than idyllic. His relationship with his divorced parents was complicated. Years later, in a painful letter addressed "Dear Dad" (dated March 23, 1949), Huncke revealed some of that complexity.[30] It included passages describing an abusive relationship:

As a young boy—I was quite frightened of you. I felt your punishments were sometimes unjust—and, incidentally, I still regard some instances in the same light; . . . When I became a young man—I no longer feared you. The predominant reaction was one of dislike. I thought you were cruel and unkind—deliberately. Now I realize that was not so—oh, of course, I don't doubt that occasionally you permitted yourself a bit of sadistic indulgence.[31]

Huncke described his relationship with his mother as being "more in the nature of an older woman and young man" than "mother and son."[32]

In his journal, Huncke described fondly the "adventures and strange experiences" he had wandering the streets of Chicago as a teenager, unsupervised, late at night where he met "lonely people—misfits—outcasts—wanderers—those on the skids—drunkards—deviates of all kinds—hustlers of every description—male and female" coming from "every section of the country."[33] Among these outcasts was one "very sick and well along toward maniacal"[34] man who lured 14-year-old Huncke into an isolated area in a park, brandished a stack of child pornography, and had a sexual encounter with him. Although, as an adult, Huncke described the event with some detached fascination, in later decades and in other forums (political, media, etc.), this kind of interaction would be interpreted for public consumption as the exploitation of a vulnerable runaway street kid.[35]

In his early twenties, Huncke moved to New York City and found "a psychic home in Times Square."[36] He described his instantaneous affiliation to the sleazy Times Square scene:

> I loved it immediately. . . . I felt as though I blended in in some way so
> that people weren't staring at me, and that I could walk down the street
> and hold my head up without having to look away.[37]

Thus he found home and community in the street subculture under the watchful eye of indigenous law enforcement agents who found reasons to arrest him periodically.

Even allowing room for the poetic license of a born storyteller, these assorted facts—Huncke's troubled home life, dropping out of high school, his early initiation to drugs and sex in street-based circumstances, his early and repeated flights from home, his attachment to the urban street scene, and his sense of finally belonging and blending in to the street subculture— are consistent with the lifestyle of runaway street youth.

Huncke, of course, never outgrew his background. In fact he reveled in it until his death. In his letter to his father, Huncke admitted his motivation for writing had "nothing to do with some vague notion of reform or of a desire particularly to change my ways. I'm too completely beat for that." The *New York Times* labeled Huncke "unrepentant, a man whose acceptance of crime as his fate bolstered his friends' views that he was a victim of a rigid, unfeeling society."[38] Of course, his adult lifestyle was consistent with everything he had learned from the age of 12. Herein is a tension that continues to exist in discussions of street youth. Are they driven to criminality in order to survive, and are therefore victims? Or are they bad kids from the start? Should Huncke have outgrown his streetwise survivalist ways simply as a matter of aging? Or was he too beat by nature? Was he the casualty or product of a rigid, unfeeling society as his Beat friends would claim?

Kerouac picked up on this tension in his understanding of the word "beat" as described by his biographer, Ann Charters:

> Kerouac was fascinated by the tone of the word "beat" as Huncke said it
> hunched over a cup of coffee in a Times Square cafeteria. Kerouac heard
> a "melancholy sneer" in the sound of Huncke's voice that Kerouac later

insisted "never meant juvenile delinquents,". . . but rather "meant characters of a special spirituality who didn't gang up but were solitary. Bartlebies staring out the dead wall window of our civilization."[39]

What the Beats attempted to capture in their writing wasn't the juvenile delinquency component of a Beat existence but rather its survivalist quality, its "spirituality," its "solitary" nature, and the social insight that came from taking stock of the world from the fringe.[40] Burroughs introduced Huncke's autobiography by saying, "The protagonist is thrown into the water to sink or swim. So he learns something about the water."[41] The point was to become aquatic, which required both art and skill. Runaway or throwaway youth who find themselves out on their own, like Huncke, must devise methods to manage survival in the street subculture. Frequently that includes engaging in assorted petty crimes and illegal behaviors.

What is particularly interesting about Burroughs's observation is that it is the "water"—the entire street subculture—that fascinated the Beats and it is what they attempted to capture in their metaphoric use of Huncke's life. They did so, however, at the relatively safe distance of being voluntary participants. Learning how to hustle, deal, and otherwise maneuver the street is a trajectory familiar to most genuine homeless street youth. For Huncke, knowing "the water" was an act of survival. He was both knowledgeable and skillful.

This is an important distinction because the Beats reinterpreted what straight society considered acts of delinquency (including prostitution, petty theft, loitering, drug-taking) as acts of survival, of spirituality, and of an alternative vantage point. Thus, a teenage prostitute or street hustler, in Hunke's day, was characterized as immoral, wayward, and delinquent. By the early 1970s this same behavior was characterized as necessary acts of survival and the public's gaze shifted to condemning those who exploit street-based youth rather than faulting youth for their own bad and immoral behavior. The shift in public perception is one the original Beats would have both approved of and been amused by.

Neal Cassady's Perpetual Motion

If Huncke named the Beat Generation, Neal Cassady must be credited for influencing its style,[42] embodying its very spirit, and providing the personal link between the Beats and the psychedelic counterculture scene of the next generation.

Neal Cassady's legend looms larger than his life. The Cassady myth is recorded in literature, poetry, music, film, and photographs. In addition to Beats Kerouac, Ginsberg, and Holmes, he captured the imaginations of Ken Kesey, Thomas Wolfe, and the Grateful Dead, among others. Perhaps the most predominant allegorical features of the Cassady myth include perpetual motion and intense velocity, a combination that suggests inevitable combustion.

Digger Emmett Grogan described Cassady as "a gypsy-traveler with no money in any bank" and as a man "who lived his life with a velocity that . . . would have killed most men twenty years younger."[43] Cassady had an "unequaled tolerance for alcohol and drugs"[44] as well as an equally insatiable sexual appetite for women and, occasionally, men. He was willing to experiment, with just about anything, any time, anywhere, with wild abandon.

Consistent with both reality and the image of a "gypsy traveler," photographers, writers, and lyricists of the period repeatedly captured or reported images of Cassady behind the wheel of moving vehicles (cars, buses, trains).[45] There are more than a few photographs of Cassady, his head slightly turned in profile, snapped by backseat passengers. He is usually described as drunk,[46] stoned, or otherwise high. For example, a Ginsberg journal entry labeled "With Neal":[47]

> . . . speeding up
> "Bloody Bayshore,"
> the ribbon of death,
> Tossing beer cans
> out of the window
> Beating on the dashboard
> smoking tea
> radio blaring among the cars.

Drinking, drugging, restless movement that included a speeding vehicle and "beating on the dashboard," flirting with "the ribbon of death"—all at a volume that seemed to dwarf those surrounding Cassady—is typical of the myth that surrounds him. Jerry Garcia of the Grateful Dead reported that riding in a vehicle piloted by him "was to be as afraid as you could be, to be in fear for your life."[48]

Even Cassady's critics, like William Burroughs,[49] confirmed his inherent passion for movement. In a letter to Ginsberg denigrating the Kerouac-Cassady cross-country adventure that became material for *On the Road*, Burroughs described Cassady:

> Neal is, of course, the very soul of this voyage into pure, abstract, meaningless motion. He is The Mover, compulsive, dedicated, ready to sacrifice family, friends, even his very car itself to the necessity of moving from one place to another. Wife and child may starve, friends exist only to exploit for gas money. . . . Neal must move.[50]

In the postscript of a letter to Kerouac dated January 28, 1951, Burroughs mused, "I can not understand Neal's passion for travel. . . . What does he do to eat?"[51] Burroughs's critique is nearly unique among the galaxy of admirers who orbited Cassady.[52]

If Burroughs did not understand Cassady's inherent, inbred need to move, Cassady's often-abandoned wife, Carolyn, did. She forgave his cross-country tripping as the inevitable consequence of his upbringing: "At the time, I thought he was deserting me, but later I realized that in his eyes he was being perfectly responsible, because he had no personal knowledge of normal family life. He didn't have the same frame of reference that most people had."[53] Overwhelming evidence for her assessment that her husband had no personal knowledge of normal family life is found in Cassady's own writing. He described his early childhood, including his warm relationship with an alcoholic transient father, his physically and emotionally abusive older brothers, and—through almost total omission—his nonexistent relationship with his mother.

In essence, Cassady began his homeless career at the age of six, when he and his father moved into the "Metropolitan," which "housed about a hundred of Denver's non-transient bums."[54] There, he said that "for a time I held a unique position. Among the hundreds of isolated creatures who haunted the streets of lower downtown Denver, there was not one so young as myself."[55] Because of this unique position growing up among "dreary men who had committed themselves . . . to the task of finishing their days as pennyless [sic] drunkards," he "became the unnatural son of a few score beaten men" (1).

Cassady slept "side by side" with his father in a "bed without sheets" in a room shared with a double amputee named "Shorty" (4, 7). He described using a communal bathroom where bums labored to shave with "the shakes" and eating meals—alone if his father was "laid up drunk"—at the "Citizen's Mission," a "Protestant church organization" where Cassady noted he "was its youngest member by a good dozen years" (8–9, 15). Cassady attended grade school, although his father was "wise enough" to provide school officials with his mother's home address. "This sort of lie," Cassady reported, "became habitual" (6). He grew up listening to the "tete-a-tetes" of "drunkard[s] whose minds, weakened by liquor and an obsequious manner of existence" represented the "collective intelligence of all America's bums" and "through sheer repetitious hearing" Cassady came to "understand as they understood" (2). Thus, like Huncke, Cassady was socialized and indoctrinated into the street subculture in early childhood. He learned how to negotiate his survival from those who scrounged, and he grew up learning to appreciate observing life from the fringe.

Cassady's father introduced his son to the art of tramping (by train and hitchhiking) when he was six and the two traveled thousands of miles, crisscrossing the country, on several occasions. They "bummed off" with "no special plan in mind" but rather "just go until stuck, work, then on again" (66). Cassady learned how to pick shelter for the night in hobo encampments ("the main thing was to be near water and wood") (34), to panhandle ("I thought the value of my presence while panhandling was overemphasized, yet I saw we always managed to eat though the others often did not") (34), and about communal existence among the community of tramps ("everyone generally agreed to get what they could" and "share it as community potluck") (34). Thus Cassady learned not only about tramping but also about the importance of communal property for survival. Burroughs complained about Cassady's adult behavior:

> I suspect he feels that others are under some mysterious *obligation* to support him. Most inveterate moochers are convinced that while they have no obligations towards anyone else ("owe nothing to anybody"—Huncke) that others have a moral obligation to supply their needs.[56]

Cassady's "inveterate mooching" could be seen as a survival skill learned in early childhood. Like Huncke, this sort of socialization, including expecting others to help support *his* freedom, started early in childhood.

In part because Cassady's father "being usually drunk, or trying to get that way" was "of necessity a bit lax in his discipline,"[57] Cassady grew up with what he calls "unorthodox freedoms" for "American boys of six" (3). The net result was that, like Huncke, Cassady learned to love the streets and explored them endlessly. "The city was to become my playground" he wrote, and he became "so bewitched" by "going Junking"—searching "trash receptacles" for "bottles and anything else of value"—that he developed his "scavengering [*sic*] into regular weekend tours" of "Denver's alleys" (33, 20). Like street youth of the mid-nineteenth century, Cassady turned this "junking" into pocket money.

Cassady described two noteworthy childhood memories. The first involved his "private ritual" of reading "all legible signatures" in the "incoming lodgers' rent" ledger at the Metropolitan in order "to guess by their sound which names were aliases" and compare the "towns and states" they registered "on the huge map" (17). The second story recounted the terrifying moment when a young Cassady found himself alone in a moving boxcar full of tramps and separated from his father, who had left the train in search of water. He wrote: "I strained to unfreeze my 6 1/2 year-old mind so as to hurdle the worry of finding the route home, yet I never formulated anything, since geographically I could hardly half plan" (39). Much to his relief, his father eventually reappeared, having hopped the moving train several cars behind. However, these two stories, read together, suggest a child who through both inclination and necessity began learning how to contemplate and negotiate traveling long distances very early in life.

Cassady's admiration for his father never dimmed, and looking back he wrote he saw a "certain bravery" even in his father's drunkenness (30). Unfortunately, from Cassady's perspective, this "happier life" (66) was interspersed with episodes of living with his mother and his "sadistic" older brothers and stepbrothers. He admitted his mother's home was "quite an improvement on the Metropolitan" except for the abuse he suffered in it (56). This abuse was physical (and included being folded into a Murphy bed and being too terrorized to scream) (57) as well as emotional (including threats of violence and demonstrations of cruelty against his father[58] and animals).[59]

By his own description, Cassady's rootless homelessness continued into his teenage years. In a letter to Kerouac he recalled: "every nite [sic] I'd sleep in some apt. bathtub and get up and find some friends place to eat then steal a car to pick up girls at school when they got out.[60] By Cassady's own— probably inflated—estimation, between the ages of 14 and 21 he had stolen five hundred cars (including a short-lived joyride in a district attorney's car when he was 15)[61] to entice girls to join him in what he called "Adventures in Auto-Eroticism,"[62] and he had been arrested ten times, convicted six times, and spent fifteen months in reform schools.[63] In a letter to Kerouac (dated July 3, 1949), Cassady provided an account of his angry and delinquent teenage years, including details about smashing a high school principal's chair, stealing chickens, stealing "anything we saw," buying a Buick (which "couldn't pass the brake and light inspection" so hitchhiking out-of-state to steal license plates), getting "accosted" en route by "a nosy sheriff who must have thought I was pretty young to be hiking," which landed Cassady in jail yet again.[64]

Cassady's childhood, like Huncke's, shared many features classically associated with runaway youth, including a substance-abusing parent, a reconstituted family, physical and emotional abuse, multiple unstable and traumatic home environments, jail time for bad behavior and delinquent acts, early quasi-homelessness, and socialization and attachment to street subcultures. Cassady's sense of justified entitlement (which so irritated Burroughs) is understandable given the fact he was responsible for crafting his own system of survival before reaching his teenage years.

Furthermore, like Huncke, the diverse constructions, characterizations, and assessments of Cassady's life (including being a psychopath, inveterate moocher, or gypsy traveler) all make sense if understood as the life trajectory of a street child. If Huncke's lifetime hustling was a natural extension of street survival skills learned in childhood, Cassady's perpetual movement, communal lifestyle, and serious drug and alcohol addictions are the life trajectory of a child socialized in the world of tramps and alcoholic bums. Like Huncke's, Cassady's life became a myth in the hands of others, and his genuine experiences served as primary source material. Since Cassady is best known for his adventures at the wheel, it is fitting he would become an updated Huck Finn and a role model, of sorts, for American Baby Boomers who were just getting old enough to leave the family nest.

On the Road

Given Cassady's passion for movement, it is not surprising that his most notable associations with two popular writers of the period involve cross-country trips. The first was with Jack Kerouac in 1949 from the East Coast to the West Coast, which provided Kerouac with his subject matter for *On the Road,* in which Cassady appears as Dean Moriarty. The second, with Ken Kesey and his Merry Pranksters[65] in 1964, was an "acid-fuelled cross-country trek"[66] from west to east.[67] The Grateful Dead recorded Cassady's role at the helm:

> The bus came by and I got on,
> that's when it all began.
> There was cowboy Neal, at the wheel,
> of the bus to never ever land.

In an interview, Kesey responded to a reporter's question about the genesis of the Merry Prankster's trip: "For a lot of us," he said, "it started when we first read *On the Road*. That's why it's so beautiful that we have Cassady driving."[68] Cassady was the embodiment of exploration, restless movement, and constant "tripping," both in the physical and in the chemically altered sense as the discussion moved from one generation to the next. For many, like Kesey, it all started with *On the Road*.

Kerouac's *On the Road* was hailed by some critics as an updated Huckleberry Finn and a significant literary contribution. Others found little to like in it, as illustrated by an entry from the *Americana* encyclopedia's 1958 annual supplement, which reported that the book recorded "the half-literate comments of a group of self-conscious delinquents, addicted to traveling at high speed between New York and San Francisco, and given to jazz, dope, and the lunatic fringe of sex."[69] Of course, therein lies much of its intrigue for youth. Furthermore, it is evidence of the great divide between characterizing the behavior as delinquency (as defined by the adult, straight world) and adventure (as conceptualized by the mobile Beat wanderers of the hip world).

On the Road immediately took its place in a genre of work on disaffected and rebellious youth of the 1950s, alongside books like J. D. Salinger's

Catcher in the Rye (1951), and movies such as *The Wild One* (1954) starring Marlon Brando and *Rebel Without a Cause* (1955) featuring James Dean. *On the Road* separated the adult world of responsibility from the wild world of the young and the reckless. Its characters insisted on absolute freedom and autonomy without guilt or responsibility. It was an anthem to perpetual motion. It modeled the image of American youth on the move. It reinvented, reinterpreted, and reinvigorated the American runaway. Almost overnight, *On the Road* became a cultural phenomenon.

On the Road could not have been better timed, or perhaps its success was due in part to its timing. First published in 1957, it was reprinted in 1959 (twice), 1960, 1961, 1962, 1963, 1965, 1966, 1968 (twice), 1969, 1970 (twice), 1971 (twice), 1972 (twice), 1973, 1974, 1975, and 1976. In short, it provided a growing-up handbook for a generation of American Baby Boomers, and the Beat message, culled from street youth experiences, was disseminated to them. If youth of the 1960s were not weaned directly on *On the Road*, they were certainly exposed to the ideas, values, and spirit it embodied. It influenced and inspired some important and vocal youth leaders of the next generation such as Bob Dylan, Ken Kesey, and John Lennon, to name but a few.

Moving On

The younger generation borrowed, reinterpreted, and expanded—as offspring are wont to do—the Beat message. Dropping out, partying, hitchhiking, bumming along, and experimenting with drugs and sex captured the imagination of hippies, rockers, rebels, and others. The Beat worldview, originally shared at poetry readings with small audiences gathered in cafes and bookstores, was repackaged in the form of rock music lyrics. The record industry capitalized on the lucrative Baby Boomer market and the affluence of the 1960s, disseminating youthful messages of movement, exploration, and life on the fringe to an even wider audience of American youth.

This new youth discourse ridiculed the straight world's notion of delinquency. To be hip in this romantic vision included viewing the world from an alternative position and under the influence of mind-altering drugs—opposing rules, challenging authority, tripping, and dropping out. At the heart of the rhetoric and behavior, however, were claims of unfettered personal autonomy.

For a brief period in the late 1960s, counterculture meccas such as Haight-Ashbury became the hotspots of this discourse as well as the host of the party. Not surprisingly, such areas temporarily attracted a mix of voluntary social dropouts—those with the "conscious desire" to be Beat—and with genuine street-acculturated runaway youth who were Beat because it was the "way they were." During this commingling of discourses (on beat, hip, independence, morality, deviance, etc.) and the intermingling of diverse populations of youth (including runaways, hippies, Beats, and the like) comes a significant transformation in public understanding and tolerance for street youth. Runaways (the youngest of these seekers) appear vulnerable and exploitable and are driven to deviant acts to meet their basic survival needs in this new environmental context. The public came to accept (or at least temporarily tolerate) the hip world's sympathy for the youngest outlaws and its reverence for those with the basic skills necessary to negotiate a Beat lifestyle successfully.

Psychedelic Social Workers
and Alternative Services

Digger Free

Power in Autonomy, Independence in a
Free City Network (1966–1968)

No one ever taught you how to live on the street
Now you're just goin' have to get used to it . . .

—Bob Dylan, "Like a Rolling Stone" (1965)

See that girl, barefootin' along . . .
. . . She's a neon-light diamond and she can live on the street

—The Grateful Dead,
"The Golden Road (to Unlimited Devotion)" (1967)

The street is a brutal parent.

—Reverend Bruce Ritter,
"Rescuing Homeless Children," *NYT* (12/25/1983)

Street-based Revolution:
Tenants of the Streets, Minor Saints of the Intersection

The epicenter of the 1960s counterculture scene was San Francisco's
Haight-Ashbury district. Influential acid rock groups like the Grateful
Dead, Jefferson Airplane, and Country Joe and the Fish as well as the popular avant-garde San Francisco Mime Troupe, and its offspring the Diggers,
added to the festivity. However senseless the acid-fueled party may have
appeared to the Establishment, amid the seemingly frivolous partying and
merrymaking, a fairly serious critique of American life and lifestyle was
occurring. The goal for at least some was social change, and the target was

the American system and its general way of life. Social rebels in the Haight disseminated their messages through the media, street theater, communication broadsides, and the underground press.[1]

In particular, the ideas and actions of the Diggers had a profound impact on the flavor of the sixties counterculture.[2] Although Haight-Ashbury was the fertile crescent of this movement, the Diggers disseminated their message and modeled their lifestyle for national public consumption. Digger rhetoric and ideology (to the extent it could be called that) spread through the underground, and Digger ideas were mimicked[3] in the United States and in Canada.

Counterculture communities in general and Haight-Ashbury in particular sounded a direct call and provided a compelling lure to runaway youth. Runaways were drawn, in part, by the utopian suggestion that an ideal kind of family could be acquired by conscious choice rather than by biological chance. Hippie colonies and communes promised peace and love to a population of youth who had little of either. They promised brotherhood and a substitute family to youth who had experienced unhappy and unstable family backgrounds. They offered alternative forms of education to children who had struggled in traditional school settings. They legitimized drug use for youth that were looking for ways to escape. They promised the freedom to "do your own thing" to a population that prematurely sought independence, yet also provided a network of adult caretakers worried about their safety. They elevated street life to an ideal worthy of pursuit to youth with few other options. Finally, they seemed to offer resources for survival and protection against traditional impediments to premature independence and autonomy, including the authoritative intervention of police, parents, and child protection agencies. Runaways responded in part because these communities seemed a compelling substitute for what they had known. They provided an attractive lure similar to the beaches, fairs, and carnivals identified earlier in the decade.

For runaway children gathering in counterculture areas, however, there was also a darker side. It included the kinds of risks always present for street-based youth trying to survive on their own, such as being subject to exploitation and victimization. A scathing Digger broadside, distributed in Haight-Ashbury in April 1967, opened with this chilling paragraph involving two minors:

Pretty little 16 year-old middle class chick comes to the Haight to see what it's all about & gets picked up by a 17 year-old street dealer who spends all day shooting her full of speed again & again, then feeds her 3000 mikes and raffles off her temporarily unemployed body for the biggest Haight Street gang bang since the night before last.[4]

While there was a group of free spirits gathering to create an alternative society grounded in communal family and brotherly love, there was the ever-present mix of those who were willing to exploit the most vulnerable and those who were there because living on the streets was the only option they had.

By the summer of 1967 there was a storm brewing with respect to the accumulation of unattended runaway youth. It was the Diggers who first felt responsible for these younger dropouts, and it was the Diggers who modeled a solution. Ultimately, even as the Digger movement withered away, their solution for providing comprehensive alternative support to street-based youth (all for free) gained a life of its own.

Diggers Defined, More or Less:
Psychedelic Social Workers, Radical Social Activism and Street Theater

In 1965 the San Francisco Mime Troupe, founded by R. G. Davis, took its socially and politically provocative performances into public parks. They soon became part of the Haight cultural scene. Davis advocated a "three-pronged program: 'teach, direct toward change, [and] change.'"[5] In 1966, twenty or so players left the San Francisco Mime Troupe and called themselves Diggers, a name they borrowed from a short-lived English utopian socialist movement of the seventeenth century.[6] The Diggers borrowed the tool of free theater and reinterpreted Davis's mission to "teach, direct toward change, [and] change." Diggers[7] took their performances beyond the public parks used by the Mime Troupe and *onto* public streets and *into* activities of daily living. They made street theater the tool of their own radical social revolution.

Diggers denied their work was street theater per se;[8] instead they claimed that the street *is* theater, consisting of ordinary events that focused public attention (i.e., "parades, bank robberies, fires and sonic explosions").[9] Players were life-actors performing on liberated ground, and the audience for an event was whatever existing crowd was hanging around. They "attempted to remove all boundaries between art and life, between spectator and performer, and between public and private."[10] Thus, public street corners, parks, and other "liberated" spaces constituted the Diggers' stage but were also their playground and battlefield. Their goal was to engage others in first contemplating, and then participating in, a new frame of social, political, economic, and cultural reference. In doing so, Diggers borrowed an outsider "frame of reference," a vantage point with its roots in being Beat, and then infused it with a social and political agenda.

Although Diggers did not produce a universal manifesto, Digger philosophy and method can be cobbled together from a collection of their writings, including autobiographies, interviews, and many contemporaneous broadsides, which were mimeographed by the hundreds by the free press arm of the Digger collective (known as the Communication Company or Com/co), and distributed on the streets of San Francisco. Chester Anderson was a self-proclaimed Digger and the cofounder of Com/co. Although others characterize his intentions as "arrogantly coercive,"[11] which put him directly at odds with the "free" participation central to Digger philosophy, in a handwritten note in the archives at Berkeley's Bancroft Library, Anderson provided a definition of the Diggers. In doing so he offers a place to start.

> [Diggers are] a non-organization of radical hippies. They believe + practice *freedom*—which includes feeding the hungry, clothing the naked, sheltering the homeless, befriending the stranger, + etc. all for free, that being their thing. . . . The diggers have Dropped Out. Abandoned the establishment + especially its values. Very radical, very active, very political. I'm one.[12]

There is much in Anderson's definition to contemplate that is consistent with commentaries by others associated with the Haight-Ashbury Diggers. Diggers considered themselves part of a "non-organization." Not only was there no organizational structure, there were no leaders. Diggers relied on the autonomous actions of a collection of anonymous individuals.[13] As a January 1967 Com/co broadside announced: "My leader is me or else I'm not a free man, and freedom is what this whole thing is all about."[14] Self-appointed or self-proclaimed leaders violated the Digger notion of autonomy because leadership resulted in imposing one's vision on someone else. Individual freedom and noninterference were central.

Undoubtedly the best descriptive label of the movement is offered by Digger historian Michael Doyle, who calls them "a freewheeling anarchist collective,"[15] which captures the individuality as well as the collective and radical spirit of the Diggers' activities. Given that Diggers were a leaderless "non-organization," it is difficult to find the right (and fair) words to describe them and even more treacherous to pick among the spokespersons—those who created historic records—as representative of collective Digger activities.[16] Certainly there were squabbles among them over who and what should be considered authentic. Nonetheless, there is also a consistent underlying thesis about the relationship between individual actors and social change. Diggers argued that the actions of individual players gathered synergy with those around them and that the collectivity of these forces could and would produce meaningful social change. The individual action could be triggered by anyone, no one was a leader (or, alternatively, everyone was a leader). So each was responsible for creating the community (and world) as they wished it to be. Peter Berg characterized this method as "creating the condition we described."[17]

According to Anderson and others, Diggers both "believed" and "practiced" freedom. "Free," as a belief system, had at least three facets. The first was personal. Free referred to unmitigated personal autonomy (i.e., freedom to do one's own thing).[18] The second was cultural and involved being liberated from any constraints imposed by social or legal norms, rules, or expectations. The third was economic and structural. It involved being free from the values driving capitalism, which included—from the Digger's point of view—an unhealthy obsession with accumulating wealth, private property, and material goods. Thus, Diggers rejected core American values upon which most of them had been raised.

Diggers, like the Beats before them, took stock of the world from outside the norms and rules of straight society. By rejecting the pursuit of material wealth, Diggers voluntarily placed themselves in a situation where basic survival was achieved through unconventional methods. They were Beat by choice and that choice was motivated by their political and philosophical beliefs. Poverty, communal living, and sharing were a central part of that life choice. This resulted in a survivalist orientation that was at the heart of Digger lifestyle.

Diggers did not reject all work, only that which they considered "dumb work" with its "dull money morality."[19] The target of Digger consternation was the internalization of material values. By living free of the capitalist economic system, money market system, and without emphasis on private property, Diggers hoped to create a meaningful alternative. It was to be a true *counter*culture.

In addition to personal declarations of independence, liberation from capitalism required creating an alternative economy for the community. According to Grogan, "One could only be free by drawing the line and living outside the profit, private property, and power premises of Western culture."[20] Julian Beck was even more forceful: "The slavery to money has to end. Which means that the entire money system has to end. A society of free goods, freely produced, freely distributed. You take what you need, you give what you can. The world is yours to love and work for. No state, no police, no money, no barter,[21] no borders, no property."[22]

Thus, Diggers "practiced free" by trying to create this alternative power base, which was to replace the capitalist monetary system with a free-flowing economy of liberated (free) goods and services.[23] It was this practice of Free that was at the heart of their anarchist radicalism. There were two phases in this Digger theater process—visualizing and taking action. In order to create the condition of an alternative power base, Diggers insisted you had to visualize an alternative and then act on it. Thus this ostensibly leaderless revolution rested on two assumptions about community interactions: first, that core members of the Digger collective would act on their own vision of alternatives; second, by creating an interesting example, others would join in and make it viable. Thus the ultimate goal of guerrilla theater was to "bring audiences to liberated territory," thereby creating "life-actors" and producing a "cast of freed beings".[24]

Taken together, the structural/political (economic independence), the personal (individual liberty), and the cultural (liberation from social and cultural conformity) created power (freedom from mainstream authority and values) through complete autonomy. Thus in its expanded and enacted form, Diggers breathed life into Gregory Corso's poetic musings about power being the ability to stand on a street corner and wait for no one.

Although Diggers had "dropped out," they had dropped out with a group of other kindred spirits who had similarly rejected traditional American values. Since practicing Free required that like-minded brothers and sisters gather and participate in the alternative vision, it was critical to the effectiveness of this revolutionary practice to collect a community of like-minded free souls. Beat elder Allen Ginsberg described Haight-Ashbury as a community experiment where "kids live together and invite others to join" and where the community operates by *example*."[25] Magnets for attracting audiences to liberated territories (i.e., public spaces such as parks, sidewalks, and streets) included free events like concerts, be-ins, and happenings, as well as free stores and other services.

Digger theater helped build community both by including the like-minded and by excluding those who refused to join in. Digger events (involving "flowers, mirrors, penny-whistles" and "mirrors held up to reflect the faces of the passersby") invited participation.[26] These events frequently carried messages central to Digger ideology; thus, Digger work started with liberating and empowering community members on, and in, the street. A broadside distributed in early 1967 and phrased as though it had been directly inspired by Gregory Corso's poem "Power" reads:

> The street belong to those who live in them. Those who live on Haights [*sic*] Street are neither loiterers [*sic*], vagrants, nuisances nor undesirables. They are the tenants of the street; angels of the corners, minor saints of the intersection. . . . To take possession of the street NOT AS AN ACT OF CHALLENGE, HOSTILITY, SHOWDOWN, WAR, BUT AS AN EXTENSION OF OUR OWN LIVES WE NEED IT TO PLAY ON[27]

The net result of fusing "art forms and life forms" into a single "social art form" was "ticketless theater."[28] For example, the Intersection Game claimed public space (liberated territory). A "game board" was formed at street intersections and the game involved "walking, somersaulting, squat-jumping, strolling in triangles and squares at public intersections." The broadside announcing this game to the public was called *Public Nuisance Nonsense*, or to be more exact, "Public Nuisance New Sence [*sic*] Nonsense."[29]

As frivolous as it may sound, these events and the street playground/battlefield created the party that the Grateful Dead urged American youth to join and provided activities around which the community bonded. The street was where autonomous freedom was asserted, and it offered the public opportunity of engaging others. Those who participated proved their membership in this action-based revolutionary community.

Digger theater also helped define community by drawing boundaries with the external world and excluding those not willing to participate (including tourists, spectators, parents, adults, straights, squares, etc.), thus creating a public litmus test. You either participated as a life player or you were not part of the movement. Coyote emphasized the importance of this forced choice for community membership: "We adhered to a one-sided vision. We excluded people who didn't see it our way. We created a dichotomous universe: us and them, good guys and bad guys. And to some degree, you define yourself, or one defines oneself, by what one's not."[30]

Drug use featured prominently in the forced choice. Drug experimentation (particularly psychedelic drugs) was one of the most important markers of membership in the youth community in general. It created a shared experience that separated participants from others. Hunter Thompson wryly reported to his *New York Times* readers that "most of the local [Haight-Ashbury] action is beyond the reach of anyone without access to drugs."[31] Youth were "utterly separated from their parents by the unbreachable gap of acid."[32] However, drugs not only separated youth from parents, they also created a communal experience that bonded the youth community together. "It wasn't just peer pressure," sixties historian Todd Gitlin argued: "More and more, to get access to youth culture, you had to get high. . . . Without grass, you were an outsider looking in."[33] Being an outsider looking in was to be excluded from the revolution altogether. In addition to creating community through shared experience, drugs united the community on the *other* side of the law. Acid rock groups such as the Jefferson Airplane made note: "we should be together, we are all outlaws in the eyes of America." Paul Krassner (the reputed "father" of the underground press) said that using LSD "meant that people trusted their friends more than the government."[34] In short, drugs served as passport and citizenship documentation for this youth community.

Finally, Digger theater captured the media's attention. From the Digger perspective, whenever the media took the time to describe Digger events, it became a player in Digger performances and helped reproduce and disseminate Digger beliefs to even wider audiences. Coyote argued that the media's insatiable appetite for news made it "vulnerable to manipulation," and Digger theater was designed to make the " 'message' absolutely clear and incontrovertible, even if they were only described in the media."[35] Thus Digger events like the mock funeral celebrating Death of Hippie Son of Media in Haight-Ashbury, or showering the trading floor of the New York Stock Exchange with dollar bills,[36] carried a Digger message to mainstream America via its own press. Together with music, literature, and the underground press, these media messages helped focus and unite a growing national community of youth around ideas. It also advertised the geographic epicenters of the counterculture movement to youth who were inclined to join the action. By operating a community by example, the Diggers' vision and rhetoric encouraged free spirits both in the local community as well as those from around the United States to participate.

To the extent that the straight world characterized the hippie phenomenon as apolitical, apathetic, and slothful, it misunderstood the work and world of the Diggers. Diggers were radical, active, and political. Thus Diggers challenged the cultural premises of American society and experimented with alternatives. The point was to transform society.

Enacting the Free City Collective: Power in Autonomy

According to Doyle, "The Diggers' principal project was to enact 'Free,' a comprehensive utopian program that would function as a working model of an alternative society."[37] When Diggers "practiced" Free they were seeking to create "an alternative power base" using street theater as a revolutionary tactic. The power derived from autonomy—both personal and economic—coupled with action-oriented Digger theater, resulted in an important (albeit short-lived) service infrastructure which supported an alternative lifestyle. It included Free services and an underground communications system (contributing to a nationwide underground network).[38] The practical result of this parallel system was that Diggers were largely responsible for "feeding the hungry, clothing the naked, sheltering the homeless" and befriending strangers, "all for free," as Anderson noted in his definition.

These Free services began appearing in the fall of 1966. By 1967 they were overrun and in disarray. Diggers quickly discovered they shared their street tenancy with other "minor saints of the intersection," including runaway adolescents. In 1968, Emmett Grogan proposed a grand plan for Free Cities which was even more comprehensive than the piecemeal experimental version enacted in 1966–67. The grand plan never got much past its blueprint stage. However, the components parts of Digger Free (free food, store, shelter, education on street survival, clinics, and referrals to other services) temporarily provided an alternative for runaway youth who had few resources of their own.

Resources for a parallel system came from the creativity and labor of individual participants who sought to liberate "society's surplus."[39] American affluence in the 1960s allowed "millions of have-nots and drop-outs in the U.S." to live off "an overflow of technologically produced fat."[40] Or, in the words of the Grateful Dead, "one man gathers what another man spills." Liberating goods involved begging, scavenging, and some theft. Diggers characterized this lifestyle as an ecology measure.[41] As urban survivalists, Diggers were "happy to live with the society's garbage" because they had "time to recycle and repair it."[42] Thus this scrounging was both survivalist tactic and political statement.

Much to the consternation of Diggers themselves, they were described by the mainstream press as a hippie sect, as psychedelic social workers, mod monks, and hip charity workers. Diggers considered their work much more important and more revolutionary than these colorful labels suggest. Nonetheless, they tried to "integrate personal autonomy with a sense of civic responsibility."[43] To the outside observer this infrastructure did, in fact, look a bit like the social service branch of the hippie community.

Free Food

In October 1966, Digger efforts began with Free Food, which eventually became a short-lived but institutional staple at 4 P.M. in the Panhandle of Golden Gate Park. Food was obtained, according to Emmett Grogan, by hitting "every available source of free food—produce markets, farmers' markets, meat-packing plants, farms, dairies, sheep and cattle ranches, agricultural colleges, and giant institutions (for the uneaten vats of food)" and by filling up "trucks with surplus by begging, borrowing, stealing, forming liaisons, and communications with delivery drivers for the leftovers from their routes."[44] This method of "liberating" food by scavenging was typical of the Digger method of stocking the shelves of Digger Free commerce.

The Diggers took responsibility for collecting, cooking, and distributing food on a daily basis. Com/co broadsides announced Free Food to the community. One broadside read:

FREE FOOD   GOOD HOT STEW
RIPE TOMATOES   FRESH FRUIT
BRING A BOWL AND SPOON TO
THE PANHANDLE AT ASHBURY STREET

4 PM 4PM 4PM 4PM 4PM 4PM

FREE FOOD   *EVERYDAY*   FREE FOOD
IT'S FREE BECAUSE IT'S YOURS!
the diggers[45]

Like all Digger services, Free Food was part of Digger theater. A large "Free Frame" was constructed and placed such that those in the Free Food line were required to step through the frame. Coyote recalled the distribution of "a tiny yellow replica about two inches square, attached to a cord for wearing" of the larger Free Frame and reported people were "encouraged to look through it and 'frame' any piece of reality through this 'free frame of reference.'" He noted that it "allowed them a physical metaphor to reconstruct (or deconstruct) their worldview at their own pace and direction."[46]

Although much Digger theater was symbolic, some services, such as Free Food, were offered in response to a real community need. It was part of acting out an alternative system that met the basic needs of its members. Grogan, for example, insisted Free Food was not merely a symbol but also was an essential service because "the young kids squatting in the Panhandle were hungry and afraid . . . [and] . . . they were on their own for the first time for no matter how long, and they wanted no material support from members of their parents' world."[47] Thus, while Grogan denied Diggers were running a funky charity, he acknowledged that the purpose, in part, was to aid youthful seekers who were establishing independence from traditional family. Free Food provided an alternative to the other, more dangerous options available to first-time runaways for surviving on their own.

The numbers of youth being fed quickly escalated while the number of daily meals offered decreased from three to one late afternoon soup line.[48]

Not to the surprise of anyone schooled in basic economic theory, the offer of *free* food quickly created a demand that was difficult to meet. The lack of viability of this system didn't escape even some self-proclaimed Diggers. Several years later, Jerry Rubin reflected: "Haight-Ashbury, the first mass experiment at an urban youth ghetto, floundered because it had a Communist ethic built upon a capitalist material base."[49] By May 1967 demand for food (and lodging) exceeded supply, and community members were beginning to record that Free Food was in bad shape.[50]

The Free Store

The Free Store[51] opened in December 1966. In keeping with Digger theater, it was originally called *Free Frame of Reference* and later renamed *Trip Without a Ticket*. The store was "brimming over with liberated goods to be shared with whoever needed them."[52] Like Free Food, the store's shelves were stocked by "liberating" assorted lost, found, discarded, deposited, and otherwise acquired property. The store served as a community resource for free clothing and other merchandise.

The Free Store functioned as Digger theater because it forced life-actors to become engaged in performance.[53] Grogan described "welfare mothers" who waited for "prize merchandise" that they could resell, but who also provided advice to their "hip sisters" about negotiating the California welfare system.[54] As was typical with Digger theater, the Free Store encouraged participation but also contributed to establishing a free-flowing information system and economy. People were encouraged to give or take from the store as they wanted. Any entrant or "shopper" was invited to take charge of the operation. As a practical matter the Free Store, like other free services, was short-lived, but it contributed to the implicit promise that the Haight community would meet the basic needs of young seekers all for free.

Free Shelter and a National Network of Crash Pads

Free Shelter was available to transient youth. It ranged from crash pads to established communes. Like Free Food, demand for free living quickly exceeded supply. Social scientists of the day reported that hippie pads existed throughout the Haight district. Most consisted of a live-in group of core members supplemented by numerous transients.[55] Diggers were responsible for hustling rent money for several crash pads, and Grogan confirmed that although a few people older than 18 managed these shelters, most of the space was occupied by "runaways."[56] Thus while older residents tended to live in communes or other relatively stable arrangements, there was also a temporary crash pad system available to younger drifting youth.

Digger shelters, crash pads, and hippie communes helped develop the sense of extended family and linked underground communities nation-wide. Available shelters facilitated cross-country movement and prolonged young people's ability to survive on their own with limited resources. Reflecting on the period, Coyote said, "We used to network from house to house. There were all these way stations where you were welcome and you were extended family. . . . There was this loose linked sense of family and sharing of resources and alliances. You'd go someplace and you'd stay for awhile, and you'd pitch in and work there and live."[57] Information about these shelters was transmitted by word of mouth, through underground press advertisements, postings in local counterculture businesses, and at times was even noted in the mainstream press.[58] Thus, a predominately youth-based communication system facilitated youth movement by adver-tising shelter locations. Children who set out on their own had places to go other than the street, and they could travel longer distances by moving strategically from crash pad to crash pad.

Free Education and "Socialization" Instruction

Counterculture members rejected traditional forms of education. It was what Coyote called "the competition to 'de-school' yourself."[59] Abandoning plastic classrooms was a theme frequently reflected in music lyrics and explicit in drug shaman Timothy Leary's message to "Turn on, tune in, and drop out." Leary called Haight-Ashbury the largest undergraduate college in the psychedelic movement.[60] Psychedelic drugs provided a method of per-sonal exploration and ways of expanding consciousness.

In Haight-Ashbury a more immediately practical form of education was offered that involved socializing arriving youth to street-based living. In 1965, Bob Dylan sang of his rolling stone ("no one ever taught you how to live on the street, now you are just goin' have to get used to it") and asked how it felt to have to "scrounge for your next meal?" However, by 1967 the Grateful Dead, a group that was at home among the Diggers and hippies of

Haight-Ashbury, were idolizing street survivalists: "See that girl barefootin' along. . . . She's a neon-light diamond and she can live on the street." The Diggers saw to it that those without the innate ability to "live on the street" were schooled in how to do it.

Diggers saw survival training as their responsibility as social revolutionaries and part of their agenda to create a free community. Street survival was not only a highly prized skill; it captured the essence of freedom. So Digger success was measured not only by their ability to "survive outside the dominant economic and social paradigm, but in one's ability to employ the techniques of theater to transmit this survival information to others."[61]

The first installment of the Haight-Ashbury "survival school" was held on April 16, 1967. According to Chester Anderson, the first session on "community, drugs and the police" drew about thirty people and was held at the Trip Without a Ticket.[62] Com/co flyers advertised the weekly survival school. In these Com/co broadsides, Diggers welcomed "newcomers & others" and promised that classes "conducted by experts, professional men & experienced street kids" would teach "six months' worth of knowledge in a mere three days" regarding "how to stay alive on Haight Street" and to "save you from becoming a psychedelic casualty."[63] Among the topics covered were "Street Wisdom: how to avoid beatings & starvation, how to survive without money"; "Drug Lore: how to keep from getting killed for kicks"; and "Policemanship: how to avoid getting busted & what to do if you are."[64]

It is unclear from the historical documents how long the actual "classroom" instructions continued; however, the basic lessons, or variations on them, were reprinted by the underground press and distributed widely. In addition, Com/co published and distributed a number of street-based educational broadsides such as "Busted"[65] (a digger advertisement for free legal help); "The Rules of the Game if Busted"[66] (which reprinted the California Penal Code's sections on disorderly conduct, arrest warrants, search and seizure, and resisting arrest, among other procedural and due process sections and offered advice on legal rights); and "Beat the Heat" (which offered "a few very simple rules to help keep busts to a neat minimum").[67]

In effect, these broadsides and activities offered training on living a Beat existence. Hard-knock experiences that honed street-survival skills among genuine runaway youth were replaced (or at least supplemented) with crash courses conducted by counterculture elders, along with articles published by the underground press. Thus, Diggers provided a formal socialization and educational structure by which to teach street-survival skills. To the extent that Diggers were successful in this educational process, they made street-living safer for inexperienced middle-class dropouts and more stable for young or more troubled runaways.

Taken together, Free Food, Free Store, the network of crash pads, the nationwide communication system, and courses (or information) on street survival created an opportunity for average American youth to experiment with being "Beat" without having to learn something about the "water" on their own. It made Beatness accessible not only to first-rate street hustlers (like Huncke and Cassady) but to average middle-class kids temporarily flirting with poverty and street life. In addition, it provided a compelling lure for those who were Beat because it was the "way they were." So although the Digger[68] movement was short-lived, its philosophy and service structure attracted runaway youth and influenced public discourse on running away. In particular, the Diggers' "practice" of Free resulted, temporarily, in creating a network of goods and services establishing a community infrastructure of social services that sustained a considerable mix of children and young adults for a brief period of time.

Runaways Among the Diggers

There is substantial evidence that runaway youth comprised a distinct subpopulation in counterculture communities although most contemporaneous texts don't routinely distinguish between runaways and hippies. Nor did counterculture members draw such a distinction themselves. Everyone was welcome as a part of the hip youth movement. Nonetheless, Diggers were particularly concerned about the vulnerability of the community's youngest members.

According to insiders, the runaway situation became critical following the January 1967 "Human Be-In" in Golden Gate Park. The Be-In (also known as the "Gathering of the Tribes") was an event designed to bring factions of the New Left and hippie communities together. It had the secondary effect of solidifying Haight-Ashbury's position at the forefront of counterculture activity in the general public consciousness. In its aftermath, the

Establishment press, the Haight Independent Proprietors (HIP)—a group of hippie business owners—and songwriters began to advertise an upcoming Summer of Love.

Public invitations to the psychedelic party were issued in various forms, including popular music. Scott McKenzie capitalized on the media hype with his pop song "If You're Going to San Francisco," released in early June 1967. The song peaked at number four on *Billboard* 's charts, and the lyrics reported that there was a "whole new generation" of "people in motion" with a "new explanation." San Francisco was a place, sang McKenzie, where you would meet "gentle people with flowers in their hair." A more hip and less pop invitation was issued to American youth by acid rockers the Grateful Dead in March 1967, who urged youth to try on their "wings and find out where it's at" by leaving home and joining the summer frolicking ("take a vacation, fall out for a while; summer's comin' in and it's goin' out in style . . . hey, hey, hey, come right away, come and join the party every day").

Hippies, "flower children," and other free spirits gathered to join the psychedelic party. This Summer of Love was a "myth," according to Grogan, that had "been manufactured to appeal to the young and they were running as fast as they could to it."[69] However manufactured the myth may have been, it created real problems for the community. At the time, one local noted that among several growing problems in the Haight, the "number one is, of course, the coming crowds of kids, all of whom will need to be fed, clothed, and housed."[70]

The Haight Diggers expressed anger at the HIP merchants and luminaries such as Timothy Leary who sent out the clarion call to youth without taking responsibility for the consequences. Grogan accused HIP merchants of generating publicity in order "to develop new markets for merchandising their crap" and argued their "newsmongery was drawing a disproportionate number of young kids to the district that was already overcrowded" with "thousands of young, foolish kids who fell for the Love Hoax and expected to live comfortably poor and take their place in the district's kingdom of love."[71]

Diggers felt a social responsibility for the arriving youth, and they were keenly aware that youngsters were arriving in the community who were unprepared to take care of themselves and were easily exploited. It was part of the Digger way to take action where they saw a need or a threat to community vision. They were also willing to include arriving youth as disciples for their revolution. A Com/co broadside dated April 1967 urged the community to take responsibility for educating the arriving youth. For example:

> The kids are on the streets, in the coffee houses, at the Trip Without a Ticket, The Psychedelic Shop, The Print Mint, Tracey's, The digger office, Haight/Ashbury everywhere. If you wait to get organized, they'll be gone. Find a kid and talk to him on your own, unled, unorganized. The future is now. Do it now.
>
> Gurus
> Wizards
> Teachers
>
> The kids are coming. The kids are here. *MAKE YOURSELVES AVAILABLE TO THE KIDS.* Seek them out. Talk to them. Go where they are and teach love. Now—these thousands of kids—is your chance to create the world as you know it should be. These kids are the future. Here and now. Please, do not wait for the future to seek you out. Go now to the kids now and teach now the way. Now.[72]

The accounts of street chroniclers, including musical artists, provided additional evidence of runaway children. Singing minstrel Ashleigh Brilliant, who performed in the Panhandle section of Golden Gate Park, referred to runaways in a number of his lyrics.[73] He portrayed the Diggers' work with them in his "Digger Lullaby":

> Hush little drop-out, don't make a peep,
> Diggers gonna find you a place to sleep
> And if your stomach stands in need
> Diggers have a big Panhandle feed
> And if of clothing you need more
> Everything's free at the Digger store

While some of these younger children assimilated, others presented problems for the Haight community and pitted its self-interests against its own philosophical beliefs. Runaways were heavy consumers of scarce resources and thus a drain on the Diggers' Free system. Nonetheless, Diggers were extremely concerned about the well-being of runaway youth. A Com/co broadside called "Unite or Die" noted: "Most of the kids that're coming in are confused & hurt & soft & inexperienced. They haven't been through this before. They can't take it but they won't go home, & the most inhuman fate is on the way if they aren't taught." And in a scathing Com/co broadside entitled "Uncle Tim'$ Children," Chester Anderson accused Timothy Leary, the underground paper *The Oracle*, and the HIP merchants of having "sold our lovely little psychedelic community to the mass media" while being "blithely & sincerely unaware of what they have done" because they are "businessmen, salesmen" and "money counters." They had, he argued, "lured a million children here recklessly & irresponsibly, & now that the children are arriving, more & more every day," only the Diggers were "acting in anything like a responsible manner." Anderson challenged them to help with the "growing tragedy" but expressed doubt: "If anyone but the diggers undertakes to feed the hungry, comfort the sick, shelter the homeless, clothe the naked & restore some measure of human dignity to Uncle Tim's children, I'll be very surprised."[74]

Anderson urged anyone who wanted "to see what the psychedelic utopia is like" to go "sit in the diggers' office for a few hours. Listen to the stories. Look at the casualties."[75] The community, particularly the HIP business community, responded angrily to Anderson's allegations that that they were responsible for attracting kids to the Haight, and Anderson expressed willingness to "concede the point"; however, he insisted that "even if the merchants aren't responsible for the kids being here . . . they still have a responsibility toward those kids, simply because those kids *are* here."[76]

Village Voice journalist Richard Goldstein took up Anderson's challenge to visit the Diggers and wrote about a Digger kitchen where one of the regular cooks, a 17-year-old girl[77] who began running away at 14, found family and a home in the Haight and was described by the journalist as ladling "out her stew" to "three girls from the New York area . . . and a freckled kid from Maine."[78] She responded to a question about Digger work: "You want to know what we're about? . . . A 14-year-old kid freaked out the other day. He was screaming 'Where's my hands?' He came to the Diggers to get food, which I guess represented warmth of his mother. He was shaking like a bastard. We had a room where he could go." The Digger Free Store maintained a large space available as a "hangout for the casualties of the so-called Love Generation" for "kids" who had been "beaten down by the mean streets."[79]

Diggers worried about the younger kids who were arriving and "creating a phenomenon."[80] They were "uneducated and stoned," according to Abbie Hoffman, making them "easy prey for sadists and pimps who set up crash pads as recruiting camps for prostitutes."[81] He asserted that "in grasping for a new family structure, many kids of the era wound up with surrogate parents more cruel than the ones they left at home."[82]

Personal advertisements in the underground newspapers hint at the breadth of possibilities for exploiting naive or desperate youth. One Com/co broadside voiced angry vigilantism and outed those who were perceived to be sexually exploiting the arriving youth:

The Psychedelic Shop's most expensive luxury is a yellow-headed sales-person that calls itself Joel.

Joel used to hang around the diggers' Free Frame of Reference on Fred-erick Street. When pretty young boys arrived looking for a place to crash, Joel would send them to the pads of elderly faggots. There is no proof that he was ever paid for this service. Perhaps it was only a hobby with him.

Nevertheless, some narsty [sic] diggers finally hung him up by his heels in a tree & put a sign on him that said PIMP & were generally rude & unkind to him, & he never went back to the Free Frame of Reference again. He moved to the Psychedelic Shop (where he may still be running his room-mate service, for all we know) & devoted himself to hating the diggers.[83]

While this broadside might be interpreted as homophobic raving, it is also consistent with evidence that exchanging sex for shelter was one way run-away youth, with limited resources and options, negotiated their living situation.

Runaways could also support their independence by begging, hawking underground newspapers,[84] or through occasional odd jobs.[85] The HIP Job Co-op (orchestrated by the HIP merchants) was a source of friction with Diggers, who argued that it primarily exploited runaways. "Sure," wrote Grogan sarcastically, "it manages to get some helpless runaway girl a job" but it is

a job in an attic sweatshop making dresses for a dollar an hour! Say it takes her two hours to make a dress. That's two dollars, right? Well, then the people who employ her—the incense-burning hippies—take that dress 'n sell it for twenty-five or thirty dollars. After a while she gets disillusioned about this kind of short action and she drops further into the street. Then we end up with her. An' that's where your HIP Job Co-op's at, motherfucker![86]

"Ending up with her" is what worried Diggers most. Runaway minors imposed a strain on limited resources. "It was a catastrophe," reported Grogan, and "there was nothing to be done except leave, or try to deal with it as best one could."[87] In fact, before the summer of 1967, a portion of the adult counterculture community began to leave, withdrawing to communes and farms outside the city limits. Those who stayed behind believed Haight-Ashbury was not only "already deep in the throes of a critical dilemma" but was "quickly approaching disaster" with "the hordes of arriving runaway youth" who were "overburdening the Digger operations" that were "struggling to meet the needs of these kids and the community."[88]

Coyote recalled the sense of responsibility that the Diggers felt toward the young people who were being "seduced" to the Haight:

[The] city was capitalizing on it and taking no responsibility for it; telling all these kids—our age, a lot of them younger—to get lost. And our feeling was that they were our kids. You know? This was America; these were our kids. We started feeding them and sheltering them and setting up medical clinics just because it needed to be done.[89]

In short, Diggers took a paternalistic interest in children who wandered into their community and who seemed to be unwanted by others and unable to care for themselves.

In spite of Digger caretaking, runaways caused problems by inviting police scrutiny. Adults who sheltered minors risked criminal charges such as impairing the welfare of a minor or custodial interference. Grogan wrote: "White middle America was outraged that their children were leaving" and "since a runaway has no constitutional rights, and is merely property of his parents, they demanded their return."[90] According to Grogan, San Francisco Juvenile Court Judge Ray J. O'Conner "became publicly irate and said that all the Digger leaders should be jailed for contributing to the delinquency of minors by harboring runaways."[91] *Village Voice* reporter Goldstein duly noted the dilemma faced by the Establishment but argued that "no one is putting the Diggers down for their brand of *loco parentis*" because "deprivation, disease and delirium are very real." Simply put, Digger services filled a serious community need and there weren't many alternatives.

In spite of the unwelcome attention runaways brought to the community, for philosophical reasons counter-culturists were unwilling to turn youth over to parents or police. Parents used the underground press to search for missing children, making direct pleas (i.e., "Mona, contact your mother"; "Debbie Blackwell—please call home collect") as well as indirect pleas to the community ("If anyone knows Georgia, please tell her to contact her mother"). Notices were posted in hippie businesses.[92] But the indigenous hippie community saw kindred spirits in runaways and reiterated the theme of taking care of its own kind. As J. Anthony Lukas documented so aptly for the *New York Times* in 1967 (see chapter 2), there was a world of worried parents whose youngsters had seemingly vanished in the underground, and there wasn't much help available for locating them.

Abbie Hoffman argued that runaways were the backbone of the youth revolution. His sympathies were clearly expressed in an essay entitled "Runaways: The Slave Revolt" (1968), in which he wrote: "A fifteen-year-old kid who takes off from middle-class American life is an escaped slave crossing the Mason-Dixon line. They are hunted down by professional bounty hunters, fidgety relatives and the law, because it is against the law to leave home (translate: bondage) until you finish your servitude."[93] Like "escaping slaves," runaways could "come down here [the East Village] or to Haight-Ashbury or to the stops in between" and find that "an underground railroad exists" in which "runaways are hidden in crash pads, communes, apartments and country communities."[94] Before 1967, this "underground railroad" consisted of Digger and hippie counterculture crash pads or communes. However, beginning in 1967, an alternative service system began to emerge that was politically and ideologically tied to "hip" communities but also sought to bridge the gap between youth and the "bounty hunters" of the straight world, including parents, police, and child welfare authorities.

Over-run, overwhelmed, and moving on

The Summer of Love of 1967 strained the resources of the fragile Digger Free system, although it did not dim the optimism of the most ardent and dedicated Diggers. In the summer of 1968, Grogan outlined an extensive plan to create Free Cities (which would accommodate both the urban and rural communes), which he outlined in a manifesto entitled "The Post-Competitive, Comparative Game of a Free City." Free Cities was conceptualized as a secondary stage of "our revolution," which demanded that "families, communes, black organizations and gangs of every city in America" coordinate and develop "Free Cities where everything that is necessary can be obtained for free by those involved in the various individual clans"; this included "establish[ing] and maintain[ing] services that provide a base of freedom for autonomous groups to carry out their programs without having to hassle for food, printing facilities, transportation, mechanics, money, housing, work space, clothes, machinery, trucks, etc."[95] The network of services Grogan envisioned included:

Free City Switchboard/Information Center
Free Food Storage and Distribution Center;
Free City Garage and Mechanics;
Free City Bank and Treasury;
Free City Legal Assistance
Free City Housing and Work Space
Free City Stores and Workshops
Free Medical Thing
Free City Hospital
Free City Environmental and Design Gang
Free City Schools
Free City News and Communication Company
Free City Events . . . Festival Planning Committees
Cooperative Farms and Campsites
Scavenger Corps and Transport Gang
Free City Tinkers and Gunsmiths
Free City Radio, TV and Computer Stations
Free City Music

Grogan outlined the responsibility for each of these services but significantly excluded parents of runaways from using the Switchboard (which was to coordinate "services, activities and aid and direct assistance" where most needed). Grogan justified the exclusion of parents, particularly those looking for runaway children, by noting that "the work load usually pre-vents or should prevent the handling of messages from parents of runaway children. . . . That should be left up to the churches of the community."

Indeed, the Diggers had already turned to local service providers, partic-ularly the religious community, for help with runaways earlier. On March 19, 1967, Com/co issued a plea "to our straight friends" asking them to "help the diggers shelter the homeless, feed the hungry & clothe the naked" and appealed to their Christian spirit: "you can help the diggers to do what Jesus told us all to do."[96] In addition, Diggers made a general plea for assis-tance, whenever and wherever they found an audience. A document dated May 13, 1967, from the Council for the Summer of Love reads: "We, indi-vidually, are meeting with religious leaders and gurus when ever we find them. . . . We are asking your action. If you have food, share it. If you have money, give it. If you have room for pilgrims to rest, open your door." Begin-ning in March before the Summer of Love, Diggers warned a group of local clergymen "that 'hundreds of thousands of young, indigent and hungry people' could be expected to 'invade' the Haight-Ashbury during the com-ing summer . . . [and] urged the religious leaders to work with the city to 'feed, house, clothe and comfort' the visitors."[97]

According to Grogan, "the apprehension generated by the approaching so-called Summer of Love also led to the creation of three other organiza-tions."[98] They were Happening House (a community center), Huckleberry House (a runaway shelter), and the Switchboard (a hotline referral service). The latter two will become important prongs in the subsequent develop-ment of the runaway and homeless youth service delivery system.

Huckleberry House was an alternative shelter arrangement—not a crash pad exactly, but not an agency that fit comfortably within the preexisting framework of California's child welfare and juvenile justice services. It was a new, alternative model that rested on a commitment to autonomy and respected youths' ability to make their own decisions. The runaway shelter operated outside law enforcement, juvenile justice, and child welfare sys-tems, and staff involved parents only with the explicit permission of the youth themselves.

In addition to Huckleberry House, the Switchboard, a community infor-mation and referral service, emerged. The Switchboard was an "answering service for messages from parents to their runaway kids. Each week, they published a long list of names in the Bay Area underground papers like the

Berkeley Barb, notifying persons that they had received messages for them."[99] According to Grogan, however, the Switchboard's "more relevant side" among other things was that it located "bed space for travelers in volunteer crash pads." Of the three new organizations, Grogan concluded that the Switchboard was the "only one of these operations that did any amount of substantial work for the welfare of the Haight community."[100] This telephone hotline for referral and counseling supplemented the more informal underground communication systems.

Taken together, Huckleberry House and the Switchboard began to replicate (as well as legitimate and nudge toward the mainstream) the underground network of services and crash pads of the counterculture for runaway youth. In short, it was a service delivery model that borrowed Digger Free services and offered them to teenage runaways but did so with the added legitimacy provided by local residents and ecumenical communities.

The Grassroots Rise of Alternative Runaway
Services (1967–1974)

One drink of wine, two drinks of gin,
And I'm back in the Ozone again.

>   —Commander Cody and his Lost Planet Airmen

The problem with institutionalizing irreverence is that it becomes a
business and thus a contradiction.

>   —Richard Rodriquez[1]

The Rise of the Alternative Shelter Providers

Huckleberry House is generally credited with being the first runaway shelter among a small group of sibling agencies having roots in geographic areas
where adolescents congregated in the late 1960s and early 1970s.[2] Gerda
Flanigan, a youth advocate from a short-lived Chicago-based program called
Looking Glass, founded in 1969, described the cluster of providers as "a
loose, undefined movement of alternative services" and estimated that by
1972 the number of initiatives in this family group had grown to between 75
and 100.[3] In addition to Looking Glass and Huckleberry House, kindred
agencies included Runaway House (1968, Washington, D.C.), Amicus
House (1969, Pittsburgh), Covenant House (1968, New York City), Ozone
House (1969, Ann Arbor), The Bridge (1970, San Diego), and Bridge Over
Troubled Water (1970, Boston).

This network of "houses" scattered nationwide were collectively known
as "alternative" services because they offered a relatively dramatic alternative to the traditional state and local social service agencies and institutions
of the day.[4] More importantly, they represented a new philosophical orientation toward serving young clients and a radical break from premises

about the relationship between adults and children that underpinned services in the state child welfare and juvenile justice systems. Historically, the state's role was protective in nature and it assumed the inability of youth to make decisions for themselves, which entitled the state to assert itself by acting in the "best interests of the child."

The alternative service agencies took a decidedly different position. At the very heart of their work was respect for youthful autonomy and an emphasis on the centrality of youth decision-making. Thus the values of the alternative agencies were deeply rooted in the youth rights movement and consistent with the counterculture discourse on power, autonomy, and freedom. In legislative testimony one provider would subsequently argue that "children represent the last vestige of slavery in this country, for no other group is so totally vulnerable to the dictates of others except perhaps those who are encarcerated [sic] in penal institutions."[5] These advocates championed nothing short of a civil rights movement on behalf of oppressed youth.

The belief that youth should be free to make their own decisions led to agencies that were different in two ways. First, youth were able to initiate services on their own, they were not "placed" in them by the state child protective agencies nor were they "ordered" into them by juvenile justice or family court judges. Second, once there, youth could make their own life choices essentially without the influence or interference of their parents, caretakers, and families. Although alternative agencies advocated family counseling and engaged parents when they could, primary and final decision-making rested with their clients.

As a result, the alternative agencies, as a generic group, situated themselves between the hip and straight worlds, acting as a kind of bridge between the two for adolescents. While young people welcomed the option, most of the alternative agencies maintained an uncomfortable relationship, in their early years, with the "straight" community.

The most radical phase of the shared history of these alternative agencies ended in 1974 with the passage of the federal Runaway Youth Act (see appendix 3). While this legislation did not put an end to all state and local skirmishes which confronted the alternative agencies, it certainly provided a mantle of legitimacy for the service delivery model by making federal grants available to programs patterned on it. Furthermore, by giving priority to programs that could point to previous experience working with runaways, funding was funneled to those agencies whose roots led directly back to counter-culture communities.

In the post-1974 context, these maturing agencies were joined by a second generation of newer shelters, and in the ensuing decades what was once a radical movement became an entrenched, fairly well-established wing of the private child welfare system in many areas of the country. There now exists a national network of runaway and homeless youth facilities and established organizations at the state and national levels to coordinate them. So the runaway shelter has become an institutional fixture and has earned a seemingly permanent place in the overall service system for young adults.

However, before legitimacy bestowed by federal legislation, those maverick alternative agencies birthed between 1967 and 1974 pushed the boundaries of legality, confronted and flaunted the rules of human services and social service departments, defied the police, challenged definitions of "professionalism" in services for adolescents, and interfered or interceded with parents (depending on one's perspective). It was a rocky road, with some contentious battles, as the program model moved from the margin to the mainstream.

In many ways, the undertaking was one of borrowing the crash pad structure (as well as a value system largely in tune with that of the radical youth community) and making it sufficiently palatable for the straight community to tolerate. The path the agencies took illuminates the uneasy transformation of a model roughly patterned on "Digger Free" to one sufficiently established, and well enough respected, to gain the endorsement of the United States Congress.

Birthing an Alternative

As the public hype over Haight-Ashbury's Summer of Love began to build in the early months of 1967, so did community concern about the impending arrival of the youngest love pilgrims. Diggers in particular and the hippie community in general were not only concerned with the lack of available resources to care for the influx of youth but also with the straight community's response to the young immigrants. In San Francisco, the police had adopted a strategy of detaining minors and turning them over to juvenile authorities.

The hip community's concerns about increasingly aggressive police measures against runaways were both ideological and practical in nature. First, police intervention offended the community's most fundamental and treasured values of autonomy and freedom as well as its sensibility about the right of youth to explore their world unimpeded. Arresting runaway minors was an affront to the notion of standing on a street corner waiting for no one or, to paraphrase Jerry Rubin, it was a direct assault on a youth's right to loiter.

On the other hand, sheltering runaway youth created practical problems for the counterculture community. Housing minors in crash pads was dangerous business for two reasons. First, state criminal laws made it illegal to harbor minors or otherwise interfere with custodial caretakers, so crash pad operators ran the risk of being arrested on criminal charges. Second, looking for missing children sometimes legitimized police searches and exposed crash pad elders to the additional risk of other contraband being discovered in the process of the investigation. Abbie Hoffman observed that the "chief causes for busts" in counterculture areas were "dope and runaways."[6] So housing runaways brought with it the additional risk of being exposed to criminal charges for drug-related offenses. In spite of these risks, the hip community was not about to ask youth for proof of age at the crash pad door, nor was it going to cooperate with authorities by turning out—or turning over—these younger kindred spirits to the police, their parents, or state child welfare personnel.

The counterculture community was not alone in its concern for these wandering younger children. Not surprisingly, progressive ecumenical organizations and liberal community residents also took an interest in the gathering young people and were offended by aggressive police action being taken against them. As Rev. Larry Beggs recalled, "Individuals in the Haight-Ashbury community decided that the intensifying runaway situation needed another alternative than police pickup."[7] It was in this environmental that the Diggers turned to the local community for help. Beggs credited the Diggers with the basic design for a new program and pointed to their "sketchy plans to provide a home for runaways in the mountains near Santa Cruz."[8] From its inception, project organizers wanted to establish a runaway house and referral center that did not "resembl[e] the standard institutional approaches" and would "experiment with new solutions to the problem."⁹ So, from the start program designers were firmly committed to an alternative framework for service delivery and a Digger-inspired model.

On June 1, 1967, Beggs was named codirector of the project, and just three weeks later, on June 23, 1967, Huckleberry House hastily opened its doors in all its experimental glory. Although Huckleberry House ostensibly was developed at a time of crisis to meet the short-term needs of the community in 1967,¹⁰ staffers discovered quickly that the need for services persisted. Furthermore, similar grassroots efforts were emerging around the country in local communities that were burdened by drifting youth. A loosely organized movement began taking shape and gaining public voice.

Rev. Doug Miller of Connecticut argued that progressive runaway crisis shelters were "a perfect project for all churches and synagogues because they can avoid the red tape of other organizations and because such a project is certainly in line with their mission and outreach functions."¹¹ Similarly, New York City's Covenant House, founded by Father Bruce Ritter, grew out of both mission and community needs. Ritter attributed his idea for Covenant House to a challenge made by his students at Manhattan College, where he was a professor of medieval theology and chaplain to the student body. He reported his teaching career came to an "abrupt end" one day following a sermon on "zeal and commitment" which entailed urging students to be more involved in the "life and work of the church."¹² At the end of the sermon Ritter was approached by the president of the student body, who accused him of not practicing what he preached.¹³ Ritter considered the challenge and requested a new assignment to live among the youth gathered in the East Village area of Manhattan. In the winter of 1968—just a year after the murder of Linda Fitzpatrick and in the same geographic vicinity—he opened up his apartment to six runaway teenagers.¹⁴ Ritter reported making "24 different telephone calls to public and private child welfare agencies," trying to find a place to deposit the kids. He recalled that "the best advice I received on how to help these children was to have them arrested. Since it should not be a crime to be homeless and hungry in this country, I decided to care for them myself."¹⁵ The six youth quickly brought friends and the agency grew from there. Of course, Ritter had discovered what others around the country were also discovering—that there was a growing population of wandering and independent youth, and the only readily available intervention featured police detainment and return home.

Not all the early runaway service organizations were associated with religious institutions. Some grew from community concerns about the adolescents gathering in the area. For example, in Ann Arbor, hometown of the University of Michigan, businesses and community residents were united in a desire to remove loitering and panhandling youth from the streets of the small university town. Together they supported the state's first runaway shelter, Ozone House.

In the earliest years, Ozone House was one prong of four "alternative" services that banded together to provide a comprehensive network of assistance to young people. The group was collectively called the Community Center Coordinating Council or C-4. C-4's purpose was to "promote the physical and mental well-being of the Ann Arbor community" by coordinating and supporting grassroots "alternative" organizations which arose to "meet a variety of needs."[16] In addition to Ozone House—which targeted its services to wandering and runaway youth—the other C-4 programs included Drug Help, the Community Center Project (which itself included a referral service called Community Switchboard and the Creative Arts Workshop), and the Free People's Clinic. Taken together, of course, this network of alternative services—drug help, switchboard referrals, crisis shelter, arts organization, and clinic—is similar in scope to other counterculture designs, including the Diggers' comprehensive Free City Collective and their proposal for Free Cities.

In Chicago, a short-lived program called Looking Glass utilized yet another method of situating itself between the hip and straight communities.[17] Like the others, Looking Glass started as a grassroots, community-based agency. It opened its doors in November 1969 and was run by an all-volunteer staff. According to cofounder Gerda Flanigan, at this point it was "technically operating illegally."[18] The fledgling Looking Glass quickly learned that it "had no authority to place children at all without securing a license from the State of Illinois as a child-placing facility" and that its "loosely organized helping service needed to be funded, legitimized, licensed and recognized in order to meet the needs of the clients applying for help."[19]

In part because of its legal problems and in part because of financial ones, Looking Glass became formally affiliated with Travelers Aid Society in 1971. Travelers Aid Society was a well-established social service agency with a half-century record of community service helping stranded wanderers. Associating with a respected agency helped smooth the road with state and local child

welfare authorities by helping Looking Glass meet state-licensing requirements; however, it also impinged on the nature and design of its services.
Thus the relationship between Looking Glass's parent organization and its
more radical youthful staff was uneasy at times.

At least one area of tension was over the notion of "professionalism" and
the relative damper radical service providers felt this placed on innovative
and "with it" service delivery. Like many of the alternative agencies, Looking Glass relied on a very small core group of paid staff and a large cadre of
volunteers who were trained, or at least acculturated, by the agency staff and
more senior volunteers. Paid staff were primarily employees of the Travelers Aid Society and had professional training. Its volunteers, on the other
hand, tended to be from the hip community, sharing political and ideological interests in youth empowerment. At the time, researchers Anne E. Fortune and William J. Reid conducted an evaluation of services provided by
Looking Glass. They commented on the tension among staff:

> Part of the ambiguity in volunteer-paid staff relations derives from a
> "working" non-written, non-oral agreement between the Looking Glass
> and Travelers Aid Society to the effect that if the spirit of one is not chal-
> lenged, the professionalism skill of the other will not be. Yet the challenge
> exists daily. Looking Glass is at present dependent on Travelers Aid Soci-
> ety for its funding and legitimization among official agencies. The vol-
> unteer staff resents such dependence yet at the same time relies on the
> professional staff in organizational as well as counseling matters.[20]

One volunteer complained that Looking Glass "is considerably more professional than I had anticipated and much more linked to 'straight agencies.'"[21] The evaluators go on to conclude that "professionalization" at Looking Glass was frequently seen as undesirable among volunteers with
extensive service."[22] Although the alternative agencies developed staff and
volunteer training programs, few of the workers had formal education as
social workers, mental health workers, psychologists, or other professional
counselors. Their qualifications tended to be political sympathy to the youth
movement and a willingness to endorse, or at least contemplate, lifestyle
alternatives for the young people they served.

Nonetheless, the associate executive director of the Travelers Aid Society
will testify before Congress in later years—and after Looking Glass had

permanently closed its doors—that this tension was a necessary and integral part of the model design. He argued that

> the young volunteer paraprofessional in our opinion is perhaps the most single crucial component to a successful helping operation. Any legislative attempt to address itself to the runaway problem should clearly address itself to supporting and encouraging the combination of young seeking an active social role and the professionals who would be wise to update their approach. We must continue to struggle to bring together the old and the young in a united effort to improve the condition of life for us all.[23]

Although each of these early agencies negotiated its survival in different ways, the basic tensions between hip and straight, between professional and nonprofessional, between community legitimacy and radical independence, and between stable and unstable funding, played itself out in the alternative agencies. It was a battle between the "spirit" of alternative and the "professionalist skill" of the mainstream. Each of the alternative agencies forged different relationships with the public and private sectors. Each responded creatively to its environment. Each operated with limited financial resources. They were united, however, in their determination to meet the needs of young people, particularly those away from home for the first time, and in their mission to do so with minimal interference from the less-than-hip institutions traditionally available to such youth.

Basic Shelter Services and Its Providers

The alternative agencies shared many characteristics, including general program design and core values. All of them provided some sort of crisis and family counseling. Services ranged from concrete offerings such as shelter, food, and clothing to auxiliary services such as legal advice and medical treatment. These services were either provided by on-site staff or were offered as referrals to other free providers in the community network. Some agencies took their brand of services to the streets and developed outreach units in which workers patrolled the community, particularly the counterculture areas, looking for youth in need of help.

The alternative service organizations were structured for the convenience of their clients. Not only were drop-in centers and offices located in areas where youth congregated, but they were open at times of the day and night when youth would be most likely to seek help. Thus, services were mostly available on-demand.[24] Indeed, some centers, such as Covenant House, prided themselves on maintaining an around-the-clock "open intake" policy. The original mission at Looking Glass was to "develop a system of self-help services for adolescents which would be available on a 24-hour a day, 7 days a week schedule."[25] Youth could get help any time of the day or night, any day of the year. Services were free and there were few or no entry requirements, so there were no impediments to receiving immediate help.

Most of these alternative organizations were touted as crisis care facilities and focused on providing short-term help or immediate referrals. The goal was to stabilize the runaway's situation by providing for his or her immediate needs (shelter, food, and clothing), and only then to begin to identify a permanent solution. In doing so, the providers situated themselves as the point of entry into the system.

Core Ideology: Autonomy

This method of delivering services to teenagers was decidedly different from those existing in the public sector, which structured interventions around an authoritative relationship toward youth, theoretically acting in *their* best interests by imposing "help" on them. In mainstream program design, adolescents were not in control of initiating or directing services.

The restless and maturing Baby Boomer cohort, however, was creating an entirely new client constituency and demanded new service models. The demographic reality was that the first wave of Baby Boomers turned 21 years old in 1967, the year Huckleberry House opened its doors. Right behind them were a large number of youth making their transition to adulthood. So not only were record numbers of young people beginning to seek independence from their family homes, there were record numbers of newly anointed and sympathetic young adults willing to share their wisdom about the process of declaring independence. Baby Boomers were both staff and clients of the alternative agencies. So it should not be surprising that old-fashioned authoritative perspectives on youth care were challenged.

At the heart of the alternative services mission was a political and ideological commitment to allow young people to make decisions about their own lives.[26] Huckleberry House characterized itself as "a ground breaking runaway housing facility and referral center . . . a program based on respect for the fundamental autonomy of young people."[27] Since autonomy was paramount in these efforts, it was afforded maximum protection. Building trust with youthful clients meant that staff members could not side too quickly (if at all) with authorities associated with the straight (and therefore suspect) world such as parents, police, judges, and child welfare agencies, or nonhip professionals.

The alternative agencies sought to provide a safe environment in which youth could make their own decisions without undue pressure or coercion from authorities (including parents) but also without risk to themselves or to the community. Given this focus on youth empowerment and the young person as client, the alternative providers argued that certain additional features were necessary to support their service model; these included providing youth access to the information necessary to make informed decisions, confidentiality assurances, and final decision-making authority, no matter what that final decision might be.

To deny young people the right to make their own decisions was, in the eyes of the advocates of alternative services, an act of oppression. Ozone House staff noted:

> We were youth advocates, which means that we believe that young people have basic rights which are sometimes denied them and that because of the general denial of these rights, young people are sometimes oppressed. It is important that all people, including young people, have the right to be heard, and that their needs are met. We do not mean by this that we would always side 100% with the youth and against his parents, because we realize it is an unrealistic and damaging position. However, we will work to assure that the youth is heard, knows the alternatives to his situation and has someone he can trust.[28]

Informed Decision-making

Early program organizers reasoned that if youth were going to trust alternative agencies, they needed to be staffed by hip guidance counselors who were in tune with youth themselves. Thus the alternative look of the agency included long-haired counselors dressed according to the fashion of the hip community and physical spaces that were homey and decidedly noninstitutional. Alternative providers saw this as integral to the process of gaining legitimacy and trust in the eyes of their skeptical youthful clients.

If this alternative look helped assure the youth being served that the service was cool, it raised suspicion in the adult, straight world. Evaluators of the Looking Glass program, for example, commented that "Looking Glass certainly does not meet most expectations of a formal counseling agency in appearance of either its offices or personnel" and speculated "this is probably more readily accepted among the youngsters than among families."[29] In the early 1970s the Ozone House handbook reflected on its own even earlier days, in which "young, long-haired counselors" were "accused of breaking up homes and indoctrinating young people" to become "Marxists, Maoists, pacifists, prostitutes and libertines."[30]

Furthermore, the counseling was unorthodox by traditional standards. In 1972, Looking Glass evaluators captured a staff member's description of his process of counseling clients:

> I try to make the kid make his decisions for himself, and I try my hardest to treat him as an adult. I usually (depending on the person) listen and get the facts of the presenting situation and try to offer alternatives of what the kid can do and let him make up his mind of what he wants to do.[31]

The evaluators, however, go on to conclude that, "Despite the preoccupation with clients' independent decision-making, it is evident that the counselors influence the client's choice of alternatives, perhaps more than they may be aware."[32] In the same evaluation study, the frustration of another staff member is captured in his answer to a questionnaire supplied by the researchers:

> Hey,—look, I'm having a lot of trouble answering these questions either seriously or in jest. . . . I guess it would be easier for me to sum up some of my personal experience here. When I first came to the "Glass" a lot of my motivation was for my own personal therapy. I think that the "Glass" provided much of the things that I felt that I needed at the time—rather than help myself directly, I more or less helped myself through helping

others. This was probably not the best of approaches but from my observations, it seems to be a common one. Most of us have come for reasons known only to ourselves, and some of us even have these reasons fulfilled. We probably help most of our clients, and even ourselves, through some sort of group process that involves all of our growing experiences as a practical approach to problem solving.[33]

Of course, at the heart of this disclosure is evidence of the fact that young adult counselors, many still struggling with issues of their own independence, were providing a sounding board and guidance to their even younger Baby Boomer siblings. Although the Looking Glass study found that volunteers ranged in age from 18 years to 54 years old, the median age was 23.[34] The alternative agencies grew out of the demographic pressures of the day and perhaps served the developmental needs of both its young staff and its even younger clients. So the alternative service design both reflected and was shaped by the developmental realities of the Baby Boomers.

Confidentiality

In addition to vesting primary authority in the youth for making decisions, alternative agencies were ferociously protective of young adults' confidences. This was based on a belief that to gain the trust of its clients, providers needed to promise that information revealed during conversations and counseling sessions would not be disclosed to others. For the most part this included keeping information from parents, police, or other suspect adult groups unless the youth specifically granted permission to disclose to these individuals or entities.

The alternative agencies claimed authority for this "confidentiality guarantee" from a number of sources, such as the privileged relationships generally afforded professionals (e.g., social workers, lawyers, and doctors). They understood the limitations to their arguments, given the fact few service providers actually had these professional qualifications. For example, an early policy and procedure manual from Ozone House set out its rules by stating that "the law says that a parent or guardian may sign release of info for a young person—BUT we don't recognize a parent or guardian's signature. We deal with young people re confidentiality just like people over the age of majority." Ozone House claimed its legal authority for trumping parental rights in federal drug-counseling provisions. Of course, counseling at Ozone House, as well as many other alternative agencies, extended well beyond drug-related issues and included a wide array of life decisions.[35]

The Right to Keep on Running

In spite of Huckleberry House's apparent roots in the Digger model, some blue-blooded counter-culturalists, such as Emmett Grogan, dismissed it as a place for "some runaway kids" who "became disillusioned with the Haight-Ashbury" to get "room and board for a couple of days, until their family made the necessary arrangements for their return home."[36] It was, in his view, a place for less-than-serious counter-culturists. To some extent, Grogan's assessment was correct. In order to shelter underage youth, alternative agencies needed parental consent so as not to run afoul of the states' criminal laws (such as custodial interference, harboring a minor, or contributing to the delinquency of a minor). Furthermore, the stated goal of many of the alternative agencies was to negotiate a safe plan for each child, and in some cases this included returning the child home. What Grogan perhaps failed to fully appreciate, however, was the steadfast unwillingness of alternative agencies to turn over the minors who *refused* to let agency staff contact their parents. Instead these youth were provided information about the risks of life on the street as well as some basic rules of survival (much like the education that was provided by Digger survival schools). They were then permitted to leave without the agency staff notifying parents or police that the youth had been there. Thus there was a subset of "runaways" who sought help, received information from the agency, left it, and returned to the street rather than deal with parents. These intermediary adults did not convey information to police, juvenile justice, or child welfare authorities. The most interesting aspect of the alternative agencies' service may be the critical role it played in protecting a youth's right to leave if he or she didn't want to play by the rules established by the straight community. In short, the alternative providers, like the Diggers and hippies before, offered aid but would not interfere with an adolescent's final decision.

For example, Looking Glass evaluators noted that, "While Looking Glass will not force a client to return home, all youngsters are told that little can be done for them unless they are willing to contact their parents.[37] The agency's only leverage with youth was in denying or withholding services—

it would *not* turn its clients over to authorities against their will. "The real failures of Looking Glass'" wrote its evaluators, "are the 12% who, rather than talk to their parents (a prerequisite for legal housing), left Looking Glass to return to the streets."[38]

The percentage of youth returning to the street as reported by Huckleberry House was even higher than that reported at Looking Glass. During its earliest years, Beggs said that youth chose "to keep running" (and not contact parents) in almost half its cases. He expressed hope that "after a few days of looking for his own place and grubbing for meals, the runaway may realize what he had at home—if only negotiations could be worked out so that there weren't so many strings attached to it."[39] So the philosophy was to let youth discover the difficulties of being on their own by themselves. The assumption was they would quickly conclude that home was a better place to be than scrounging on the street.

Of critical note, of course, is the complete deference to the young client in making the final decision, even if that meant he or she returned to the street and attempted to negotiate survival on his or her own. The purpose of the alternative agency was defeated if the end result of its work was that youth were turned over to parents, police, or child welfare authorities against their will. Thus for youth who wanted to use the program to negotiate with parents, they could. But for those who wanted to just move on, they could do that, too, without the threat of being identified to, or turned over to, authorities.

The question of age complicated matters for service providers. Clients who were above the state's age of majority posed no problem because they had the legal authority to make decisions for themselves. Underage youth, however, were another matter altogether. In general, working with minors required parental consent or the endorsement of police, juvenile justice, or child welfare authorities. In the eyes of the alternative community, such cooperation constituted untrustworthy adult behavior, jeopardized youth's autonomy, and threatened youth confidences. Like the crash pads of the counterculture, there was no lower-age boundary at which the rules changed. So the alternative agencies were faced with the dilemma of being trapped between their ideological commitment to a service delivery design based on self-determination and the legal and social rules of straight society.

Alternative agencies were in the position to act as bridge between child and parent, facilitating the youth's return home, but they also took a firm position against acting as a conduit of information to authorities. Minors were permitted to continue to drift outside the realm of adult care if they so chose. In this important way the alternative agencies aligned themselves with the values of the counterculture and of the youth rights movement.

Walking the Line Between Hip and Straight

The Board of Directors for Ozone House identified one of its program's major features as its "two-way interpretive task between 'straight' and 'hip' cultures."[40] In the early years, the alternative agencies walked a fine line between both the "hip" and the "straight" communities, constantly attempting to maintain their status with the former while establishing sufficient credibility to survive with the latter.

Digger Emmett Grogan complained that "Huckleberry House . . . was as lame as its name" and characterized it as a "nice, mild, safe, responsible way for the church to become involved in 'hippiedom.'"[41] However, Grogan's characterization of the alternative services as a safe and sanitized alternative for runaways missed the boat with respect to appreciating the difficulties and obstacles these alternative agencies faced with the straight world. Like the risk to crash pad operators in the hip community, the risk to the alternative providers involved the fact that most states had criminal laws against harboring a minor or interfering with custodial rights. For example, in the early 1970s, the Michigan law read:

> No person shall knowingly and willfully aid or abet a child under the age of 17 to violate an order of a juvenile court or knowingly and willfully conceal or harbor juvenile runaways who have taken flight from the custody of the court, their parents or legal guardian.[42]

It didn't matter if the persons doing the aiding or abetting were hippies, alternative service providers, family friends, or children's schoolteachers. Alternative providers were no more immune from police raids and legal sanctions than any of the others. Thus alternative service providers, like counterculture Diggers and hippies who operated crash pads, faced the very real prospect of police raids and staff arrest.

Beggs recalled discussing bail money at the very first organizational meeting of Huckleberry House.[43] The planners were anxious about their legal vulnerability, and they were right to worry. On October 19, 1967, several months after opening its doors, the police raided Huckleberry House, arresting all the youth (for being without parental supervision) and their adult caretakers (for contributing to the delinquency of minors).[44] At issue was Huckleberry House's failure to obtain parental consent for sheltering a 15-year-old boy.

It quickly became apparent that the State of California's primary concern rested in questions of legal authority, and its primary objective was to force Huckleberry House into an accountable slot in the public child welfare system. The state's position was that Huckleberry House was a child care agency within the statutory definition and needed to be licensed as such in order to provide service to those under 16. In contrast, Huckleberry House maintained that providing emergency shelter was merely incidental to returning the runaway home, and therefore Huckleberry House was not a child care agency nor was it subject to state regulation. The state forced a choice: apply for a license or cease housing youth under 16 years of age even *with* parental permission.

Beggs complained that this was where bureaucracy stifled innovation, because licensing was designed for traditional child welfare services and not for this new breed of runaway shelters. For example, if one followed the rules of the state's mandated intake policy, it could take several weeks to complete. Huckleberry's clients stayed on average two or three days. Although state representatives were generally cooperative and Huckleberry House struggled to comply, the alternative staff was particularly unhappy with the notion of licensed foster care for those under 16 because it was these very youth, they argued, who were in greatest need of emergency housing service. Without Huckleberry House, youth in this age group could only get shelter by turning themselves into the state-run Juvenile Hall or by going underground. Huckleberry House maintained that neither parents nor youth preferred these two options over its unique brand of crisis care service. Nonetheless, Huckleberry House eventually complied with the state in order to stay in business.

Ozone House faced similar hurdles in Michigan as it confronted the straight community but selected a different organizational strategy to address the core problem of how to handle underage clients, parents, and police. In its earliest years, it devised and adhered to a three-tiered approach to sheltering youth: crashing, fostering, and moling. As suggested by the labels themselves, these approaches reflected various levels of compromise (or not) with the straight community.

Crashing was defined as housing youth over the age of 17. Since these youth were over the age of majority, no parental consent was necessary and the policy did not run afoul of the custodial interference law. Ozone House did not operate an independent "crash pad" as suggested by the terminology. Instead, it maintained a list of sympathetic individuals and families in the Ann Arbor community who were willing to take in visiting youth. Thus it referred its crashers, on an individual basis, to private homes. Staff understood the risks associated with this strategy. The program's reputation rested, in part, on the good will of those community members willing to house long-haired wandering youth. It threatened the whole operation if these referred youth ended up being poor houseguests. For this reason, the staff of Ozone House suggested using the screening question "Would you feel comfortable crashing this person in your own home?" as the threshold for making a placement determination. This system was all but abandoned by 1973 as the agency turned its primary focus to younger children.[45]

The second housing alternative used by Ozone House was *fostering*. Like other alternative agencies, Ozone House faced state-licensing problems if it wanted to house underage clients even temporarily. So, by the early 1970s it had established a relationship with Catholic Social Services (CSS) and instituted a procedure for fostering youth which entailed referring them to state-licensed foster homes through CSS. This conveniently shifted legal responsibility to CSS for whatever took place in the foster setting. Parents had to consent to this kind of care and were asked to contribute a small sum for their child's upkeep although children were not denied services if parents failed to pay.

What was unique about this strategy was that the youth, rather than the parents or the state, initiated the service. Ozone's fostering system allowed the youth to trigger a "time-out period" away from home, as long as parents consented. So the net result was to provide short-term (two-week) crisis care and safe shelter without involving courts, judges, or child protective services.

The homes themselves were relatively unique by the standards of the child protective services and included single students and unmarried couples who "share Ozone's belief in a young person's right to self determination."[46] It was necessary, Ozone staff making those referrals were told, to "reassure young people that Ozone Foster Parents are not going to be like their parents, but that they are simply more Ozone people."[47] Even in foster homes, however, the alternative provider's policy on confidentiality was maintained. Parents received a "short non-identifying description of what the foster home is like"[48] if they requested it. However, Ozone House staff refused to disclose the whereabouts of children to their parents, although they were willing to relay messages.

Ozone House acknowledged the limitations of its fostering initiative almost immediately. By 1973 it was having trouble finding enough foster care homes to deal with its clients. In addition, and perhaps more importantly, it recognized that the runaway had to "expend energies adjusting to a new family which should be directed toward solving his own familial problems."[49] Thus, staff were worried that children had to devote unnecessary personal resources adjusting to yet another home environment on a short-term basis. Ozone House began to consider opening its own shelter. With federal funding for this sort of thing just down the road, this was what it eventually did.

Ozone House's third housing option was called *moling*, a term that captured its radical youth advocacy and antiestablishment nature. Moling was illegal because it involved housing a minor (under 17) without a parent or legal guardian's consent. Mole homes were used "when a young person cannot get parental permission for Foster Care, the young person refuses to contact his/her parents, is an institutional runaway, or in other special circumstances."[50] So while Ozone House attempted to obtain parental consent, it didn't necessarily turn away minors if either the parents or the child were uncooperative. All parties involved (staff, mole parents, and youth) incurred the risk of criminal charges for harboring minors without parental consent or state approval. The mole homes were not licensed.

Ozone House used mole homes cautiously and with full understanding of the risks involved. Staff was adamant that mole homes were not to be used by the youth as an excuse for avoiding personal or family problems—they were to be used in real crises situations when there appeared to be no other immediate alternative. Before deciding to mole a youth, counselors were urged to ask a series of responsible questions such as *are there alternatives?* And, *will moling help . . . in a way that s/he cannot be helped otherwise?* In addition, they asked more practical ones like *does this young person's parents have any friends or relatives who are law enforcement officers?* Perhaps the most interesting question on the list has to do with moral authority: *if we were caught, would we be able to justify our actions from a moral, if not legal standpoint?*[51] The debate about youth and youth rights was an ideological and radical one for the family of alternative service providers. "This is political to us because it involves change and new directions to the present system. Youth advocacy is political-radical because we are working from a unique position by believing in the rights of youth and change to a system that oppresses them."[52] Thus, ultimate authority for their policies and actions were derived from the providers' own ideas of moral authority but also held true to the Beat–Digger notion that autonomy was power.

Ozone House devised ways to minimize the risks, or at least to circumvent police, by creating a procedure that used backup volunteers to make the moling arrangement so that the placement was not made by the child's primary Ozone House counselor. According to the policy manual of the day, this procedure was instituted so that the child's primary counselor could honestly respond to those asking about the child's whereabouts by saying; "I do not know where s/he is. I did not find him/her housing."[53]

What is particularly interesting about Ozone's early strategy is that it illustrates so clearly the accommodations and adaptations alternative agencies made in order to promote their mission of youth autonomy while bridging the gap between hip and straight communities. Furthermore, Ozone House's tripartite strategy for dealing with housing youth is interesting for the language selected in describing it: *crashing* from the counterculture, *fostering* from the world of public child welfare, and *moling* suggesting the influence of the underground. It is indicative of the practical problems faced by alternative agencies trying to devise strategies consistent with their radical agenda to advocate for youth while confronting the real-world conditions and constraints presented by the straight community.

The Nomenclature Debate and Sanitizing the Service

Ozone House's struggle over what to call its temporary housing services illustrates the difficulty in characterizing and capturing a publicly acceptable label, and underscores some of the issues inherent in crisis sheltering. The press coverage of these alternative providers also reflects this struggle. For example, the YMCA in New York's East Village is said to have obtained an *apartment* and created a *commune*, but it also posted a sign on its door reading: "This is not a *crash pad*" (emphasis added).[54] In Philadelphia, a program called Voyage was described as "*hous[ing]* those whose needs are greatest and *crashes* others for a night or two" (emphasis added).[55] In Westport (Connecticut) a program called Phone-a-Home was characterized as "a volunteer *foster home*" program giving "*temporary lodging* to youngsters" on an "*emergency basis*," but "youngsters passing through the community who think Phone-a-Home would be a cool '*crash pad*' were *turned away*" (emphasis added).[56] In Fairfield County (Conn.), alternative agencies were reported as providing "*two halfway houses*" and were said to have "opened their doors to all youngsters who need *temporary homes.*" The program "*sheltered*" youth "for periods ranging from overnight to lengthy stays" (emphasis added).[57]

This struggle in labeling the service (crashing, lodging, sheltering, housing) and defining the temporal nature (halfway, crisis, temporary, overnight, lengthy) was important for two reasons. First, it suggested distancing from the counterculture's "crash pad" terminology, thus legitimizing the service by relying on more widely acceptable providers. Second, it illustrated the precarious nature of temporary housing, which filled the gap between the "street" and "home" environments. Public discourse began to reflect both dimensions of this intermediary position.

Runaway *shelters* were useful in "saving" youth both from bad homes and from the street. This was reflected in headlines describing runaways and runaway shelters: "Where Runaways Can Find a Haven";[58] "Priest's Shelter Tries to Salvage Times Sq. Youths";[59] "Two Houses Run by Church Offer Runaways Haven in Fairfield";[60] "An Oasis for Runaway Teen-Agers Appears in a Pornographic Desert."[61] Children could be described as finding a haven from violent and troubled home environments, reflecting a growing public willingness to attribute children's behavior on bad parenting and to focus on the innocence and vulnerability of youth. For example, youth seeking help in Connecticut were described as "coming from homes which are 'so intolerable that they have either fled or been told to leave.'"[62] Others were described as needing "time away from such family problems as divorce, violence, alienation, alcoholism and drug abuse."[63]

Shelters also provided resources and services to street-based populations. Philadelphia's Voyage was said to "supplement or replace the 'street' as the controlling factor in the lives of runaways."[64] Volunteers were described as searching Times Square in order to "reach new arrivals before the pimps do," and to "offer escape to those who have already fallen" into what one service provider called "'the bleak nether world of exploitation.'"[65] A youthful client from an East Village program called Project YES confirmed that if it wasn't for the program he would be "walking around the streets saying 'excuse me, mister, do you have a quarter?'"[66] From the media's perspective, then, the alternative service providers were protectors of children on all fronts, providing shelter from bad homes, from the street, from victimization, from exploitation, from starvation, from exposure, and from juvenile delinquency. Thus the runaway shelter could appear to be an appropriate solution for any number of different rhetorical constructions of public and private childhood problems.

Threats to Runaways and the Hotline Response

In addition to the runaway shelters of the late 1960s, yet another counterculture-based service response emerged to meet the needs of runaway youth in the early 1970s. It too functioned outside the mainstream of the child welfare service delivery system, privileged the values of the youth movement, served a practical function for autonomy-seeking youth, and addressed the rhetorical concerns about runaway children being raised in the media. It was the runaway "hotline."

In mid-August 1973 a grisly story dominated the front pages of newspapers nationwide as Americans read of the discovery of a mass grave outside Houston, Texas. The gruesome process of locating the badly decomposed bodies of dozens of teenage boys took over a week and was reported in multiple stories. First there were seventeen, then by August 11 twenty-three,[67] and by August 23 the number had climbed to twenty-seven, making it the largest serial killing in American history up to that time.[68]

An eerie tale emerged of a "polite 33-year-old Houston utility worker"[69] who had once owned a candy shop but "didn't seem to act his age."[70] It turned out this odd and childish one-time candy store owner, Dean Allen Corll, was a brutal, sadistic, sexually perverse, and ritualistic murderer. Furthermore, as the story unfolded it became apparent that most of his victims were runaway boys. Even worse, from the vantage point of a worried public, many of the boys had been reported missing from home by their parents. The case not only brought the issue of vulnerability and exploitation of runaway youth to the fore but raised questions about the ability of police to intercede or to protect them.

For at least a three-year period, Corll had played "sugar daddy" to a number of estranged runaway boys. He lured them to his home by hosting "parties" supplying drugs and providing food and other goodies to boys who were both hungry and needy. Corll subsequently handcuffed his victims to a specially designed board and sexually assaulted, sodomized, and tortured them before killing them. Corll paid two teenage boys, 17-year-old Elmer Wayne Henley and 18-year-old David Owen Brooks, $100 to procure youth—mostly hitchhiking runaways—for him. Corll eventually made the strategic mistake of threatening Henley directly. Henley murdered Corll and then led local authorities to all the bodies. Like the Linda Fitzpatrick murder in 1967, "Houston" would color the runaway discourse for the next few years, serving as a shorthand reminder of the dangers that could befall vulnerable runaway children.

On September 11, 1973, one month after the discovery of Corll's victims, a group of volunteer organizers—with the help of the Holiday Inn (which donated two rooms) and the support of Texas governor Dolph Briscoe—established Operation Peace of Mind, a local telephone "hotline" created as a service to "worried parents who feared their children had become victims of a mass murder ring" as well as to runaways who could confidentially relay messages to their parents or receive counseling.[71] Within months, Operation Peace of Mind had set up a nationwide WATS number.[72] An early poster advertising the program showed a scruffy long-haired teenager hitchhiking with a sign to "Anywhere" and a poster tag line which read: *Are you still alive? Let somebody know.*[73] One of Corll's teenage procurers had told reporters "to warn children against hitchhiking" because he had "picked up many victims that way."[74] The poster capitalized on this connection in advertising the hotline service.

Runaway hotlines shared many features and values with the alternative shelter movement. First, service was available 24-hours a day, so it was readily available to meet youths' immediate needs. Second, hotlines were operated primarily by volunteers with a small core of young, paid staff. Third, hotline service was confidential. Youth could obtain information, and parents did not need to be notified unless the youth requested or permitted it. The hotline had several service objectives. It was a way for runaway children to call family or friends and let them know they were safe. These messages or "safety calls" could be passed along to parents confidentially; youth did not need to provide information to phone operators about their whereabouts. Staff insisted confidentiality was necessary, and volunteers could assure it "without deception" because "we truthfully don't know where the kids are when they call and we don't ask."[75] So "no matter how much parents may pry for the information," there was little information that hotline operators could convey unless the youth had requested that they do so.[76] This was not unlike Ozone House's approach of shielding primary counselors from knowledge about where children were "moled" so they could honestly deny knowing this if confronted by authorities.

The hotline provided "immediate help" by passing on "information to runaways to assist them finding shelter, food, and other services, in cities throughout the nation."[77] Thus the runaway hotline supplemented the alternative shelter system because it helped youth locate temporary housing and other youth-friendly services. The once-held belief that local police could intercept runaways was replaced by the growing public acceptance that it was incumbent on runaway adolescents to seek services voluntarily.

One consequence of "Houston," then, was the emergence of a national runaway hotline. This helpline, crisis line, or hotline model had bubbled up from underground examples like Haight-Ashbury's Community Switchboard. Before the Houston discovery, helpline efforts were mostly local and referred youth to services within communities. Following the Houston murders, concerned community members recognized the need and utility of a national system. Thus began efforts to compile data to permit runaway youth to access information about safe, temporary shelter in cities across the nation. In addition, hotlines permitted youth to convey information to parents without revealing their whereabouts. The hotline, like runaway shelters, purported to protect youth from the negative outcomes of living on the street or being on their own by helping them find resources, but it did so without threatening their autonomy, betraying their confidences, or invoking law enforcement or juvenile justice systems. In the end, the entire package—the national hotline system that referred youth to crisis shelters anywhere in the country—replicated and legitimized the underground communication system and network of crash pads of the 1960s counterculture.

Legitimization and the Irony of Maturity

Taken together, the runaway shelter and the runaway hotline as service responses to the runaway problem came to the attention of federal legislators in the early 1970s. This, coupled with increasing legitimacy, acceptance, and tolerance by local and state authorities, created a crisis of conscience for alternative service providers.

For example, in 1974 Ozone House noted that the local "straight" community had grown to accommodate the alternative agencies, or as captured in Ozone House files: "the police/juvenile court/institution 'block' [sic] seems to be more tolerant toward Ozone and its style of services." Although the providers wanted to stay true to their radical roots and their youth advocacy mission, the Board of Directors acknowledged a pragmatic problem: "Ozone needs money to survive."[78] The opportunity to compete for federal funding was soon to be a reality.

Many of the alternative providers viewed contracts with the federal government suspiciously. It was a dance with the devil. Federal funds came with rules, regulations, oversight, supervision, and requirements of public accountability. Taking funds from the Establishment meant trading in their freedom to operate outside the system. Nonetheless, generating sufficient funds to stay in business had been a constant struggle for these grassroots organizations. A group of Ozone House's in-house policymakers tackled the issue directly: "how much of our 'alternativeness' are we willing to sell in return for funding?"[79] But in the true spirit of an agency forged in the radical community it also asked, "How do we get the $ with the least amount of strings attached?"[80] The issue was debated fully at Ozone House, as in other alternative agencies nationwide. The staff of Ozone House contemplated the scope and structure of critical services and the agency's core identity, including where they might be willing to compromise. They even pondered the possibility—remote as it may have seemed to some—that federal accountability might actually result in better service. For example, some suggested that program evaluations might lead to greater emphasis on the quality of service and on client outcomes. Furthermore, they acknowledged that government money was enticing because it permitted staff to experiment with "more diversified models of delivering service to runaway youth."[81]

Buried in a folder of Board of Directors minutes from a meeting held on October 14, 1974, is an intriguing note: "The program can't drift back underground after developing legitimacy in the community."[82] Therein lies a particularly telling truth: radicalism can't survive indefinitely. By the mid-1970s the struggle to earn legitimacy, which had been part of the radical mission, had mostly been won. The only two paths that seemed available were toward extinction or toward the mainstream.

So the direction surviving shelters took, for the most part, was toward the mainstream and a stable place in the network of acknowledged youth services. The agencies surviving into the next decades, including Covenant House, Ozone House, and Huckleberry House (renamed Huckleberry for Youth), necessarily traded at least some of their "alternativeness" to gain legitimacy in their respective communities.[83] Over time the rhetoric about children receiving services at shelters has changed, and the focus now includes those who are homeless, shoved out, or thrown out of family homes. Furthermore, children served come from diverse ethnic and socio-economic backgrounds. Services have expanded to included outreach, transitional living, and aftercare. In addition, the National Runaway Switchboard, based in Chicago—which received a government contract in preference over Operation Peace of Mind following the enactment of the Runaway Youth Act of 1974—is well established (1–800–621–4000). Nonetheless, the roots of this package of alternative runaway services (shelter and hotline) can't be denied; they are deeply intertwined with the missions and values first introduced by the counterculture communities that spawned them in the late 1960s.

Policy and "Runaway" Youth

Shifting Institutional Structures

From Moral Guidance to Autonomous Denizens

(1960–1978)

Public Institutional Responsibility and the Role of Juvenile Courts

In the early 1960s, California and New York led a reform movement that created legal distinctions between *juvenile delinquents* and *status offenders*. Over the next decade other states followed suit. The idea was to create two distinct categories of legal actions against children—one for youth whose offenses would be criminal if committed by an adult (delinquency), the other for those whose chronic behavior made them difficult to supervise. The adjustment in state law seemed harmless and logical enough, in the abstract. Yet it had profound impact on the institutional rules regulating runaway behavior and triggered complex dilemmas. New York State serves as an excellent example of the ripple effect of this structural change.[1]

In 1962 the New York State legislature created a uniform statewide family court system that replaced or supplemented a mosaic of existing rules which had been laid down piecemeal during the preceding fifty years for dealing with troublesome children, including runaways.[2] None of the Family Court Act's provisions was completely new. However, by reorganizing and modifying existing rules, the New York State legislature articulated a

---

Box 6.1

New York State

WAYWARD MINOR ACT / *CODE OF CRIMINAL PROCEDURE* § 913-A:

Any person between the ages of 16 and 21 who either

1. is habitually addicted to the use of drugs or the intemperate use of intoxicating liquors, or
2. habitually associates with dissolute persons, or
3. is found of his or her own free will and knowledge in a house of prostitution, assignation or ill fame, or
4. habitually associates with thieves, prostitutes, pimps or procurers, or disorderly persons, or
5. is willfully disobedient to the reasonable and lawful commends of parent, guardian or other custodian and is morally depraved or is in danger of becoming morally depraved, or
6. who without just cause and without the consent of parents, guardians or other custodians, deserts his or her home or place of abode, and is morally depraved or is in danger of becoming morally depraved, or
7. who so deports himself or herself as to willfully injure or endanger the morals or health of himself or herself or of others may be deemed a wayward minor.

The interstate compact on juveniles shall apply to wayward minors to the same extent as to minors below 16 years of age except that the provisions of article four of said compact shall apply only to wayward minors included within (6) hereof.

---

new philosophical vision and set the policies and procedures for dealing with youth into considerable flux. It would take the next decade for these changes to settle into predictable patterns. However, during the process of institutionalizing the reform, serious practical and structural problems became evident, particularly when dealing with chronic runaways.

To appreciate the unfolding institutional drama, it is useful to remember some of the modifications the Family Court Act imposed on the preexisting rules for dealing with adolescents (see chapter 1). The provisions of the Wayward Minor Act were housed in New York State's Criminal Procedure Code (see box 6.1). These applied to young adults (ages 16–21) and covered a wide range of *morally* suspicious behavior. The moral jurisdictional base of the statute included concern for those who endangered the morals or health of

---

Box 6.2

The New York Statute of 1924 (Chapter 254)

DELINQUENT CHILD DEFINED

The words "delinquent child" shall mean a child over seven and under sixteen years of age who violates any law of this state or any ordinance of the city of New York, or who commits any act punishable otherwise than by death or life imprisonment; who is incorrigible, ungovernable or habitually disobedient and beyond the control of his parents, guardian, custodian or other lawful authority; who is habitually truant; who, without just cause and without the consent of his parent, guardian or other custodian, deserts his home or place of abode; who engages in any occupation which is in violation of law; who begs or solicits alms or money in public places; who frequents any place the maintenance of which is in violation of law; who habitually uses obscene or profane language; or who so deports himself as willfully to injure or endanger the morals or health of himself or others.

---

themselves or others. The statute covered past behaviour, but it served as a prevention and intervention tool for future behavior as well. The delinquency provisions, on the other hand, commingled noncriminal behavior (such as leaving home without cause, cursing, or being habitually disobedient) with criminal behavior (such as violating state law) (see box 6.2). In either case, punishment for wayward or delinquent minors was essentially the same. Children could be sent to state reformatories, state training schools, or private agencies for indeterminate amounts of time. Although they were not supposed to be housed in facilities with adults, that prohibition was not absolute and an explicit exception existed to "prevent escape." So it was permissible to incarcerate children—particularly those with a propensity to run away or otherwise elope—with adults.

Taken together, the state's reach over minors was considerable from the 1920s into the 1960s. It included regulating criminal and noncriminal behaviors. It included youth up to the age of 21. It included intervening on moral grounds for actual behavior or potential behavioral problems. It permitted imposing sanctions ranging from probation to indeterminate sentences in reformatories for any of these activities. The state could exercise broad discretion and justified doing so in arguments about public morals, safety, and the welfare of both youth and the community.

Significant Restructuring of Policy Frameworks:
A New Conceptual Organization

The Family Court Act of 1962 (FCA) rewrote the rules. First, it created three conceptually distinct categories. In addition to juvenile delinquency[3] and status offenses—known in New York as Persons in Need of Supervision,[4] or PINS[5]—it added a third category: *abused and neglected children* (FCA, art. 10). The final category targeted parents who either abused, failed to supervise, or otherwise neglected their children.

On its face, the FCA appears merely to rearrange the conceptual framework of regulations already present under earlier provisions on wayward minors and delinquents, but this is not the case. There were critical differences. Specifically, it deleted all references to morality, it reduced the age of intervention from 21 to 18 for girls and to 16 for boys, it excluded criminal offenses from the delinquency provisions, and finally, it appeared to require different treatment plans for status offenders, delinquents, and abused and neglected children. Each of these factors had a profound practical effect on the state's ability to conduct its business with children, particularly those who ran away from home.

Relinquishing Moral Authority and Running Away

Although the state's responsibility for the moral education of its young citizens was essentially written out of the PINS statute, the earliest decisions reflected the long-established role of courts in safeguarding public morals. More importantly, however, the Wayward Minor Act continued to be used until 1971. Thus the courts' moral reach over children, particularly girls, was slowly extinguished during the decade of the 1960s. By the early 1970s it was gone completely.

Two things happened in 1971 to end the judiciary's reign of moral supervision. First, the New York State legislature simply permitted the wayward minor law to expire on August 31, 1971. That seems final enough; however, in addition, the U.S. Supreme Court affirmed a lower court's ruling that the Wayward Minor Act was unconstitutional.[6] The statute had withstood constitutional challenges in New York's highest court twice before, once in 1966 and again in 1968. In the third attempt, even though the law was set to expire, the Court of Appeals retained jurisdiction on behalf of those children who would have remained sentenced to custody, parole, or probation after its scheduled expiration.

The case, *Gesicki v. Oswald*, involved three girls (Esther Gesicki, Marion Johnson, and Dominica Morelli), each of whom had been committed with indeterminate sentences of one to three years to a New York State reformatory under the Wayward Minor Act. Each was convicted because of her "moral depravity," and all three girls had histories of running away. The basic facts of their individual cases are telling.

Esther Gesicki had been living on her own following her mother's institutionalization in a state mental hospital. She was expelled from school because of her alleged sexual promiscuity. She was committed to the state reformatory for violating her probation by running away from a foster home. The petition alleged she had sexual relations with fourteen men, calling into question her morality and the soundness of her judgment.[7]

Marion Johnson had lived in foster homes since the age of five, and was adjudicated a wayward minor at 17 when she refused to sign adoption papers for her out-of-wedlock child. She ran away from foster care after being denied permission to visit the baby's father. She was charged with being willfully disobedient and in danger of becoming morally depraved.[8]

Dominica Morelli also grew up in a troubled home—her mother had remarried four times. One stepfather had sexually abused her. She was placed in a foster home after her alcoholic mother was found unfit, but she ran away and was ultimately charged with violating probation when she "journeyed" out of state "without her mother's permission."[9]

One of the critical issues before the court involved the constitutionality of the provisions regulating morality. In a district court opinion, Judge Morris E. Lasker put the issue in historical perspective, writing:

> Whatever the significance of the phrase "morally depraved" may have had at an earlier date of more absolute standards, the mistiness of its contemporary interpretation is such as to make it unusable as a standard of conduct, and certainly such as to raise a substantial question as to whether it is not unconstitutionally vague.[10]

He went on to argue that if "morally depraved" was problematic language, then "in danger of becoming" morally depraved was even worse. The three-judge appeals panel agreed, concluding that the "concept of morality has occupied men of extraordinary intelligence for centuries, without notable progress (among even philosophers and theologians) toward a common understanding."[11] The court held that the provisions of the Wayward Minor Act were unconstitutionally vague.

The facts in *Gesicki* suggest just how far the State of New York had been willing to go in its intervention with young people. It played an unapologetic role as protector and enforcer of public morals, and was willing to discipline its youthful citizens by restricting their liberty. On the other hand, the girls did not present easy cases. They came from deeply troubled backgrounds and had long histories of family problems. *Gesicki* is also useful in foreshadowing the kind of factual patterns that will appear before the new family court. Yet this new court had greatly restricted reach over children with histories like those of Gesicki, Johnson, and Morelli.

Gender-based Age Distinctions and Running Away

A year after the *Gesicki* decision, a more specific gender-based challenge brewed in New York State. The original 1962 PINS statute had permitted intervention with girls and boys at different maximum ages (18 and 16, respectively).[12] In 1972, in *Patricia A. v. City of New York*,[13] the New York Court of Appeals struck down the age differential as it applied to girls as an unconstitutional violation of the equal protection clause.[14] In doing so, it drastically diminished the state's reach over its children. Thus the maximum age of regulating behavior (boys or girls) dropped to 16 and, as a practical matter, to 15 since jurisdiction was lost on the child's sixteenth birthday. This new maximum age limit applied to all PINS behavior, including running away. The net result was that a child could run away (even repeatedly) with impunity at 16.

The decision and resulting shift in policy did not go unnoticed. About three weeks after the *Patricia A.* decision, Stanley Gartenstein, a Bronx family court judge, complained that the equal protection argument might better have been made on behalf of boys between 16 and 18 who had a right to treatment, than to girls between 16 and 18 who didn't.[15] In the case before Judge Gartenstein, Gregory, a minor, had assaulted his father, who subsequently obtained an order of protection against his son. The order barred the boy from entering his family home. Using the word "unfortunately" twice to describe the resulting situation, Gartenstein observed: "Gregory is under age and cannot wander the streets on his own." Yet the court lacked PINS jurisdiction, that "having been lost on his 16th birthday."[16] The result "leaves Gregory outside the home and unsupervised." In vacating Gregory's PINS warrant, the court "acknowledge[d] its helplessness" but hoped that "the Legislature may yet save potential youths similarly situated, trapped by circumstances over which they have no control, whose right to self realization may well be contingent on the existence or lack of it of jurisdiction of this court."[17] In short, the judge argued it would have been better to raise the age of PINS jurisdiction to 18 rather than lowering it to 16. He was not alone. The argument made by Judge Gartenstein was also being made by police officers and service providers as well, but it fell on deaf legislative ears for decades.[18]

In short, between 1971 and 1972 the demise of the Wayward Minor Act and these PINS cases drastically altered the state's authority. The combined effect was twofold. First, there was a precipitous drop in the age (from 21 to below 16) for which behavioral misconduct could be regulated. Second, it created a particular problem for 16- and 18-year-olds. Since the state lowered its age of majority to 18 in 1972, the judicially rewritten statute left a jurisdictional vacuum for those who were out of reach of the PINS law at 16 but not yet fully vested with the rights of adults until 18. From the youth's perspective, these alterations meant he or she could decide to leave home, skip school, avoid curfew, and perform any other act of willful disobedience at relatively younger ages. Conversely, from the state's perspective, it meant it lost much of its ability to control and discipline youth on and after their sixteenth birthday. To the extent that parents turned to the juvenile courts for help with ungovernable teenagers, this meant that parents also lost a tool for interceding. Beginning in 1972—as the Baby Boomers were still aging through their teenage years—16-year-olds, both boys and girls in New York State, could freely roam.

One Nonviolation or Many Behaviors? More Jurisdictional Seepage

New York State not only lost control of runaways because of the age provisions in the PINS statute. Substantial authority was also ceded to youth as the courts attempted to bring meaning to the legislative decision to separate PINS from juvenile delinquency proceedings. It would take more than a decade of judicial activity to work out the basic rules. As courts struggled to establish these rules, judges repeatedly complained about the consequences and practical implications of their decisions and advised legislators to reconsider some basic flaws in the structure of the FCA itself.

The first problem involved excluding petty criminal activities from the juvenile delinquency provisions. In order to proceed, the petition had to allege acts that would be criminal if they had been committed by an adult. Built into the statutory definition of *criminal* was reference to New York State's Penal Code, and also a problem. Felonies and misdemeanors were included, while *offenses* were not. (This is in direct contrast with the delinquency provisions of the 1930s, which which included all these infractions within the delinquency statute.) Offenses consisted of such commonplace violations as disorderly conduct, public intoxication, harassment, loitering, trespassing, and prostitution (as well as the more historically dated bean-shooting, peddling, and stone throwing). So unless the predicate incident constituted a crime (i.e., misdemeanor or felony), it did not amount to a delinquent act. More than a few family court judges were incensed by the exclusion.[19] "Are we now to say to a child that you may commit an act labeled an offense with impunity?"[20] Judge Richards W. Hannah of Kings County asked rhetorically.

While one problem rested in the fact that the juvenile delinquency statute omitted offenses, the general problem was aggravated by the PINS statute's requirement that the child had to engage in *repeated* bad behavior. Unlike delinquency jurisdiction (which could be predicated on a single incident), PINS required allegations of habitual or chronic behavior. Judge Hannah complained in his written opinion that "this petition again directs attention to a serious lack of jurisdiction in this court; namely, its lack of jurisdiction over offenses."[21] He queried: "Are we to say to the public that you must wait until a child commits a crime or falls under the definition of a person in need of supervision before the court can exercise its jurisdiction and extend its facilities of rehabilitation?" And further commented: "it is my opinion that the welfare of the community and the child demands that this immunity for children who commit acts termed offenses be removed and the court have the power to deal with such acts even if a single violation of law."[22] In short, judges who once had a great deal of discretion in dealing with children suddenly felt constrained.

During the 1960s, New York's appellate courts repeatedly grappled with the distinction between delinquency[23] and "in need of supervision"[24] cases. The matter was finalized in 1971 when the state's highest court held that a

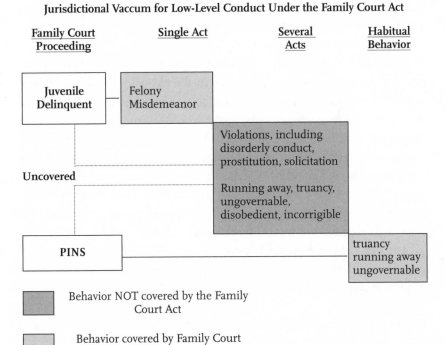

Figure 6.1

Jurisdictional Vaccum for Low-Level Conduct Under the Family Court Act

Family Court Proceeding	Single Act	Several Acts	Habitual Behavior
Juvenile Delinquent	Felony Misdemeanor		
		Violations, including disorderly conduct, prostitution, solicitation	
Uncovered		Running away, truancy, ungovernable, disobedient, incorrigible	
PINS			truancy running away ungovernable

☐ Behavior NOT covered by the Family Court Act

☐ Behavior covered by Family Court Jurisdiction

single act of harassment (an offense) was not a sufficient predicate to sustain a delinquency petition, and that more than an isolated incident was necessary to support a determination of "in need of supervision."[25]

In the end, running away once or twice, or perhaps even more, wasn't subject to regulation under either the delinquency or the PINS sections of the FCA. A child had to be away from home chronically or habitually before the court could intervene. While it might intuitively and conceptually make sense to delay intervention until a pattern was established so as not to intervene too early, as a practical matter it meant a child had an opportunity to stray—physically and emotionally—quite far from home before receiving attention.

Furthermore, by removing violations from its jurisdictional reach, the legislature excluded activities that served as a bridge between "criminal" behavior on the one hand and mere "misconduct" on the other, thus widening the distance between delinquency and PINS categories (see fig. 6.1). This had a direct impact on runaway youth whose behavior frequently fell into the ensuing vacuum. In fact, offenses such as prostitution, disorderly conduct, loitering, or trespassing were the very ones most commonly associated with running away.

Ironically, habitual truancy and chronic running away, the allegations at the heart of most PINS petitions, permitted children to avoid two primary institutions of socialization and education (family and school); at the same time, the state (through its courts) was abdicating its role as guarantor of the moral and civic training of children. In short, as the state waited for an accumulation of habitual acts it also subsidized the youth's ability to circumvent these socializing institutions. Therefore, chronic runaways, acculturated street children, throwaways, homeless youth, and children with histories of mental illness or serious behavioral problems were among those whom the state had delegated greater freedom through its own diminished role.

The net result was that it is possible, even probable, that children like prostituting 12-year-old Veronica Brunson could become well entrenched in street life before triggering significant state intervention.

Enhancing Constitutional Protections of Minors

In addition to jurisdictional gaps, and in keeping with a line of U.S. Supreme Court decisions during this period, New York was also applying increasingly stringent constitutional due process protections for youth in family court proceedings. Areas that received attention included adequate representation of counsel,[26] the right to remain silent,[27] the right to a fair hearing,[28] and safeguards against admissions of guilt.[29] In terms of runaway behavior, perhaps the most important protection involved increasing the burden of proof necessary to sustain a PINS finding from *preponderance of the evidence* to *beyond a reasonable doubt*.

The court had routinely applied the lower standard—preponderance of the evidence—in the 1960s.[30] The proper evidentiary standard continued to be contested in New York State[31] even after the U.S. Supreme Court had seemingly resolved the issue in its 1970 ruling in *In re Winship* (which raised the standard to beyond reasonable doubt). The matter of the appropriate evidentiary standard in PINS cases was finally settled by New York State's highest court in 1974 when it held that proof beyond a reasonable doubt was constitutionally required for adjudication of a minor as a PINS.[32]

The net result of this constitutional activity was twofold. On one hand, adolescents received greater protection from arbitrary judicial discretion, and their civil rights and liberty interests were protected. On the other, the state's authoritative role was diminished and with it the reach of parents and the state to intervene with adolescents based on their behavior.

Available Interventions

There remained one final but very serious issue: what should the court do with a PINS youth once it had one? It was a political as well as practical problem, and it caused New York's family court judges untold irritation and heartache.

Historically, youth with behavioral problems had been incarcerated together with delinquent youth. However, New York courts reasoned that if the legislature had gone to such great lengths to separate PINS and juvenile delinquency at the outset of the legal proceedings, then certainly it must have intended that children be treated differently at the other end of the process. Greatly complicating the problem was the fact that New York State's Department of Social Services (DSS) had assumed primary responsibility for abused and neglected children and had built a foster care system in response which relied, in part, on contracting with private agencies to provide placements. Concurrently, New York State's Division for Youth (DFY) had assumed primary responsibility for delinquent youth and ran training schools and other secure and nonsecure facilities. However, to the enormous frustration of family court judges, neither DSS nor DFY seemed particularly eager to deal with PINS cases. Furthermore, the private sector, which the legislature had assumed would fill the gap in service for these nondelinquent youth, had not done so in sufficient force to abate the crisis.

The judicial process of spelling out the letter of the law—while discovering the reality that services were neither in place nor forthcoming—was a painful one. The placement debate had three facets. First, what treatment was appropriate for children needing supervision? Arguments focused on whether PINS could, or should, be confined to state training schools and reformatories like delinquent youth. Second, which public agency, DFY or DSS, should take primary responsibility for PINS? In other words, should PINS be placed under the jurisdiction of the agency that primarily dealt with delinquent youth or the one that dealt with abused and neglected children? They reflected fundamental differences in treatment philosophy. Third, what was the appropriate role of the private sector?

By the late 1970s it was clear to anyone in the know that facilities or treatment centers for chronic runaways were lacking. The problem got even worse if you coupled chronic ungovernable behavior with other complications such as pregnancy, teen parenthood, mental or emotional health issues, mental retardation, or developmental delays. By the time Veronica Brunson plunged to her death in 1977, there was a near-complete void in service for children like her; so, wayward girls who until 1971 had been locked up for their "moral depravity" had by 1978 virtually no place to go but the streets. But this time they did so, essentially, with the blessing of state legislators.

What Kind of Treatment?

From the start, the legislative plan for treating children in need of supervision was not well conceived. In 1964, New York's highest court faced its first challenge, in fairly dramatic fashion, when the superintendent of Westfield State Farm, a women's reformatory operated by New York State's Corrections Department, simply refused to accept the court-ordered placement of a 17-year-old girl who had been adjudicated a PINS.[33] Westfield's position was that it was only authorized to accept females placed under the Penal Code and not girls "in need of supervision." While endorsing Westfield's position and overruling the lower court's order, the Court of Appeals drew a distinction between the word "placement," found in the dispositional language of the PINS statute, and "commitment" found in the language of the delinquency statute. Westfield was not an authorized agency within the meaning of the PINS statute because it amounted to a commitment rather than a placement. The court reasoned that sending PINS to "penal institutions . . . would be at cross purposes with the underlying design of the new Family Court Act."[34]

The decision precipitated a crisis. What to do now? Legislators responded with a stopgap measure that permitted placement of PINS in state training schools. It was a provision that was supposed to be temporary, but it was reauthorized for four successive years (from 1964 to 1967). In 1968, rather than revisit the underlying philosophical issues which had created the dilemma in the first place, the legislature simply authorized this disposition permanently.

That was not the end of the friction. In 1968, state training schools began refusing to accept pregnant girls, thus precipitating a variation on a theme of the underlying problem. In one compelling article, the *New York Times* described the appearance of a weeping, 7-months pregnant 14-year-old who was "a chronic truant and runaway" before a judge who ordered her placed in the custody of New York City's Commissioner of Social Services. Describing the scenario as "typical" of the 4,382 PINS cases the city courts had handled in the preceding year, the order illuminated the problem that DSS had "no facilities for caring for such children."[35] Children adjudicated as PINS were sometimes spending months in limbo waiting for permanent placement, and the problem was even worse for children with additional complicating problems. This case, of course, raised a secondary problem. Not only was it hard to know in what kind of facility to put PINS-adjudicated youth, it was unclear which agency was responsible for the most difficult placement cases.

Department of Social Services (DSS) or Division for Youth (DFY)?

In the first half of the 1970s, New York State's highest court and its two most overburdened and critically loquacious judicial departments (First and Second) engaged in a four-year judicial dialogue on appropriate PINS placements. In the process, not only was black letter law articulated, but the judiciary, in uncharacteristically acrimonious dicta, repeatedly recorded complaints and warnings about the impending crisis and scolded legislators, politicians, and agency administrators for their inaction.

For three consecutive years (1973–1975)[36] New York State's highest court was confronted with critical cases involving placement issues as they bubbled up from the active appellate courts. Before the first of these cases, a frustrated First Department ("frankly, we also are at a loss")[37] openly sympathized with its lower court judges ("there is little doubt that . . . the learned Family Court Judge was doing the best that he could . . . in a well-nigh impossible situation and one with which he never should have been faced")[38] and laid blame on legislative inaction ("the provision of proper facilities is the responsibility of the Legislature and the legislative failure in that regard does not warrant circumvention of the statute").[39] The press called the opinion "an unusual display of exasperation" and the attack on legislative inaction "caustic."[40]

The facts of the case triggering this hostility dated back to 1967 and the placement of a 12-year-old boy in the custody of DSS as a neglected child. His stay in placement, according to the cynical court, was "more a matter of official notation than actual residence" since he "constantly eloped to his mother's home and remained there for extended periods."[41] Repeated attempts at placement in both private charitable institutions and foster homes had met with failure. In frustration, the lower court judge, looking for some measure of control, converted the case from one of parental neglect to PINS and ordered the boy confined in the Otisville Training School for a period of up to eighteen months. The appellate court, while sympathetic, held that this conversion was not warranted and—without hiding its annoyance at the system—went on to write: "the court obviously cannot provide a facility where none exists."[42]

As disgruntled as the First Department was, it paled in comparison to the irritation expressed in a string of opinions issued by the Second Department between 1970 and 1972.[43] First, it overruled a PINS placement order that sent a girl to a training school for up to eighteen months and remanded her to the Commissioner of Social Services for more suitable placement. While recognizing the difficulties, the court found the distinction between PINS and delinquents "useless where, as here, the treatment accorded the one must be identical to that accorded the other solely because no other adequate alternative has been provided" and noted that "this case points up again the increasingly urgent need for proper facilities to provide adequate supervision and treatment for infants found to be persons in 'need of supervision.' "[44]

In another case, it located the genesis of a girl's "propensity for absconding from home" in the "unwholesome and often bizarre home environment and family tensions to which she has been subjected since she was seven or eight years of age," and rejected the notion that her commitment to a training school was acceptable because there were no other alternatives.[45] The court rejected "as defeatism, the premise that children in need of supervision, such as appellant, must be confined as quasi criminals because allegedly there are no viable alternatives."[46]

In a third case, the court reversed an order confining a PINS to a DFY training school for up to eighteen months, finding that it did not meet the treatment needs of the boy in question.[47] Finally, the court's frustration seems at its greatest in a case involving a 13-year-old girl committed to a training school after being adjudicated as a PINS. It remanded the case for further exploration of more suitable treatment options. Although the court openly sympathized with the lower court's judge and his lack of options, the higher court concluded that, "The obligation of society to this young girl is to rehabilitate her" and warned that sending her to a "facility with those confined for misconduct of a criminal nature" was to admit the "abject failure" of "our judicial system."[48]

New York State's highest court, the Court of Appeals, faced with such truculence in the courts below it, first weighed in on the acrimonious placement debate in a case known as *Ellery C.*[49] Ellery had an IQ of 69, placing him on the border of mental retardation. Ellery's mother had originally petitioned the family court in 1971, when her son was 14. At that time, allegations of his misbehavior included skipping school, avoiding curfew, fighting with his siblings, disobedience and petty theft from home. Following his adjudication as a PINS, Ellery refused to stay where he was sent. According to the appellate court, "every effort" at placement in a "non-structured" facility had ended in Ellery's running away. So the court confined the 15-year-old to a state training school.

In overturning that placement decision, the Court of Appeals found a "vital" distinction in the statutory language on dispositional hearings.[50] In delinquency hearings, the court was to determine whether the youth required "supervision, treatment or confinement" while PINS statutory language referred only to "supersivion or treatment." The court reasoned that the omission of the word *confinement* from the PINS menu "was no mere oversight."[51] It noted that lower courts had "severely condemned" the practice of placing PINS in the same institutional settings as juvenile delinquents and worried that doing so would result in PINS-adjudicated youth becoming "well tutored in the ways of crime."[52] Furthermore it would not be consistent "with the implied, if not explicit" intent of the legislation to confine PINS with "adjudicated juvenile delinquents in a prison environment."[53] Historically, the argument against incarcerating children with adult criminals was that it gave rise to dangerous socialization; here the argument is extended to include the commingling of children adjudicated as PINS with children convicted of delinquency.

The Court of Appeals quoted the dissent of the lower court and its worry about the effect of mixing PINS and delinquent youth in a single facility:

[C]onfinement in the training school, along with juveniles convicted of committing criminal acts, "can hardly, in any realistic sense, serve as 'supervision' and 'treatment' for him. On the contrary, it may well result in his emerging from his incarceration well tutored in the ways of crime."[54]

The dissent laid blame where it saw fit: "I do not believe that the State or City of New York may default in its duty under the statute to provide a minor with supervision and treatment suitable for his needs." The court rejected the notion that the training school was "the only facility available which could possibly help this boy become a constructive member of society."[55]

The concerns of the court about children becoming "well tutored in the ways of crime" dramatically and tragically foreshadowed events of just a few months later. A troubling story appeared on the front page of the *New York Times* under the headline, "Court May Have Freed Slaying Suspect, 16." It expressed concern that, "A 16-year-old youth arrested for a murder in a subway station . . . is believed by officials to be the youngster who was sent home from a state training school last July after a landmark decision by the state's highest court."[56] Indeed, *Ellery C.* became known as Ellery Coleman, who stabbed a 14-year-old boy to death in the Utica Avenue IND subway station. Officials called it "a classic example of the revolving door" and of our "failures to help troubled kids."

A lawsuit against New York State brought by the victim's father for negligence made a series of arguments about the state's failure to provide appropriate services for Ellery.[57] Among other things, the father argued that Ellery had not had appropriate rehabilitative supervision, and had been placed improperly, where he was educated further in crime. Finally, he argued that the state had failed to protect the public. Not unexpectedly, the claim was dismissed, but not before the court pointed out that because children in need of supervision had not engaged in criminal-like conduct, a PINS "cannot be categorized as a direct threat to society."[58] In historic context, the argument is interesting because it stands in stark contrast with the earlier position that wayward youth, particularly those in danger of becoming morally depraved, *were* a direct threat to public welfare and therefore intervention was justified. Furthermore, it is interesting because it reflected the notion that children who engaged in criminal conduct and those who engaged in behavioral misconduct were two entirely different species. It is a fallacy that persists in statutory construction to this day.

The Ellery ruling generated considerable confusion. It wasn't immediately clear exactly what constituted acceptable treatment. It appeared as though the court might have intended to bar the institutionalization of PINS altogether. The proliferation of conflicting decisions warranted yet another review of the issue. In 1974 the issue returned to the highest court in an appeal that consolidated two cases—one from the First Department and one from the Second.

The facts of the two cases were similar. They both involved youth who had been incarcerated in DFY state training schools for up to two years, largely because they had backgrounds of running away, thus making them difficult for nonsecure facilities to control. In the First Department case,[59] a mother had filed a PINS petition against her daughter, Lavette, when she was 13 because she ran away from home continually. Lavette was remanded originally to a shelter run by DSS but was transferred to a DFY voluntary group home in South Lansing. She continued to run away. Following two additional attempts at private placements and the refusal of South Lansing to readmit her, the family court ordered Lavette confined to Hudson State Training School, which was allegedly an "all PINS facility." A deeply divided appellate court affirmed the placement.

The Second Department case involved Maurice C., an orphan with "a long history of elopements from foster homes and other unstructured facilities" (although he had never committed a delinquent act).[60] He was diagnosed as suffering from "childhood schizophrenia, poor judgment and lack of insight."[61] The initial PINS petition was filed by his foster care social workers and recited a long list of his runaway episodes which included such destinations as Washington, D.C., Chicago, Cleveland, and Fort Lauderdale. In exasperation, the trial court judge ordered 14-year-old Maurice placed in a PINS-only facility, the Tryon State Training School.

The Appellate Division was not satisfied that PINS-only really meant, "PINS only." It insisted it would have been "content to reverse the order" and remand it to the family court for placement "in a more suitable environment" if it hadn't been for the "self-serving declarations" found in DFY's *amicus* brief and assertions made by New York City's Corporation Counsel that "segregation of the two types of children has already been accomplished."[62] The court opined that in spite of "commendable efforts of the

Division for Youth to improve conditions in the State training schools and of the voluntary agencies in developing new programs" that "too little has been done."[63] In particular, Maurice needed "care and psychiatric treatment in a more therapeutic setting than has thus far been achieved in the training school program."[64]

The decisions in *Lavette* and *Maurice C.* were in direct conflict, and given the contradictory holdings at the appellate level, the state's highest court once again took up the issue of PINS placements in a consolidated appeal in 1974.[65] The key issue was whether PINS placements in training schools were unlawful, *per se*, under *Ellery C.* The potential significance of the outcome led both DFY and DSS to file *amicus curiae* briefs.

In an opinion that ended up being more confusing than helpful in many ways, the court pontificated on a number of relevant factors without setting very clear standards. First it pointed out that it would be inconsistent with a PINS child's right to "supervision" and "treatment" to place him or her in an institution where juvenile delinquents were also confined. However, it held that placement in training schools was not prohibited, per se. There was a catch, however. The court was willing to permit PINS placements in training schools *unless* there was a clear showing that the facilities were not up to the task of adequate treatment. The right to treatment, said the court, amounted to a constitutional interest if the child's liberty was at stake. It wrote:

> Where the State, as *parens patriae*, involuntarily places a PINS child in a training school, it is for the purpose of individualized treatment and not mere custodial care. Whatever the altruistic theory for depriving the child of his liberty, if proper and necessary treatment is not forthcoming, a serious question of due process is raised.[66]

In short, the determinative issue was not the characterization of the placement but "the adequacy of the supervision and treatment" it provided. The court concluded that determining "adequacy" was not within the court's purview but that assuring "the presence of a bona fide treatment program" was.[67]

Furthermore, the court cautioned that "lack of staff or facilities" would not justify unsuitable placements. So while the court acknowledged that it was "well aware of the current preference for expanded use of community agencies, community residential centers and similar shelters for the treatment of nondelinquent children who are beyond or without parental supervision," it was willing to see youth confined in training school if (and only if) his or her rights to adequate treatment were not violated.[68] In short, the court seemed to permit limited commitment in PINS-only facilities, if something beyond custodial care was being offered.

The Hope of the Private Sector

The New York State legislature had counted on private agencies stepping forward and providing flexible and innovative services for PINS-adjudicated youth. The appellate courts remained hopeful that the private sector would be able to devise appropriate nonrestrictive and therapeutic treatment facilities. However, these programs were not sufficiently forthcoming in the 1970s to abate the crisis. Henry Saltzman of the Citizens Committee for Children of New York noted that many agency staff were "not ready to grapple with the behavior of these adolescents a number of whom are angry and street-wise and much more difficult. The bulk of adolescents who are disturbed and a serious jeopardy to themselves and the community are wandering the streets. There aren't enough facilities to cope with them."

The problem of finding adequate treatment for PINS was aggravated both by the economic recession and by the sharp increase in demand for foster care for adolescents. The demand was driven, in part, by demographic pressures. By 1975, 46.7 percent of New York City's applicants awaiting foster care placement as abused and neglected children were over the age of 12. Thus homes and facilities for adolescents, be they funneled through abuse/neglect or PINS proceedings, were in short supply. The problem was even worse for the most mobile and troubled children, such as chronic runaways and those acculturated to street life.

Particularly painful evidence of the placement problem is seen in yet another appeal to the state's highest court.[69] Although the legal issue had to do with a young girl's constitutional right to be present at her own dispositional hearing, the dissenting justice, Judge Matthew J. Jasen, seemed more troubled by the fact that *had* she been at the hearing (in which she was ordered placed in a secure training school), she would have been subjected to "a recital of no fewer than 23 rejections of placement by private agencies made on her behalf."[70] The dissenting judge noted: "it should be perfectly obvious how emotionally devastating such rejection testimony would have been upon this 13-year-old girl." The majority took the opportunity to complain, in a footnote, that the case "calls attention to the societal problems posed by the nonavailability of facilities . . . which impedes even heroic efforts by our courts to place them in authorized nonsecure agencies before commitment to more controlled settings."[71]

Lower courts continued to deal with the conundrum without any real hope that a solution would be forthcoming, legislatively, politically, or administratively. Yet they persisted in recording their complaints in judicial opinions. For example, in 1978, in the case of Felix, who had run away from several nonsecure short-term diagnostic and treatment programs and had also been rejected by a series of private institutions, Judge Jerome M. Becker wrote that the situation was not unique:

> He is but one of many youngsters appearing before the courts each day who are suspended in this unfortunate state of limbo. Undeniably, the needs of Felix in this proceeding are real. Yet our society, through the Department of Social Services and the Division for Youth, nonchalantly asserts that there is no way to meet them. Were the courts an executive agency with power to provide the services required by youngsters like Felix, the court's task would be simple. It is not. That is the province of either the Department of Social Services or the Division for Youth.[72]

By the second half of the 1970s, the placement options for troubled and mobile runaways was in extreme crisis.

PINS and Prostitution

Given the mess in New York's family courts, it seems remarkable that in 1977, when confronted with stories in the *New York Times* about the "Minnesota Pipeline" and the link between child prostitution and runaway youth, that New York City officials announced that they had a solution to the teenage prostitution problem (see chapter 2). New York City's Corporation Counsel, W. Bernard Richland, reportedly was "apparently reacting to recent disclosures of the growing teen-age prostitution problem" and announced "a new prosecution strategy" which "will be a powerful tool" in "rehabilitating runaway minors who are drawn into lives of prostitution[73]." Mr. Richland announced the solution involved having "the girls processed in Family Court as PINS." He explained: "After being classified as PINS, the girls could be sent to rehabilitative institutions upstate for as long as two and half years."[74]

Ironically, the Wayward Minor Act—used since the 1920s to incarcerate "morally depraved" girls—had been declared unconstitutional just five years earlier. Thus Mr. Richland's proposed solution to the teenage prostitution problem looked a lot like an attempt to resurrect this expired statute under the PINS provisions. Mr. Richland, while addressing the topic in the context of the political and media discussion on prostitution, was apparently unaware of the dismal state of affairs in the family court system, the unhappiness of its judges, and their complaints about legislative and administrative inaction in creating suitable PINS placements.

Given the dire reality of the placement situation, it is not surprising that there were critics of Mr. Richland's plan. Among them were detectives and officers from the police department, and Father Bruce Ritter, founder of Covenant House, which had grown from its radical 1968 roots into the largest runaway service provider in the state. Ritter summarily, and publicly, dismissed the Corporation Counsel's policy plan as "virtually meaningless." Embedded in his colorful comments ("God help us, the laws are crazy. . . . We have many more girls 16 and 17 who are street walkers and who are in far greater jeopardy but who will continue to be treated as adults and who can't get any kind of help") is a basic, very recognizable complaint. The PINS age limits made the policy ineffective. Ritter argued that 16- and 17-year-olds, who fell outside PINS jurisdiction, represented the largest numbers of children on the street, and those were the very youth who had no services available to them. They were, after all, no longer subject to state regulation and did not yet qualify for social service help that might be available to adults.

The second proposed solution to the teenage prostitution problem involved the runaway shelter model itself. It appealed to the public (and the press). In an article published in December 1977 under the headline, "Priest's Shelter Tries to Salvage Times Sq. Youths," Covenant House is featured as a service alternative to the street.[75] This article was one of many that began to focus on programs serving runaway youth that offered a lifeline to children while they were on the street. The journalist referred to Ritter as "a symbol of the effort to salvage the wandering youths of Time Square." Ritter argued that the youth themselves "often wind up in prostitution 'because they have no choices,'" especially when they have been "pushed out" of home, cannot get work, have no schooling to speak of, and—if they are over 15 years old—are abandoned by public agencies that "refuse to take responsibility for them." He said, "People really don't know, they think these kids are bad, rotten punks who are leaving good homes. They're not street-hardened toughs, although many are forced into criminal activity in order to survive." The proposed shelter solution offered resources to entice runaways away from pimps, life on the street, and to protect them from physical danger. So while Ritter was speaking of real institutional holes in the family court system, the press found some romance in telling the story of private service providers who were on a mission of rescuing children from the street pursuant to this new social construction of the "runaway" youth.

A Band-Aid Solution: New York's Runaway and Homeless Youth Act of 1978

Given the crisis, it should not be surprising that in 1978 New York State's Runaway and Homeless Youth Act (RHYA) moved swiftly, and without opposition to passage,[76] nor is it surprising that it had the support of a number of public[77] and private constituents.[78] The legislation had political and practical appeal although it was certainly not a meaningful solution to the overall problem. However, it was legislation that removed any remaining doubt about the legality of initially radical alternative shelter services, such as Covenant House, in New York State.

The RHYA permitted crisis shelter for runaway and homeless youth, and additional concrete services (e.g., food and clothing), as well as counseling, medical care, and other emergency services. The residential facilities were approved by DFY and operated in accordance with DSS and DFY regulations. What was unique about the shelter option was that it didn't involve judges, police, or parents in placements. Furthermore, shelters like Covenant House had an open intake policy and refused to turn away any youth seeking help, including pregnant teenagers, teenage mothers, youth with emotional problems, and others. The service was available, on demand, by the child directly. The hope was that the shelter provided an attractive alternative to street life. As such, shelters were not a placement option for the courts, nor were they a solution for DSS or DFY's facility problems. Nonetheless, they diverted public attention and seemed to provide an emergency lifeline to children most in need.

From the shelter's perspective in New York State, there were only two real requirements under the RHYA. First, staff had to notify parents within seventy-two hours that children were safe (although in keeping with its counterculture roots and values, shelters were not required to disclose the actual location of the children). Second, if staff believed the child had been abused or neglected, they were required to report that abuse. Otherwise, the shelter system operated outside the departmental settings of juvenile justice, family court, law enforcement, and public social services.

The crisis shelter alternative was appealing on many grounds. It was consistent with the youth rights movement and respected youth liberty and autonomy interests. Children who entered runaway programs did so voluntarily and could leave without consequences or accountability. It was an option that came with a potential federal funding stream (through the federal Runaway Youth Act of 1974) at a time when the state had limited funds to invest in adolescent programs (see chapter 7). It appeased public concern that children were being forced into prostitution because they lacked resources and alternatives. It provided the allure that children would be returned home without law enforcement or family court involvement. However, it ignored the reality that at least some of these more incorrigible children had already decided that home was not an option. Thus the shelter design, birthed in a milieu of counterculture crash pads for temporary middle-class dropouts, may not have been the best model for care of chronic runaways who arrived with multiple and complicated personal and family problems.

The justification section of the memorandum of support accompanying the RHYA legislation noted that there were "few services available" for runaway youth and that "when they do come in contact with the State, it usually results in judicial processing and the child being placed outside his own home in institutional care." It goes on to make the link between running away and prostitution and specifically points to Veronica Brunson:

> [T]housands of teen-age runaways as young as 13, are working in massage parlors, live-peep shows and prostitution houses. The Committee also

was told of large numbers of male youth loitering the streets for the purpose of prostitution, a situation referred to as a "chicken and hawk" relationship. The problem of youth prostitution is widespread, most dramatized with the grim death of 12 year old Veronica Bronson, [sic] (who either jumped or was thrown from the window of a building known to be frequented by prostitutes) in New York City last summer.

The memo argued that it was "time to recognize this new class of youth—described as 'urban nomads'—who range from twelve to twenty-one and . . . without recognition and assistance . . . fall prey to criminals and violence, and often become criminals themselves."[79]

Interestingly, the legislators lump all children wandering alone between the ages of 12 and 21 under the label "urban nomads." Thus the shelter system was offered as a solution to both younger children (below 16) who would (or arguably even should) be under auspices of the family court as well as to older youth (16 and above) for whom the state was no longer responsible. Voluntary crisis shelters like Covenant House provided an expedient and publicly palatable solution to both problems without examining the broader contextual picture carefully. Although service design flexibility was a great asset for alternative providers, realistically crisis shelters could not and would not fill the structural and institutional holes that had been dug over the previous decade.

In the pre-1960s era, runaway child prostitutes were characterized as immoral individuals and threats to the general public welfare. Yet the population of children who had once been locked up in secure facilities as wayward had lost room in the public treatment care system. Shelters seem a humane response and even had some romantic appeal because they met the immediate needs of children in crisis, while seducing them back to the mainstream. A bigger question remained as to whether such shelters served as a true alternative system of care or merely as a bubblegum patch for a leaky boat.

A report issued by a judicial committee appointed to study family court services in 1972 found that

Contrary to some misconceptions . . . behind "incorrigibility" as behind the "delinquent act" one finds a long history of a troubled child who has been left without help until he becomes so troubling that a crisis situation forces parental or community action. A high incidence of persistent truancy, failure in school, late hours, poor peer relationships, involvement in drug abuse, narcotic addiction, emotional disturbance, and in some cases mental retardation or mental illness are present in both types of children.[80]

One of the consequences of separating PINS, juvenile delinquency, and abuse and neglect was that different institutional systems of care were established and delivered to children based on the procedure used to funnel the child into the system in the first place. In creating these separate, specialized domains, the state's ability to evaluate the totality of the child's circumstances may have been diminished. Runaways, standing at the categorical boundaries, had the most to gain—or to lose—in the process.

Legitimization Through Legislation— The Runaway Youth Act

National Attention to the Runaway Problem

(1971–1974)

> There was a time when those in power need not have worried about alternative services. . . . Such is no longer the case . . . no matter what the rhetoric of the large traditional youth serving organizations, young people who are runaways come to us. They know that their rights as individuals will be respected and that we assume a youth advocacy role.
>
> —Gerda Flanigan, Looking Glass[1]

If state legislatures were busy tinkering with their conceptual frameworks for dealing with youth in the 1960s, it took the U.S. Congress until the mid-1970s to seriously begin enacting youth-oriented legislation. In 1974, President Gerald Ford signed two important policy initiatives into law—the Child Abuse Prevention and Treatment Act (CAPTA; P.L. 93–247), and the Juvenile Justice and Delinquency Prevention Act (JJDPA; P.L. 93–415). In 1975, Congress passed the Education of all Handicapped Children Act (P.L. 94–142), and three years later the Indian Child Welfare Act of 1978 (P.L. 95–608). It was an astounding burst of legislative energy around child welfare issues. Taken together, a central theme of all this legislation was youth rights, including the right to protection, to treatment, to education, and to cultural identity (at least for Native Americans).

CAPTA and JJDPA were significant for many reasons, but among them because they created a conceptual framework for the child welfare and juvenile justice systems at the federal level much like that seen at the state level. These two different prongs of intervention—the child-abuse protection side and the juvenile delinquency side—represented the long-standing tensions in designing child and youth public policy over determining whom to blame and thus whom to hold accountable. Child protection orientations faulted parents, and interventions were intended to keep children safe. Juvenile justice orientations blamed youth, and interventions were intended to reform, retrain, or punish (depending on the philosophical dogma of the day).

The significance of the bipartite system cannot be underestimated. Our present-day public systems of child welfare and juvenile justice have descended from these initial conceptual frameworks. At the federal level, they are administered and funded through different departments (Health and Human Services and the Office of Juvenile Justice). At the state and local level there are different service delivery structures, policies, procedures, regulations, and the systems are staffed by different personnel and are located in different institutional settings. In colleges and universities, faculty specialize in one area of expertise or the other but rarely, if ever, in both. Scholars, students, and practitioners in the areas of child welfare and juvenile justice read different research journals and attend different professional conferences. In short, the division between child welfare and juvenile justice is systemic and entrenched.

Noticeably absent from this two-part federal framework—at least when compared with New York State's tripartite system—is the "status offender" category. Conceptually, there wasn't a clearcut obvious fit within either protective services or juvenile justice. When it came to behavioral problems, it was possible to blame the parents for an intolerable home environment or to blame children for acting out and behaving badly. Consequently, it was possible to fashion an intervention that punished the child or to design one targeted at saving him or her. In short, it was possible to place "runaways" within either of these two jurisdictions.

So the problem became, how to classify or where to put runaway behavior? Congress embedded the Runaway Youth Act (RYA) as Title III of the JJDPA. It was thus housed under the juvenile justice umbrella and framed as a delinquency prevention measure. Of course, the RYA and JJDPA themselves did not emerge in a vacuum. Beginning back in 1961 with the passage of the Juvenile Delinquency and Youth Offenses Control Act, Congress had sought new ways of preventing and controlling juvenile crime. More importantly, perhaps, it was focused on preventing delinquency while sorting out those children who seemed to need supervision or guidance rather than punishment.

In 1967, President Lyndon Johnson's Commission on Law Enforcement and the Administration of Justice produced a report on juvenile delinquency and its prevention. The report recommended four basic strategies:[2]

- decriminalizing status offenses;
- diverting youth from the juvenile justice system to community-based alternatives;
- deinstitutionalizing status offenders; and
- increasing due process protections.

Arguments about decriminalizing status offenses and distinguishing children with behavioral problems (e.g., running away, truancy, curfew violations) from those who committed criminal-like acts were already being made in many states. In addition, the commission recommended *diverting* youth from the court system altogether. It was better to keep minors out of the juvenile court, training schools, and other public institutions than to have them acculturated into such environments. The commission favored prevention strategies that avoided state intervention. It also recommended *deinstitutionalizing* youth. This approach was focused on substituting community-based programs and residential facilities for incarceration in training schools. Again, several states had already headed down this road, but others were urged to follow (although of note is that states such as New York struggled mightily over what to do with these youth: see chapter 6). Finally, the commission recommended extending *due process* rights to juveniles who ultimately ended up in court settings in spite of diversion efforts. The commission's report led to passage of the Juvenile Delinquency Prevention and Control Act of 1968 (JDPCA), which favored these various strategies.

In keeping with the spirit expressed by the president's commission, the due process protections afforded children were increasingly being safeguarded. During this period the U.S. Supreme Court entertained a series of important cases and handed down decisions that essentially established the parameters of children's civil rights in family or juvenile court proceedings for decades to come.[3] These cases, as a whole, guaranteed youth greater due process protection than they had had in the past, and shielded them from the unmitigated discretion of family and juvenile court judges. On the other hand, juveniles were not afforded the complete legal protections of adults.

But by curtailing the discretion of authorities, interventions with children were less arbitrary. Of course, it also became more difficult to control runaways by using legal tactics than it once had been. Altogether, the overall strategy favored less public and social control of runaway children.

While Congress tinkered with how best to administer and structure the juvenile justice system, it is perhaps not surprising that the voices of alternative service providers began to rise in the din. Crisis shelter and counseling programs such as Huckleberry House, Covenant House, and Ozone House addressed many of the major congressional concerns. These alternative shelters were not linked to law enforcement, diverted youth from the juvenile justice system, and respected youth rights. By 1971 such programs were receiving serious attention and support from important political friends in Washington.

Background on the RYA Bill

The Runaway Youth Act was at least four years in its gestation. It was first introduced on November 9, 1971, by Senators Birch Bayh (D-Ind) and Marlow W. Cook (D-Ky) as Senate bill 2829 (S. 2829 in appendix 1). One of its primary purposes was "the establishment, maintenance and operation of temporary housing and counseling services for transient youth." Thus the bill focused on youth in crisis.

The RYA situated the "runaway" problem within the juvenile delinquency framework and touted runaway shelters as juvenile delinquency prevention measures. To the extent the bill purported to save youth from the evils of the street, it also protected them by diverting them from problems associated with being on the street. It differed from the child welfare system in that the responsibility for initiating services rested with the youth themselves. In fact, by design the RYA supported services that were outside the law enforcement, juvenile justice, and child welfare systems.

The initial Senate bill was justified as based on six broad congressional declarations of purpose:

(1) the number of juveniles who leave and remain away from home without parental permission has increased to alarming proportions,

creating a substantial law enforcement problem for the communities inundated, and significantly endangering the young people who are without resources and live on the street;[4]

(2) that the exact nature of the problem is not well defined because national statistics on the size and profile of the runaway youth population are not tabulated;[5]

(3) that many of these young people, because of their age and situation, are urgently in need of temporary shelter and counseling services;[6]

(4) that the anxieties and fears of parents whose children have run away from home can best be alleviated by effective interstate reporting services and the earliest possible contact with their children;[7]

(5) that the problem of locating, detaining, and returning runaway children should not be the responsibility of already overburdened police departments and juvenile justice authorities;[8] and

(6) that in view of the interstate nature of the problem, it is the responsibility of the Federal Government to develop accurate reporting of the problem nationally and to develop an effective system of temporary care outside the law enforcement structure.[9]

The bill's purpose was to provide federal grants to applicants to "establish, strengthen, or fund an existing or proposed runaway house, a locally controlled facility providing temporary shelter, and counseling services to juveniles who have left home without the specific permission of their parents or guardians".[10] The bill required that applicants submit a plan to Health, Education, and Welfare (HEW) that met several requirements; among these was that there be an adequate plan for contacting parents and an adequate plan for insuring proper relations with law enforcement. Funding priority was to be given to "private organizations or institutions that have had past experience in dealing with runaways".[11] The first-generation alternative service providers (including Huckleberry House, Ozone House, and Covenant House) were well situated to meet these priorities. Of course, this scenario—stable funding in exchange for following federal guidelines—was hotly debated within the alternative service community by staff who worried about trading their "alternativeness" for financial stability (see chapter 5).

The first bill received unanimous support in the Senate but was ignored in the House during the 92nd congressional session. It was reintroduced by Senator Bayh in the next congressional session.[12] Less than five months later (June 8, 1973), the Senate passed it unanimously again. The following month the bill was introduced in the House (H.R. 9298) (see appendix 2). This time, it moved forward and was folded into the JJDPA, which was signed into law by President Gerald Ford on September 7, 1974 (see table 7.1; see also appendix 3).[13] It is significant that, between the initial introduction of the RYA and its final enactment three years later,[14] there occurred the serial killings of runaway boys in Houston.

Houston: Police Inadequacy and Runway Vulnerability

The Houston tragedy had several notable consequences, not least the public outrage and criticism over local law enforcement's inability to deal with runaway children. Although the press and public may not have been particularly sympathetic to the police in general during the early 1970s, law enforcement officials nonetheless voiced some legitimate structural, practical, and bureaucratic concerns that hindered their efficiency when it came to dealing with stray children.

After the Corll murders, local police departments were called upon to explain, and at times defend, their procedures in regard to runaways.[15] The police attempted to appease the public, sometimes not very successfully. For example, in the immediate aftermath of "Houston," Capt. Francis Daly of the NYPD's Youth Aid Division reported that the mass murder of runaway children in New York City was unlikely because "You can't bury very much in this city without being seen by somebody."[16] This questionable statement could hardly be considered reassuring words for parents concerned about absent children.

In any case, police departments generally offered three common (and reasonable) defenses. First, missing persons procedures were inadequate in providing the kind of comprehensive intervention that the public seemed to expect when it came to runaway children. Second, state law—and in particular the "in need of supervision" statutes—hampered police. Third, while mobile runaways could cross jurisdictional boundaries, local law enforcement agencies were not sufficiently linked with police in other areas to make interventions effective. Clearly, local police were not prepared to deal with the national scope of the runaway problem.

Table 7.1

		Legislative History of the Federal Runaway Youth Act, Title III of the Juvenile Justice and Delinquency Prevention Act of 1974
Year	Month/Day	Action Taken
1971	Nov. 9	S. 2829 Runaway Youth Act introduced by Senators Birch Bayh and Marlowe Cook. (Bill unsuccessful.)
1972	Jan. 13, 14	(Senate in Committee) Hearings on S. 2829 "a bill to strengthen interstate reporting and interstate services for parents of runaway children; to conduct research on the size of the runaway youth population; for the establishment, maintenance, and operation of temporary housing and counseling for transient youth" before Subcommittee on Juvenile Delinquency.
1972	Feb. 8	Senator Bayh introduces S. 3148 "a bill to improve the quality of juvenile justice in the US and to provide a comprehensive, coordinated approach to the problems of juvenile delinquency and for other purposes."
1972	May 15, 16 & June 27, 28	(Senate) Hearings on S. 3148 before the Senate Judiciary Committee, Subcommittee to Investigate Juvenile Delinquency. This version does not include the RYA.
1972	July 27	(S.Report 92–1002) Senate report recommends passage of S.2829 "to authorize HEW to provide assistance to local groups to operate temporary shelter care programs in areas where runaways tend to congregate" and "strengthens interstate reporting and interstate services for parents of runaway children and authorizes research on the size and composition of the runaway youth population."
1973	Feb 22; Mar. 26, 27; June 26, 27	(Senate in Committee) Hearings on S. 821 before the Senate Judiciary Committee, Subcommittee to Investigate Juvenile Delinquency. This version does not include the RYA.
1973	March 23	(Senate in Committee) Testimony by Hon. Jerry J. Miller, Mayor of South Bend, Ind and Mr. Patrick Gallagher, Director of Public Safety. They submitted a report on the juvenile delinquency problem in South Bend and a statement (prepared by Jim Statzell) on the Runaway Problem in St. Joseph Country. (See Note A below.)
1973	June 4	(Senate Report 93–191) Recommends passage of S. 645 "to strengthen interstate reporting and interstate services for parents of runaway children; to conduct research on the numbers and characteristics of runaway youth; to provide for temporary housing and counseling services for transient youth , and for counseling of the runaway and his family after he has moved to permanent living facilities." (Bill is similar to 92nd Congress Senate-passed S. 2829.)
1974	March 5	(Senate in Committee) Subcommittee to Investigate Juvenile Delinquency unanimously reported S. 821, as amended, the full Judiciary Committee. This version does not contain the RYA.
1974	May 8	(Senate in Committee) Full Judiciary Committee considered S. 821. Senator Hruska offered an amendment in the nature of a substitute which was accepted by an 8–5 vote, and the amended bill was reported to the Senate.

Table 7.1 (continued)

		Legislative History of the Federal Runaway Youth Act, Title III of the Juvenile Justice and Delinquency Prevention Act of 1974
Year	Month/Day	Action Taken
1974	Mar–May	(House in Committee) Hearings before Subcommittee on Equal Opportunities on H.R. 6265, the Juvenile Justice and Delinquency Prevention Act (parallels S. 821), H.R. 13737, to amend and extend existing juvenile delinquency legislation, and H.R. 9298, the Runaway Youth Act, in L.A. and Washington, D.C.
1974	May 30	(Senate Floor) Senator Bayh introduces S. 821.
1974	June 6	(House in Committee) Subcommittee on Equal Opportunities favorably reported a clean bill, H.R. 15276, the Juvenile Delinquency Prevention Act of 1974 to the Committee on Education and Labor. This does contain RYA.
1974	June 12	(House in Committee) Committee on Education and Labor ordered H.R. 15276 reported to the House, by a vote of 28-1. This does contain RYA.
1974	June 12	(House Floor) Representative Hawkins introduced H.R. 15276. This does contain RYA.
1974	July 1	(House Floor) House floor debates and passes H.R. 15276. This does contain RYA.
1974	July 18	(Senate Floor) Senator Bayh introduces amendment No. 1578 to S. 821, an amendment in the nature of a substitution to S. 821 as reported by the Judiciary Committee. This bill does not contain the RYA.
1974	July 25	(Senate Floor) Senate floor debate and passage of S. 821 with three amendments. This bill does not contain the RYA.
1974	July 31	(House Floor) House considers S. 821 as passed by Senate and substitutes the language of H.R. 15271.
1974	August 8 & 15	(Conference Committee) Compromise bill includes "establishment of an independent Runaway Youth Program to be administered by HEW."
1974	August 19	(Senate) Considers and approves Conference Report (including RYA).
1974	August 21	(House) Considers and approves Conference Report (including RYA).
1974	Sept 7	President Ford signs Juvenile Justice and Delinquency Prevention Act of 1974.
1976	June	National Statistical Survey on Runway Youth Part I issued. The study was authorized under Title III of the JJDPA (1974). It was issued to meet the requirements of Congress to report by June 30, 1976. Part B of the Runaway Youth Act mandated a comprehensive statistical survey to define the major characteristics of the runaway population and determine the areas of the nation most effective.

After the Corll murders, Houston's police chief, Herman Short, argued that his department accepted missing persons reports from the public *only* as a matter of "public service, without the protection or authority of the procedural laws of arrest of Texas."[17] He was quick to point out that Texas did "not define running away as illegal."[18] Police jurisdiction under missing persons provisions ended when the child was found and the parents advised that the youth was no longer missing; it did not extend to reunification nor did it necessarily require disclosing the location of a child to a parent. Obviously, the missing persons procedure by itself was not an adequate response to the problem of runaway youth.

The outcome could be different if there was a preexisting warrant such as one that might be issued in an "in need of supervision" case, which would then give police the authority to take a child into custody. In order for this option to work, however, such a warrant had to be issued in the first place.[19] Furthermore, if there was a preexisting warrant, not only did the police have to know about it and have to have an idea where to look for the child, but also the child had to be within the department's jurisdictional reach.

The *New York Times* provided a graphic illustration of how the intersection of the "in need of supervision" statutes and missing persons procedures created barriers to police effectiveness in runaway cases. It reported that of the 28,000 missing persons cases filed in 1972 in New York City, 13,000 involved children under 16 (and were therefore at least theoretically within New York State's PINS jurisdiction), while the majority of the remaining 54 percent involved 16- to 21-year-olds for whom no runaway jurisdiction existed.[20] Realistically, then, there was little incentive for the police to expend resources on these cases.

Finally, in the wake of the Houston horror, police departments around the country argued that both the interstate and national nature of the runaway problem made it impossible for local authorities to deal effectively with missing youth. In New York, police pointed out that, as had been the case historically and was true now, "most local juveniles return home after a few days," but they also suggested that "the real problem" was "out-of-state teenage runaways, who numbered about 10,000 last year".[21] It is unclear where this figure for out-of-state runaways came from or how it was derived; nonetheless, the underlying argument was that youth were often traveling long distances and were moving across city, county, and state lines. The fact that large numbers of young adult Baby Boomers were taking to the roads and hitchhiking across the country did not make life for the local police any easier. Police had to contend with the interstate nature of youth travel without access to a national tracking system or infrastructure that could facilitate the flow of information between local law enforcement units.

Such defensive police counterarguments, emerging in light of the Houston tragedy, hinted at the practical problems associated with their work with runaway children. At the time, however, such subtleties in regard to law enforcement's point of view were mostly lost on a worried public more generally willing to believe the arguments put forth by youth advocates that runaway children should *not* be the responsibility of the police at all.

Hearing Testimony (1971–1974)

Yet another major impact coming out of the Houston story was that it focused public attention on the vulnerability of runaway youth and the dangers that could befall them. The horrors of the Corll murders were never far from legislators' minds during the second set of congressional subcommittee hearings on the Runaway Youth Act and served as an omnipresent backdrop. Both sponsors for the separate Senate and House bills opened their statements with references to "Houston." Sen. Birch Bayh noted that "the recent tragic multiple murders of juveniles in Houston has underlined the desperate situation of youth on the streets."[22] Less than a month later, as he introduced the House version of the bill, Rep. Augustus F. Hawkins said, "I need not dwell on the tragedy which befell these youth in Houston, Texas, last year."[23]

An impressive cast of fairly predictable characters came forward to testify at the various Senate and House hearings on the Runaway Youth bills. The alternative service community was represented (including individuals from Huckleberry House and Looking Glass)[24] and brought runaway clients with them. Police officers,[25] traditional private service providers,[26] and assorted others offered their expertise. Parents of runaway children were notably absent.

For the most part, testimony before the committees was not contentious and was very supportive of the alternative community service delivery model. A few police officers, traditional service providers, and one lone unhappy government official from HEW (Philip Rutledge) opposed some parts of the measure. In the end, the tension was resolved mostly in favor of the alternative service community.

The Children and Their Living Situations

The Findings and Declaration of Policy portion of the proposed Runaway Youth bills relied heavily on characterizing runaway children as vulnerable and exploitable. There were two references to the condition of children. First, both the Senate and House versions noted that children "who leave and remain away from home without parental permission" had "increased to alarming proportions," with the result of "significantly endangering the young people who are without resources and live on the street." Furthermore, the legislation was justified based on the stated concern in both versions of the bill that "many of these young people, because of their age and situation, are urgently in need of temporary shelter and counseling services." Thus the Senate and House versions capitalized on a portrait of resource-less and therefore exploitable children in crisis and on their need for temporary services.

Testimony about the dangers facing runaways was colorful and reminiscent of Abbie Hoffman's characterization of runaways as fugitive slaves.[27] One alternative service provider reported that "the life of a runaway is fraught with danger" and that runaways were "forced to live like escaped convicts."[28] Girls were said to find themselves in "the middle of new, unknown types of street culture where human predators move about in a friendly guise."[29] Runaways were reportedly "often the victims and the perpetrators of criminal acts" and are "frequently subject to exploitation of streetwise persons."[30] Capt. Francis Daly, of New York City's Youth Aid Division of the NYPD, confirmed that troubled and vulnerable kids were "fair game for the smooth and slick-talking pimps and the gentle persuasions of drug pushers and degenerates, with their kindly offers of a handout, a meal, a night's lodging or a job."[31]

Child witnesses vividly reiterated these themes for the legislative subcommittees. In fact, they painted horrific pictures of their homes and life on the street. They described leaving abusive home environments at 14 and 15, and being raped, arrested, or committed to psychiatric wards. They talked about living on the street and informed lawmakers that their survival was aided by repeated visits to runaway shelters, which they said they learned about from advertisements in underground newspapers of the countercul- ture. The youths' stories varied, but they told of serious abuse at home, mul- tiple episodes of running away, unstable living conditions, criminal arrests, drug experimentation, precarious living on the street, and homelessness. In the end, the young people testified that runaway shelters had become nec- essary for their survival. Of course, these children representing "runaway" youth were neither weekend thrill-seekers nor little adventurers out for a lark; they came from seriously troubled families. Interestingly, there was no testimony to the contrary presented by parents, nor did parents appear at the hearing to testify about the benefits or usefulness of runaway shelters. In fact, there were no parental spokespersons at all.

Relationships Between Shelters and Police

It is not surprising that one major point of contention was the role of police in dealing with the problem of runaway children. The stated purpose of both the Senate and House versions of the bill was to divert runaways from police intervention. The Findings and Declaration of Policy portion of the bill included the concern that runaways presented a "substantial law enforcement problem" and that the problem of "locating, detaining, and returning runaway children should not be the responsibility of already over- burdened police departments." Of course, this was exactly the way the alter- native service community wanted the problem framed. The police them- selves were divided on the issue.

Police who appeared at the hearings, mostly officers who specialized in working with runaway children, testified about their experiences with youth . and with alternative service providers. The alternative service providers offered their own guarded opinion about their relationship with law enforcement. Senator Bayh located the inherent tension in the fact that "police are by law the adversary of runaways," yet "they are virtually the only group which deals with them on a regular basis."[32]

Law enforcement agents argued that it was useful to have a place to refer troubled youth, but that alternative providers were sometimes uncoopera- tive and occasionally even impeded the effectiveness of the police. The police pointed to attitudes and philosophies held by some of the service providers as being unnecessarily "anti-cop." Furthermore, they expressed concern about the agencies' views on parents and voiced frustration that the police were often caught between worried parents and defiant providers.

The NYPD's Captain Daly conceded that the Runaway Youth bill was useful to the extent it would ensure the existence of shelters to which police could refer youth safely.[33] On the other hand, Daly also noted that "we have had problems with these type of agencies. As you may know, different agencies have a different philosophy about dealing with youth."[34] He expressed concern and frustration with the lack of cooperation in respecting the front-line role of law enforcement. When questioned by committee members about the language in the proposed House bill, which required service providers to develop "an adequate plan for insuring proper relations with law enforcement personnel," Captain Daly responded: "Some of the agencies . . . are not what you call propolice, and they would rather have police not involved in this situation. . . . I can't picture any real accomplishments being made, or any real dealings with runaway youths without the police having to be involved in the initial stage, identifying."[35]

In contrast, supporters of the measure argued that police ought to be relieved of the burden of dealing with runaway youth. The House committee's chairman, Rep. A. F. Hawkins, opened hearings by suggesting that not only were local law enforcement officers *overburdened* by the problem of runaway youth, but that their "energies [were] siphoned off by the scope of this problem."[36] Not surprisingly, advocates for the alternative providers were equally vociferous about the unnecessary involvement of police officers. Brian Slattery, from Huckleberry House in San Francisco, spoke *on behalf of* the police when he testified that the "patrolmen almost unanimously think that runaways should not be a police problem" and that arresting and detaining youth was a "waste of police manpower."[37] He concluded that it was a process that didn't help "the runaways, their families, or the police."[38] Similarly, John Wedemeyer, director of The Bridge in San Diego, argued that runaways should be considered a "social problem, not a law enforcement problem."[39]

Some police officers concurred. John A. Bechtel, head of the Investigations and Services Division of the Montgomery County Police Department in Maryland, reported that he was speaking for police officers from "East Coast to West Coast and north and south" when he said they were "somewhat stuck with the situation" of runaways.[40] He noted that "we are the ones that are dealing with them, right off the street" and asked rhetorically, "when a police officer picks somebody up, what is he really going to do?"[41] He testified that he had "never heard of any . . . patrols that went out specifically looking for runaway juveniles" and assured the committee members that arresting runaways was certainly *not* any police officer's idea of "a big day."[42]

Bechtel's position was challenged by his counterparts from New York City. The NYPD had in fact created a Runaway Unit two years earlier in 1972 whose primary responsibility was to look for runaway juveniles.[43] The New York officers repeatedly emphasized the importance of their role as part of the overall solution. Captain Daly described the work of the Runaway Unit as "primarily an outreach program" with the "specific function of seeking out runaways by patrolling" the places "runaways tend to frequent."[44] He and other officers in the NYPD argued that the local police department was better situated than any other institution to protect and supervise street youth. Calling on the historic role of officers as the first line of defense in spotting runaways, Daly argued: "The bill points out that this is not a police problem, or suggests that the police should not be burdened with this problem. I don't see how the police can be relieved of the problem. It is the only agency nationwide that is on the street and can identify runaway youths."[45]

Although Captain Daly acknowledged that his position was contrary to that of others, he argued that there were good reasons that "recovery of runaways" was a "legitimate police function."[46] Relying on the juvenile delinquency prevention arguments of the umbrella JJDPA, he suggested that the early intervention function played by police meant that "each runaway recovered minimizes their exposure to the streets and the possibility of their becoming crime victims or engaging in delinquent or anti-social behavior."[47] Furthermore, it was "a positive aspect of police work, in that we are out on the streets, seeking out runaways and returning them, in many cases, to distressed but grateful parents."[48]

In his testimony, Daly made four important points. As he indicated, police already had the role of patrolling the streets and, like it or not, they were the local public watchdogs. Second, they could intervene faster than any other organization or institution. Third, given the ability of local law enforcement to detect runaways, the interstate runaway problem was best solved by linking local law enforcement units and sharing information to create a national network. Fourth, at the very least, law enforcement and alternative service providers needed to cooperate.

Captain Daly's position at the hearing was met with some skepticism. In particular, concerns for minors' civil rights were raised. "It seems to me you would be stopping a lot of them who are *innocent*, who are not actual runaways," commented Representative Hawkins. "How many are merely questioned who are not runaways?"[49] Daly assured Hawkins that the police had "developed expertise in identifying" runaway youths and then deferred to his frontline officers to explain what that meant. One of them, Officer Warren McGinniss, conceded that many youth were questioned and discovered not to be runaways. So the direct answer to Hawkins's question turned out to be that a significant (although unspecified) number of "innocent" youth were stopped. However, continued the officer, police only looked in areas known to be populated by runaways, and they looked for children who "appear lost," are "dirty, ragged looking," who carry clothes in "shopping bags" and "apparently [have] no goal, they are wandering about."[50] It was only at that point, he assured the congressman, that "we approach them."[51]

Hawkins's concern about the violation of the rights of non-runaway youth who were questioned or detained unnecessarily is telling. Historically, police authority went mostly unchallenged and was considered an acceptable feature of police interaction with street youth. Although Hawkins moved on with the hearing, in the context of the constitutional, youth rights–based movement of the era, McGinniss's concession that police temporarily detained and questioned youth who turned out to not be runaways might have seemed suspicious.

Alternative service providers voiced concern but also some optimism about their relationship with local police. Flanigan, from Chicago's Looking Glass, characterized this relationship as "difficult" but not "insurmountable."[52] Treanor reported that, "Every runaway project has to overcome community and police suspicion and hostility."[53] Most reported that some sort of truce had been achieved with local law enforcement. For example, Ray Ben David, executive director of Focus Runaway House in Las Vegas, reported, "there was a time when the police were stationed down the street from us and would watch us through binoculars. That doesn't happen anymore."[54] In the end, providers seemed willing to concede that most police officers could be taught to leave them alone.

To Network or Not?

Perhaps the single greatest point of contention at the hearing involved the notion of communication. At the heart of the issue was who should be talking to whom about runaways. Questions arose over whether information could or should be shared between police departments, between police and shelter staff, and between shelter staff and other public or private service providers. Finally there was the question of parents. Who should be allowed, or required, to tell parents what? And when should the information be conveyed? Of course, this discussion pits the notion of youth autonomy and independence against the rights and responsibilities of parents and of the state.

The alternative service providers bristled at the idea of being linked or associated with traditional public institutions or parties that might scare runaway children away or deter them from seeking their services; this included parents and police as well as child welfare or juvenile justice authorities. Others argued for communication of one sort or another. In general, the alternative community favored an isolationist policy. In the end, it mostly got its way.

Police concern over sharing information took three forms. Information should flow between law enforcement and the alternative agencies. Second, information should flow to parents from somebody. Third, information should flow between law enforcement agencies. Jerry Wilson, chief of police from Washington, D.C., argued that

> There should be complete cooperation and open communication among the agencies concerned, namely, the police, the court and the runaway houses with the welfare of the child and his family always in mind. A procedure to notify all agencies concerned of the identity of the child being housed would not only alleviate parental concern, but would also insure the speedy resolution of the children's problems[55]

Daly returned several times to the importance of enhancing the information network between police departments in order to increase effectiveness. He argued in favor of a "national registration center" where police officers could "put information" and/or "get information." The registry, he suggested, "should facilitate the reporting, identification and recovery of interstate runaways" and should also help "in developing statistics, patterns, etc. of runaway youths which can assist all police departments in planning programs for recovering runaway youths and preventing delinquency, along with the other related problems."[56] He pointed to the problems stemming from not having uniform procedures. "Many jurisdictions do not send a missing person alarm across the country on a runaway youth," and the net result is that "we don't have records to back up our 12,000 out-of-town runaways in New York."[57]

The value of the preexisting police network for monitoring the runaway problem was also mentioned by Dr. Martin Gold, program director for the Institute for Social Research at the University of Michigan. Although he admitted to speculating in the absence of data, he worried that

> to release police enforcement authorities from the burden and power of apprehending youngsters, containing them when they have run away will mean that there is no agency which has a vast enough network from community to community and from State to State to handle that small percentage of youngsters who do go far from home and who would stay there unsupervised and unprotected unless some law enforcement agency could pick them up.[58]

Philip Rutledge, a HEW official, warned against the federal government's subsidizing alternative outlets to responsible parenting and family stability and worried that the bill "doesn't deal with the total problem of youth and families," which he argued called for a "comprehensive program." Under agressive and sometimes hostile questioning by Senator Bayh, Rutledge finally summarized his position on service integration: "Now, I am merely suggesting, Mr. Chairman, that we need a variety of approaches, and they need to be linked and tied in with what the cities and States and other units are doing, and they should not be a categorical program standing by itself."[59]

Dr. Rhetta Arter, from the national YWCA, a traditional provider, complained about the "patchwork" of services and advocated greater communication ("a systemic network") between *providers*. However, her position favored the temporary exclusion of parents. She asserted that, otherwise, minors would decide to keep running. She noted:

It is not unusual for one YWCA to call another YWCA to say, "Tell her mother she is here." You may or may not have the girl's permission to say exactly where she is, but we usually are successful in extracting at least agreement that the other YWCA can say that she is still alive and well. Then it takes time to get her to the point where she will agree to having her exact whereabouts known.[60]

The contentious issue of parental notification was included in Dr. Arter's argument for a well-connected service network. Informing parents that their children were safe, without specifying their location, was consistent with the crisis shelter and hotline movements.

From the point of view of the alternative service community, an integrated approach to service delivery was the problem, not the solution. The notion of tracking or overarching surveillance of runaway youth offended them. They argued that protecting the youth's rights, and particularly his/her confidentiality, was the very contractual bond that enticed the youth to the alternative service in the first place. The notion of networked or integrated services was at odds with the providers' skepticism of the Establishment—the whole point was to be a true alternative to the Establishment and its existing services.

The Problem of Parents

Significantly, the only major changes between the draft legislation and the final enacted version of the Runaway Youth Act had to do with parents. Clearly, by the time the bill reached its final form, lawmakers had heard about the need to minimize parental involvement while maximizingthe flexibility of alternative service providers and the independence of runaway youth. Alterations in language regarding parents came in two places.

First, in the original Senate and House versions, one of six major justifications for the proposed legislation rested on the notion that "the anxieties and fears of parents whose children have run away from home can best be alleviated by effective interstate reporting services and the earliest possible contact with their children."[61] This idea is dropped completely in the final version of the act. This is significant because, after the deletion of this clause, the bill's Findings and Declaration of Purpose section focused entirely on the vulnerability and needs of youth. The parental perspective is removed from the equation altogether. Furthermore, the final legislation eliminated the foundation of an "interstate reporting system" to identify runaways and to serve parents (as had been advocated by Captain Daly). So the national networking of authorities was not to be.

Second, applicants for funding under the original versions of the bill would have been required to "develop an adequate plan for contacting the child's parents and insuring his safe return according to the best interests of the child."[62] This mandate was significantly altered when legislators added two additional clauses. First, they diluted the federal requirement that providers have a plan to contact a child's parents by stating that this was necessary only if "such action is required by State law."[63] Second, they added the requirement that plans "for contacting local government officials pursuant to informal arrangements established with such officials by the runaway house, and for providing for other appropriate alternative-living arrangements" be included in their proposals.[64] Thus there was some early recognition by Congress that not all youth could return home and that alternative living arrangements would be necessary for some. However, alternative service providers were required only to make "informal arrangements" with state officials, so for the most part they were permitted to operate independently of parents and child welfare systems.

This was indeed the position favored by the alternative service community. There were two separate issues at stake relating to parents: parental notification (simply letting parents know their child was safe), and consent for sheltering or treating youth. In general, the alternative providers favored delaying safety calls to parents until the youth was ready to place such a call him or herself. For example, Ray Ben David of Focus from Runaway House in Las Vegas (Nevada) testified: "a kid comes in and we allow him 48 hours in which to make a decision."[65] Of course, within that time a youth could also decide to leave the shelter without notifying parents at all.

At the hearings, Brain Slattery of Huckleberry House argued that runaway houses needed greater flexibility and freedom from regulations that hindered child and youth services in the public sector. In particular, Slattery argued for a three- to seven-day stay from contacting parents. Alternative providers were adamant that contacting parents too early would drive youth away from safety and back onto the streets. When asked what happened in cases where parental consent could not be obtained, Slattery replied that the runaway "is informed as accurately as we can of the consequences of living on the street, some of the alternatives, survival techniques for living on the street, but he is certainly in no way obstructed from returning to the street."[66] This alliance with the youth and a willingness to educate the young person and permit him or her to continue on their own is consistent with the youth-focused counterculture mission and contrasts with that of traditional service providers.

The role of parents divided alternative runaway agencies from other experts. The constituency most often caught between these providers and the parents of runaways were law enforcement agents. Bechtel confirmed the dilemma posed for police: "One thing we have had with runaway houses that probably causes the most problem . . . [is] pressure exerted on us by parents whose children were in Runaway House. . . . They go down to get their children out and their children do not want to come out. They exert a lot of pressure along this line.[67] The policies of runaway shelters in regard to parental notification provided the dividing line for the New York City Police Department. It refused to deal with alternative providers it felt were failing to deal adequately with parents. As Captain Daly noted: "One agency will not notify a parent, whereas another agency will. As police officers we feel we have a responsibility to contact parents and notify them of the whereabouts of their children. One agency that hasn't done this, it just so happens we haven't been using that agency in New York to any great extent."[68]

So the battle lines around the Senate and House versions of the Runaway Youth bill were predictably drawn. Police argued for a role with runaways and expressed concern for parents. Alternative agencies argued for independence from traditional rules (and roles) of child welfare and the maximization of youth autonomy.

The Runaway Youth Act of 1974

Questions of youth autonomy, independence, and freedom were clearly evident in the arguments over confidentiality, parental notification, police authority, and the scope of information networking. These tensions—including the degree to which runaway shelters should cooperate with police departments and parents, and the degree to which information was linked nationwide between law enforcement agents and/or service providers—go to the heart of service design. The more providers were permitted to shield runaway children from parents and police, the more they resembled the counterculture model of care.

The final enacted version of the Runaway Youth Act was based on some key premises:

- that runaway children were victimized and vulnerable because of lack of resources associated with a street-based existence;[69]
- that the most appropriate response was provided by "alternative" shelter services, functioning outside the juvenile justice and law enforcement systems;[70]
- that runaway shelter plans needed to make only "informal" arrangements with local child welfare officials;
- that a national data collection system be established in order to understand the runaway problem but not for the purposes of aiding law enforcement[71] or facilitating parental notification;
- that parental contact need only be assured where state law required it.

As a group, runaway shelters—that loose-knit community of alternative providers which had operated on the fringe of legality and maintained uneasy alliances with parents and police since 1967 when Huckleberry House first opened its doors in the midst of the youthful pilgrimage for the Summer of Love—had at last found favor in Washington. The Runaway Youth Act itself would incorporate a host of counterculture values, including

- providing "crisis" shelter;
- protecting minors' liberty interests;
- permitting minors to avoid parental or state contact, thereby undermining authorities' efforts to control or supervise them;
- replicating a network of underground resources, referrals, and support;
- providing survival skill education; and
- putting them in touch with adults and youth advocates sympathetic to their liberty interests.

In short, the RYA legitimized (by offering federal grants) the delivery of basic resources (shelter, food, clothing) to at-risk street-based youth founded on the argument that lack of resources made them vulnerable to crime and victimization. This situated the "runaway problem" squarely within the framework of juvenile justice delinquency prevention. This model respects the youth's rights to be in control of the decision to seek services, to continue with services, and to contact home.

Taken together, these steps increase the relative power of youth to make independent decisions, while the integrated authority of parents and the state to intervene, control, and supervise youth was decreased. With this rights-based approach toward youth comes some abrogation of authority (parent and state) to define adolescent care, its conditions, and its rules.

Conclusion

In closing the first round of hearings of the RYA, Senator Bayh asked Brian Slattery one final question:

> SENATOR BAYH: Just as an aside, I had a chance to see Haight-Ashbury for myself the first time this summer. It is not what used to be, is it? Has it lost a lot of its glamour?
>
> MR. SLATTERY: I do not think it ever had very much.
>
> SENATOR BAYH: Maybe that was just the way it was described to some of us here, a whole nation away. . . . Mr. Slattery, I appreciate very much what you are doing there in Huckleberry's and for giving us your expertise in substantiating our need for this bill.

It was undoubtedly an accurate assessment of the Haight-Ashbury experience: it wasn't "glamorous." However, few revolutionary movements questioning the core premises of a dominant culture and advocating radical social change are glamorous. Nonetheless, there is some irony to the fact that the glorified Beat lifestyle, as adopted and adapted by Diggers and institutionalized by privately sponsored runaway houses operating on the fringe of counterculture communities, was on its way to receiving the seal of federal approval and funding to boot. In the end, the Diggers successfully established an infrastructure to support freedom for independence-seeking youth outside the dominant institutional, cultural, and social systems of our society. The Runaway Youth of 1974 is still in place today. Thus this "crash pad service-delivery" model, albeit legitimized and sanitized, has long outlived the flamboyant youthful cultural revolution that produced it, yet it continues to survive as part of its legacy.

Conclusions

Where We've Been, Where We're Going, What We've Learned

Natural Extensions—Problem, Services, and Policy (1974–)

History is just one damn thing after another.

—Attributed to Winston Churchill

Where We Have Been

At the outset one of the questions I sought to answer was, *How do the interactions between key players, individual events, and social movements influence problems, policy, and programs?* (See foreword.) This complex question was tackled in three parts in this book, first by looking at the way social problems are constructed (from the perspectives of the media and the counterculture), second by looking at grassroots service providers (Diggers and alternative providers), and finally by looking at policy formulations and responses (status offenses and runaway shelter legislation). Nonetheless, when the three parts (and the individual case studies within them) are pieced together they begin to provide a layered answer to this question about the complicated relationships between social actors and movements, their ideas and actions, and also the way the problem is constructed as well as service delivery and policy. Each of these individual narratives has its own longitudinal (historical) rhythm, but they share some critical moments of intersection. None may be more significant in the evolution of ideas on "runaways" than the year 1967. Consider the following tangle of separate incidents and ideas from that single year. In 1967,

- Baby Boomers first saturated every year statistically, from when they entered their teens at 13 through to the then-age-of majority of 21;
- Acid rockers (such as the Grateful Dead) invited American youth to "come join the party," and pop singer Scott McKenzie advised youth that, "If you're going to San Francisco," be sure to "wear flowers in your hair";[1]
- Diggers organized Free Food, crash pads, a street-survival education, and worried about the young children being drawn to their alternative community;
- Huckleberry House first opened its doors;
- Haight-Ashbury hosted a Summer of Love;
- Linda Fitzpatrick and her hippie boyfriend were brutally murdered in the East Village in New York City;
- J. Anthony Lukas wrote about the Fitzpatrick death for the *New York Times* (winning a Pulitzer Prize) and immediately followed it with a "case study" on a "runaway flower child";
- The police raided Huckleberry House, shutting it down (temporarily) as an illegal child care agency;
- The U.S. Supreme Court handed down *In re Gault*, a landmark decision that increased constitutional due process protections for youth (see chapter 7 at note 3); and
- President Johnson's Commission on Law Enforcement and the Administration of Justice urged the diversion, decriminalization, and deinstitutionalization of status offenders.

This list provides evidence of the dramatic shift in the construction of the social problem of runaway youth—from one in which little boys' adventures were celebrated to one that was concerned with the dangers that befell runaway girls in counterculture areas, thus setting the stage for the problem to be reconstructed as one that would embrace the street-based, survivalist version of the runaway child. Second, we witness the birth of the first alternative service provider (patterned on the values of the Digger's Free City Collective and experimenting with a new shelter model) as well as the struggles of that fledging shelter with regard to law enforcement and traditional public providers. Finally, it is a year in which jurists and federal policymakers become firmly committed to a path of striving to increase the civil rights protections of youth and diverting status offenders (including runaways) from traditional institutions such as child welfare and juvenile justice, but leaving open the question of the best kind of alternative treatment. All this was happening; of course, in the context of the Baby Boomers growing up and the pop culture they were fueling. Both because it changed what had come before and anchored future pathways, the year 1967 would be pivotal and defining. In other words, it was a year in which the cultural, demographic, individual, and institutional forces influencing and shaping runaway discourse began to converge.

Of course, history never stands still. The Baby Boomers grew up, became parents, and are growing older. New generations of radical youth displaced their Beat, hippie, and Digger elders and have found their own cultural spokespersons. But what became of runaways? Even today, the "runaway" problem continues to evolve after the 1970s, as did the services and policy frameworks.

Runaway Children: Lost in the Rhetoric of the "Missing"

In general, we no longer speak as sympathetically about runaways as we once did. They are sometimes now dismissed as being merely *voluntarily missing,* falling under the larger rubric of "missing" children, which includes those kidnapped by noncustodial parents or abducted by strangers.[2] Missing and exploited children have gained visibility on milk cartons, shopping bags, and as a "charitable contribution" category automatically available on federal income tax returns.

Within this newly constructed problem of "missing children," public concern has morphed into public hysteria and has become focused with particular intensity on abductions by strangers. Although these cases are small in number, they are high in drama, such as those of Adam Walsh, Etan Patz, and Elizabeth Smart. Or consider the spectacle of watching an "Amber Alert" on CNN cable. Amber Alerts now invite the public to engage in active surveillance to aid police in child-snatching cases, thus bringing renewed public vigilance and sophistication to the process of retrieving missing youth quickly. So while the plight of innocent children nabbed by (usually) complete strangers captures the attention of cable and network news, the vulnerability of resourceless runaway youth living on city streets is now sometimes overlooked or overshadowed.

Federal Legislation: The Missing Children's Act

The concern for "missing" children makes sense as an extension of the runaway problem as posited in the 1960s and 1970s. At the time, the "runaway" child was mostly constructed from the perspective of youth themselves. Their autonomy and independence was at the forefront of public discussion, in part because the Baby Boomers put it there. However, this perspective diminishes the voice of parents, particularly those who are genuinely frantic or worried. Since parents were mostly omitted from the equation as the runaway problem was framed, services designed, and policy enacted, they needed to find their way back into the public discussion. A separate and independent parents-initiated movement became the predictable and logical response. Parents framed their concerns around this new rhetorical construction of "missing children," including those who were taken by ex-spouses or strangers.

Exactly a decade after the initial Runaway Youth Act, Congress enacted another piece of legislation entitled the *Missing Children's Assistance Act* of 1984.[3] In the United States Code—a codification framework which topically arranges *all* existing federal law—both acts are inserted under Title 42, *Public Health and Welfare*, and within Chapter 72, the *Juvenile Justice and Delinquency Prevention Act* (JJDPA). However, the *Runaway and Homeless Youth Act* is Subchapter III, and located right next to it as Subchapter IV is the Missing Children's Assistance Act. There is some irony in the fact that these two policy and service frameworks are codified side by side as distinct legislative initiatives—one for "runaway" children and the other for "missing" children; one framed with youth rights in mind and the other privileging the rights of parents. For example, each act has established and now supports its own independent telephone hotline. The National Runaway Switchboard (1-800-621-4000), first founded in 1971 and supported under the Runaway Youth Act of 1974, is a continuation of the service that had its roots in the counterculture. The National Center for Missing and Exploited Children has its own hotline (1-800-THE-LOST), established primarily for the parents of missing youth. Although the National Center is mandated legislatively to "coordinate" the operation of its telephone hotline with the one funded under the Runaway Youth Act,[4] they are in fact two separate service entities and their host home is situated in two different subchapters of the United States Code.

Crossover with the Child Welfare Discourse

Concern for "missing" children has also spilled over into the arena of child protective services, and in doing so has implicated runaway youth. Of course, by definition children who are involved with the child welfare system have come from troubled families (troubled enough for children to have been declared by a court to be "abused" or "neglected" and removed from their homes). So children who opt out of the child welfare system (or run away) are asserting their independence, in part, by rejecting the state's offer of substitute family-living arrangements. In general, however, public attention has focused on system failure with respect to missing teenagers rather than on the plight or circumstances of individual children who have left the system.

In 2002, in a case that received considerable public attention, the state of Florida "lost" a five-year-old child, Rilya Wilson, who was supposed to be in its foster care system.[5] The aftereffect of this story was to put pressure on states nationwide to attend to their foster care records and to account for their own "missing" children. The media covered these disclosures. In August 2002, for example, Michigan declared 302 children "missing" from the Family Independence Agency (FIA), its state-run child welfare system.[6] FIA promptly borrowed techniques similar to those used by groups advocating for missing and exploited children. FIA posted the names and photographs of its missing charges on an official state Web site. In essence, it invited the public to help track down the system's missing children.[7] On careful inspection, most of these youth proved not to be "lost" young children like Rilya Wilson but rather teenagers who were missing "voluntarily" (in other words, had run away) from foster care.[8] In an exposé on Michigan's "missing" children on the NBC Evening News, the segment opened with an illustration showing how the news team was able to track down one of the system's AWOL teenagers—a 17-year-old who had been gone for two entire years—in a matter of hours. When confronted by reporters, her response was, "I'm glad they lost me. I don't have to look at their face every day."[9] Clearly, at the age of 15 this young woman had decided she no longer wanted a home provided and supervised by the state.

But the public problems of Michigan and Florida paled in comparison to that of California's gigantic child welfare system. In 2002, NBC News reported that 740 children were "missing" from Los Angeles alone. Of course, as in Michigan, most were runaway adolescents. NBC featured the story of one girl, Desiree Collins, who entered the foster care system at 12, "suffered serious mental problems," and had run away from state-provided care "fourteen times in one eight-month span, sometimes living on the streets."[10] A month after her final flight from foster care, she was lost permanently to the system at the age of 14, when she was found murdered. Before her disappearance, relatives had written a letter to Los Angeles County's Department of Children and Family Services asking that it "lock her up to protect her from herself," and saying that the girl had already been "raped, stabbed, and beaten."[11]

Experts in California called Desiree's death "tragic" but not an "isolated" case.[12] During questioning on the news program of John Oppenheim, the deputy director of the Department of Children and Family Services, the following exchange took place:

> OPPENHEIM: We knew exactly where these kids were until the day that they were either abducted or ran away.
> REPORTER: And now?
> OPPENHEIM: Absolutely, I don't know where they are.
> REPORTER: So, they are in fact missing?
> OPPENHEIM: I don't deny that. But I think the significant difference is that we knew where they were—and that's why we know that they've ran away [sic], or we know they had been abducted.[13]

While the reporter and state official quibbled over whether the general problem was one of *missing* children, *runaway* children, or *abducted* children (which presumably would lead to different attributions of responsibility or accountability), the specific facts of Desiree's case pointed to a runaway recidivist with serious problems who had repeatedly fled the state's child welfare system, and then found her way to the street. Once she was on the street, it is reasonable to conclude that her options for survival were limited. Runaway shelters—which are available in the Los Angeles area—may have been her only alternative to the help offered by acquaintances who might have befriended her while living on the street. Which raises the question: In regard to runaways, what has happened to federal policy and services?

Evolution and Expansion of the Federal Runaway Youth Act

Another place to look for the evolution of the runaway problem, including services and policy, is in the amendments to the 1974 federal Runaway Youth Act. As is often the case with legislation—once enacted—it gets incrementally and repeatedly expanded with each reauthorization. Each amendment provides trace evidence of that evolution of the problem in public discourse as it unfolds longitudinally (historically). The Runaway Youth Act is no exception. It has unfurled in three directions. First, it is reaching more varied populations of youth. Second, it is providing a wider array of services. Finally, legislators have called upon providers to act as an "alternative" to an increasing number of public institutions.

Population Expansion

In 1977, just three years after the Runaway Youth Act's initial enactment, it was amended to include "otherwise homeless youth."[14] In 1980 the legislation was renamed to reflect this new focus, and it became the Runaway and Homeless Youth Act (RHYA).[15] In 1994 the law's scope was extended to include "street youth" (defined by Congress as "a juvenile who spends a significant amount of time on the street or in other areas of exposure to encounters that may lead to sexual abuse").[16] It was also expanded to include "early intervention service (such as home-based services) . . . to prevent runaway and homeless youth from becoming involved in the juvenile justice system."[17]

The addition of "home-based" services indicates a move to strengthen interventions within the youth's natural family in order to prevent running away; however, the other additions to the list seem to acknowledge that basic runaway shelters were serving a much more estranged and street-acculturated group of youth (homeless and street youth) than the original word *runaway* apparently captured. Certainly, I have myself argued here that these kind of street-based youth were folded under the rubric of the original "runaway" label in 1974. However, the simple service response of providing shelter, providing counseling, and then expecting youth to return home was clearly not sufficient to meet the needs of some youth seeking services. New labels describing the youth population emerged, as services expanded to support and reach truly homeless and/or street-based youth who needed much more extensive help than just room and board for a couple of nights.

Service Expansion

Today, for administrative purposes, the services funded under the RHYA are organized in three basic categories. In addition to the runaway shelters (generally now called the Basic Centers Programs), there are two additional prongs—Traditional Living Programs (TLPs) and Street Outreach Programs.

Basic Centers Programs provide the same services they have since the 1960s, such as food, clothing, shelter, and medical care referrals as well as counseling and recreational programs. TLPs are designed for those youth aged 16 to 21 who cannot return home and need longer-term assistance—up to eighteen months—than crisis shelters can provide. These TLP programs can be structured as group homes, supervised apartments, or placements with host families. In 2003 this section of the RHYA was amended to add "maternity group homes," which are designed to provide transitional living for pregnant and parenting young women. Services can include classes in parenting, child development, health, nutrition, family budgeting, and other topics useful to young parents.[18] Street Outreach Programs target youth deemed to be at-risk for sexual abuse and/or exploitation. They include crisis intervention and counseling, housing information and referral, health care service referrals, as well as advocacy, education, and prevention services for alcohol and drug abuse, STDs (including HIV/AIDS), and physical and sexual assault.

Yet another addition folded in with the 2003 amendment was reference to providing "linguistically appropriate" services, suggesting that Congress is concerned about the ethnic diversity of youth seeking services at runaway and homeless youth programs.[19] Given this addition, coupled with that of maternity group homes, it is possible to add to this list (of youth populations specifically mentioned in the act), pregnant and parenting teenagers as well as ethnically diverse clients. In short, both the list of specifically included populations and the list of potentially available services have grown dramatically since 1974.

Alternative to an Increasing Array of Public Institutions

The third way in which the RHYA has expanded is that it is now expected to provide an *alternative* to an increasing variety of traditional systems of care. In the original legislation, shelters were introduced to relieve responsibility from "already overburdened police departments and juvenile justice authorities." Congress found it was incumbent on the federal government to develop "an effective system of temporary care outside the law enforcement structure."[20] By 1992, Congress provided grants for runaway shelters to deal with youth in a "manner which is outside the law enforcement system, the child welfare system, the mental health system and the juvenile justice system."[21] Furthermore, the 1992 amendments stated that "runaway and homeless youth have a disproportionate share of health, behavioral and emotional problems," and that they "need opportunities to complete high school or earn a general equivalency degree."[22] This pattern suggests that the shelter system and its extensions are being asked to serve as an alternative to a variety of other institutions, including law enforcement, juvenile justice, child welfare, public schools, and mental health.

The Net Effect?

Taken together, this incremental legislative tinkering offers evidence that the original "runaway" policy is expanding in three directions—population expansion, service diversity, and as an alternative to an increasing number of other institutions and systems. While each incremental adjustment may make sense, as a conceptual matter—that is, taken as a whole—it should raise some concerns. The assumption (or expectation) is that the private sector will respond with an increasingly comprehensive package of services (crisis care, transitional living, outreach, etc.) for a population of youth with multiple complicating factors (homeless, street-acculturated, pregnant and parenting, mentally ill, undereducated, etc.). An alternate way of framing this idea is to wonder if the public institutions (law enforcement, juvenile justice, child welfare, public schools, and mental health) in this expanding array are being excused from their responsibilities in the care, discipline, treatment, education, and socialization of many of society's most difficult and troubled youth.

In light of the historical ground just traveled in this book, and the root assumptions embedded in the original policy design, it is worth pausing to consider the current scenario. The alternative runaway shelter movement of the 1960s favored youth autonomy, confidentiality, and working outside public institutions and systems of care. Services were triggered when youth asked for them directly and did not require the intervention of courts or police. Services were not, therefore, imposed against the will of youth; they could come and go from programs as they wished.

This continues to be the general service design. However, today the type of youth the policy invites the alternative community to serve includes those who are avoiding both of our basic and traditional institutions of child and youth socialization—the family (or foster care) and schools. In addition, these youth possess a combination of characteristics (e.g., runaway recidivists, sexually active, perhaps mentally ill, come from troubled families, have been involved in criminal activities, have failed at school) which suggest that they are more difficult, rather than less, to engage. Yet we are expecting them on their own to find their way to alternative services, voluntarily ask for help, and stay involved with the providers for long enough periods of time to produce good outcomes. One suspects that the responsibility for these troubling cases are now being placed at the doorstep of the alternative community, which is expected to provide catchall services for youth who don't easily fit anywhere else.

Again, given the evolution of federal policy, it would seem that three assumptions are currently being made which are worth considering in light of the original construction and design of alternative services. The first assumption is that alternative services are available in all the communities in which they are needed. The second is that these alternative providers offer a full and comprehensive range of services (street outreach, crisis intervention, transitional living, education, mental health, etc.). And third, that the alternative providers have enough secure funding to provide the full range of services even though they have no legal mandate to do so.

Although there are many programs scattered across the United States, the actual service offerings vary dramatically from community to community.[23] Of course, unlike the child welfare system—where there is a legal mandate to provide public care for abused and neglected children—there is no such legal mandate for these alternative providers. To the extent the alternative community is providing supplemental kinds of services, this may make sense; however, to the extent they are being asked to provide for the basic needs (food, clothing, and shelter) of children who have been lost by other public institutions, this may be an undue burden. Furthermore, while alternative providers can compete for some public funding, most must also look for other ways to support their work, including soliciting donations from private individuals, foundations, and corporations. Yet courting donors for programs serving high-risk youth takes concerted effort and a set of skills that are very different than the ones needed to engage and serve youth in the first place. It requires developing expertise in writing grants, fund-raising, or other forms of scrounging for money. It also takes learning how to "sell" their message in ways donors find compelling. It is asking a lot of the alternative community to absorb a variety of troubled youth, be creative in service delivery, and find ways to stay financially solvent.

Given the evolution of these policies and the demands being placed upon the alternative community, it is possible to posit two different outcome scenarios for youth. The first is that the alternative community becomes successful in providing for adolescents who otherwise fail in, or are being failed by, our other institutions. This scenario assumes that youth will find the services, when and where they need them, and will use them as a true alternative. The second possible outcome paints a less rosy picture. It is that runaway shelters will temporarily support children who will eventually graduate to adult homelessness while public authorities are absolved from their caretaking responsibilities. If the most difficult youth are permitted to drift off, be expelled, suspended, or otherwise lost by the public systems (such as schools, mental health institutions, foster care) because they are difficult to work with, then the existence of the alternative services community may salve the public's conscience, but expecting it to save these children is asking a lot—indeed, probably too much.

All of these considerations raise a fundamental question: is this approach really a solution for those youth who need help or are we abandoning kids without the proper support and guidance they should receive earlier on? The troubling truth is that after forty years of legislation, service, and research, we don't really know the answer to that question. Only in the most recent years have researchers even begun to turn their attention to the question.[24]

The National Network for Youth estimates that between 1 and 1.3 million youth run away from home each year.[25] While the body of social science research on runaway children has grown significantly since the 1970s, much of it has been devoted to identifying the family and personal characteristics of runaway youth and the risk factors associated with running away (see Selected Bibliography). This research literature has been complicated by the lack of consensus on population definitions. Researchers have studied "runaway," "homeless," "street youth," "throwaways," "shoveouts," and others, yet frequently their conceptual frameworks overlap, making it difficult to figure out what we really know about any given group. Very little has been done in the way of evaluating the success or failures of alternative services, and virtually nothing has been done to evaluate policy. In part this is because these children are difficult to study. At least some of them lead such unstable lives it makes them hard to locate and track. They "cross over" between systems (such as juvenile justice, foster care, home, friends, mental health), making it difficult to design studies tracing their movement from system to system. Furthermore, policies of the Institutional Review Board (IRB), which generally require parental consent to conduct research with minors, can place additional burdens on researchers studying vulnerable populations. This often makes it difficult to study independent, high-risk, street-based youth whose parents are not readily available to sign consent forms. There are, in short, plenty of disincentives—both practical and systemic—in regard to studying this mobile, parentless, system-crossing, premature independence-seeking group of wandering minors.

Historical Vision and Current Problem-Solving: The Case of Nicolette R.

On September 15, 2004, Leslie Kaufman wrote an article for the *New York Times* which should sound eerily familiar to anyone who has read through this book.[26] The story ran under the headline "Finding a Future for a Troubled Girl with a Past: Is the Answer to the Growing Problem of Child Prostitution Forced Counseling or Incarceration?" The story is interesting for its construction of the child prostitution problem, the characterization of the alternative service community, and its reporting of the clashes in court over what to do with this one troubled girl. More to the point, it serves as a useful source of comparison for this study on the construction of the runaway youth problem as well as on services and policy. How much progress have we made over the last four or five decades?

The journalist traces the story of one girl, Nicolette R., while placing her life in the broader context of unsubstantiated claims by professionals that the child prostitution problem is on the rise. Some of the core facts in Nicolette's case, as reported, include that she had been arrested for prostitution twice by the age of 12. Her family life—beginning at the age of six—had been unstable and her caretakers were no longer active participants in her life. She had probably endured years of sexual, physical, and emotional abuse by multiple caretakers. It is unclear if or when she ever attended school. She was a drug user if not abuser. She was angry and capable of violence, but also inclined to suck her thumb. She began running away at the age of ten.

The facts of Nicolette's life are similar, in many respects, to those of Veronica Brunson or Karen Baxter, who served as the poster girls for the "runaway" problem in 1977 (see chapters 1 and 2). They are also similar to those presented in the cases of Esther Gesicki, Marion Johnson, and Dominica Morelli, the lead plaintiffs in the class action suit challenging New York's Wayward Minor Act in 1971 (see chapter 6). These girls really represent variations on a theme: Esther, Marion, and Dominica; Veronica and Karen; Nicolette (and perhaps Desiree)—wayward, runaway, PINS, missing, prostitute, the same sad story through the 1930s,1960s, 1970s, and to the present day.

There are four features in the story construction and circumstances of Nicolette's case that are worth pondering in light of the historical material presented in this book. The first has to do with the reporter's characterization of the runaway shelter, Covenant House. Nicolette found her way to this alternative provider and Kaufman describes that encounter:

In 2001, at age 11, she ended up at Covenant House, the primary city residence for teenage runaways. It is a magnet for the troubled and unprotected, and the sidewalk outside Covenant House is a notorious recruiting ground for pimps. It was there that Nicolette, in her words, "met a guy who would take care of me."

She ran away with her pimp for a week at first before returning to her aunt's Bronx apartment, but then she left for increasingly longer periods of time.[27]

So Covenant House, once described in the press as an "oasis" for runaway teenagers,[28] is now referred to as a well-established "magnet" for troubled

kids and hence offers a "notorious recruiting ground for pimps." In its earliest days, the shelter model was sold to the public as a refuge from the street
and a lifeline *off* the street. Kaufman's story construction reverses the
sequence of events. By first offering a place for runaways to go, the shelter is
now described as an entrance point *into* street life. Of course, an alternative
provider such as Covenant House cannot lock up or restrict the movement
of any child seeking its services, including the youngest ones (although
undoubtedly her counselors would have asked her to stay inside as a condition of her case plan). Furthermore, as a "mandated reporter," a child care
facility like Covenant House undoubtedly would have notified the state's
central registry of abused and neglected children about Nicolette's case (if
such a case was not already open and active). Nonetheless, if Nicolette
decided to walk out the shelter door and select her own substitute family—
even in the form of a pimp—rather than agreeing to work with shelter counselors on a plan that would have probably sent her into the foster care system, there was nothing shelter staff could have done about it.

A second item of interest in the story's construction is the characterization of Nicolette herself, who is described as a "prostitute" with a history of
running away. Her running away is itself provided mostly as tangential
information, with experts expressing concern that her past behavior will be
repeated if she isn't placed in a secure, restrictive facility. In the 1970s Nicolette might well have been described primarily as a runaway child who had
been driven to prostitution as a form of survival sex. Today the labels are
switched and the emphasis is reversed. Now the problem becomes what to
do with a prostitute (who has a history of running away) rather than what to
do with a runaway (who has been involved in prostitution). Note that the
conceptual design of providing shelter makes sense when you rhetorically
construct the problem as one in which a youth runs away from home and
needs an option other than prostitution for survival. On the other hand, if
you describe a child like this as a prostitute, you have vested her with some
agency to choose that lifestyle. In doing so, a situation is created in which
the matchmaking between troubled kids and pimps can take place on the
sidewalks in front of the shelter itself. It reverses the order of choices. Nicolette can leave a safe shelter for the caretaking of a pimp instead of the historically made assumption that she would flee her pimp for the safety of a
shelter.

The third point of interest is the reference to the growing problem of child prostitution, although no concrete data are offered to support this assertion. "No one" wrote Kaufman, "from child welfare experts, to social workers to the police or politicians concerned about the problem—are willing to hazard a guess as to how many children are, on their own or against their will, selling their bodies for cash."[29] She goes on to report, "Nonetheless, in recent years, there has emerged a shared alarm among many public defenders, prosecutors and child advocacy organizations that child prostitution is on the rise."[30] This assertion (without supporting data)—that there is a large and growing problem of child prostitution—is also familiar. The story of Veronica Brunson was a case study within newspaper articles that reported on the widespread problem of runaway youth. Furthermore, arguments that the "runaway" problem had increased to "alarming" proportions without any empirical support are specifically articulated and embedded in the legislative findings of the Runaway Youth Act of 1974 (see chapter 7).

This point is not made to dismiss or diminish the genuine concerns of child advocates, nor to question their observations, but it is important to consider how fueling public panic about unsubstantiated growth of an alarming problem focuses public attention and permits individual cases (such as Veronica's or Nicolette's) to serve as illustrations of newly discovered social problems.[31] This helps raise public awareness and may galvanize public support. However, it also invites the question as to whether we are repackaging an old problem under a resuscitated label and treating it as news.

Finally, the story is interesting for the factual information it provides about the "clash of approaches" over what to do with Nicolette once authorities finally had her in family court. As Kaufman wrote: "The wrangling would play out over a full year in Family Court, drawing in prosecutors, judges, dueling therapists, court-appointed lawyers, child welfare authorities, a representative of the state's juvenile jails, and a private organization that provides housing for troubled adolescents."[32] This list is interesting, of course, because it includes all the representatives that would be expected. According to Kaufman, "each had strong opinions about the girl" but "none had easy answers for dealing with her or helping her" (27). Yet the arguments made from each of the constituencies are entirely predictable. Among those reported in Kaufman's article were the following:

- The prosecutor argued she was "a hardened child who lacked remorse and who would return to her life on the streets unless she was imprisoned" and, furthermore, if placed in a nonsecure facility would runaway "at the first chance" because children like Nicolette "are in the lifestyle" and will "not participate in treatment unless they were compelled" (27).
- Nicolette's lawyers said she was "too young to have consented to sex and should be set free" or, alternatively, should be "seen as a victim of sexual exploitation" and provided medical treatment. Locking her up, they argued, would be "both counterproductive and needlessly punitive" (27).
- The family court judge believed that what Nicolette needed was time in secure juvenile detention, in part to get "proper moral principles" (27).
- A child welfare official reported that "finding places to send young children with as active a sexual history as Nicolette is a challenge. Foster homes do not want them, and specialized homes currently exist only for girls over 16" (28).
- A psychologist argued she was dangerous and advocated incarceration in order to protect others (27).

So there are some recurring lines of debate. Was she a "hardened" criminal or a "victim"? Was she "in the lifestyle" or "too young to consent" to sex? Was she bad by nature or was she driven to her current condition? Was she emotionally disturbed or morally depraved? Was she in need of guidance, treatment, or punishment? Should our focus be on protecting her or protecting the public? Did she belong in foster care or some other system? How coercive or restrictive should be our intervention?

One troubling aspect of these arguments is their dichotomous nature. Adversarial, judicial intervention certainly invites these kind of either/or choices. Each side is attempting to persuade the judge that it has the more correct version of the truth about Nicolette. Yet pitting one constructed version of the truth against the other does a disservice to the complexity of the lives of individual children like Nicolette.

What if children—particularly those asserting independence prematurely like Nicolette—wields a knife *and* sucks her thumb? Or shows signs of resilience *and* appears emotionally disturbed. Is both sexually active *and* sexually exploited? What if she is both child *and* adult? What if she is good *and* bad; healthy *and* disturbed, victim *and* perpetrator? Those kinds of complications make treatment, service, and policy much more difficult to arrange.

When individual children "cross over" in our social constructions, they blur boundaries and don't neatly fit within our existing institutional structures.

It would seem that embracing the complications and contradictions rather than denying them might be a more honest approach to problem-solving. Presumably such a holistic and contextual approach would require more individual discretion, which carries with it the inherent danger of being less vigilant about civil rights. Supreme Court cases from the 1960s and 1970s, such as *In re Gault*, sought to protect youth (whose liberty interests were at stake) from the unfettered discretion of family court judges acting in their "best interests." Nonetheless, somewhere along the line we may have lost sight of the fact that a full year of adult quibbling is a relatively long time in the life of a 12- or 13-year-old child like Nicolette. Perhaps this combination of civil rights protections, stereotyping children into discrete categories (abused, neglected, delinquent, status offender), and positing dichotomous constructions of their behavior within these categories has splintered real children into too many pieces.

A second troubling aspect of these arguments is their repetitive nature and lack of historical vision. Each of the parties involved makes predictable arguments based on their institutional roles and ideological views. Yet these are the same sets of arguments that have been made over the past four decades (at least). By losing track of the historical repetition, we are destined to place the same kind of professionals around the same kind of metaphorical tables (or court rooms) in order to make the same predictable arguments with limited ability to move beyond those boundaries in a timely fashion for the benefit of the child at issue.

So what happened in the real-life story of Nicolette? At the trial court level the judge ordered that Nicolette be placed in a secure detention facility which, Kaufman observed, "is the most common approach in New York City," in part because "there are few practical or attractive options" (27). This approach essentially resurrects the effects of the long-defunct Wayward Minors Act of the 1930s. However, in a move that Kaufman describes as unusual, Nicolette's lawyers appealed the decision. On appeal, the family court judge's placement decision was overturned and Nicolette's attorneys "won the right to have her transferred to a residential treatment center for emotionally disturbed children" (27).

Of note is the fact that only one out of the six private agencies contacted in regard to her placement was willing to accept her, and none had "expertise in sexual abuse, much less prostitution" (27). Opponents of Nicolette's placement expressed concern about the agency, in part, because other "youngsters had temporarily gone missing from the home 150 times in 2003 and about five had run away altogether" (27). In other words, it was a private, nonrestrictive facility housing high-risk youth and it lost some. Kaufman wrote that, "Surprisingly, Nicolette's lawyers were helped in their arguments by the state detention center itself. In a highly unusual move, a representative testified that the facility could offer her only drug treatment, not counseling for sexual abuse or prostitution. Nicolette 'would be better served' by a private facility, the representative testified" (28). In short, both the official of the child protective services, cited above, and the official of the state detention center cited here, take the position that its facilities cannot handle Nicolette. Neither public-sector system is willing or able to provide for her, which leaves only innovative alternative programs to care for her.

Here, then, is another battle with historical precedence (see chapter 6). What kind of treatment or care/custody does she deserve? Who is primarily responsible for a child such as this—the public or private sector? Furthermore, how cohesive should treatment be or, alternatively, how protective should we be of Nicolette's liberty interests? In 1975, *In the Matter of Cecilia R.*, twenty-three private placement agencies were approached about taking Cecilia and none would do so (see chapter 6).[33] In Nicolette's case, finding one out of six sounds like an improvement. Nonetheless, if the private sector is going to be made primarily responsible for these children who cross boundaries and present such dilemmas for public caregivers, we need to think about how we can entice them to engage in this kind of work in sufficient force (and funding) to provide meaningful service, in the right geographic locations, for all the youth who need help. These adolescents take up a lot of time and resources. They may not always appear sympathetic to the public. They can cause disruptions to the regular order of things. They are defiant, strong-willed, and independent. Ensuring that there are sufficient providers out there willing to handle them has been a recurring problem.

Conclusions

In the 1860s, Jacob Riis described New York City's vagabond street youth as "bright and sharp as a weasel," but as "acknowledging no authority," raising

a "grimy fist against society whenever it tries to coerce him" but also possessing "sturdy independence, love of freedom and absolute resilience."[34]
Therein lies a uniquely American dilemma: in a country that values individual freedom and independence above all else, cultivating those qualities
in its rebellious children will always conflict with the realities of children's
lives on the street and on the run. There is an inherent tension between hon-
oring self-sufficient autonomy and being dismayed at rule-breaking delinquency which may endanger children or others.

As noted at the beginning of this book, youth like Veronica (and Nicolette) may serve to illustrate the individual price of freedom as we struggle
to get the balance right. For the moment, Nicolette's case stands frozen in
time and space, hanging in history. It serves as a useful metaphor. At the
time of Kaufman's story, Nicolette had spent a month in her placement, but
she "still has not bolted."[35] So she is already doing better than her historical
counterparts Veronica and Karen. Nonetheless, she is in a precarious position. We are hoping that she will act dependently even though she can
assert her independence. If she wants, she can walk out the door—either
temporarily, like those 150 youth did in 2003, or permanently like the four
other young girls before her. Nicolette sits poised on the cusp of success and
failure. If she chooses to leave, the adults around her know that risks to her
life and health increase. Street life may be her only option; it is what she
knows best, so it is where she would likely return. Of course, once there she
might remember that she has other options and find her way back to an
alternative shelter, using it as a means to escape the street. All these pathways are available to her. In time, she will have to choose her own way. And
perhaps this is the best we can hope to do for children in our free society.
We can argue and we can worry but, somehow, coercing and incarcerating
sturdy, resilient, independent adolescents doesn't seem to be quite the right
approach. Ultimately, we may have to hold our collective breath and trust
that these fragile but determined children use their freedom wisely.

Closing Note
Lessons Learned and Conveyed

. . . if I'd a knowed what trouble it was to make a book I wouldn't a tackled it and ain't agoing to no more.

—Huck Finn

Of course, if an exercise such as this history on runaways, services, and policy is to be of any general use, larger lessons can and should be drawn from
it. Certainly my work with this material over time has profoundly influenced my understanding of social problems, grassroots service responses,
and policy. Nothing seems quite as linear, quite as neat, nor quite as easily
presented and understood as I was once willing to believe. Given my post at
a university and my responsibility for teaching a next generation of social
work advocates something about social problems, services, and social policy, I've found that the lessons I've learned in the process of producing this
work have invariably seeped into my classroom and have influenced my
instruction. Not all the lessons are entirely new; nonetheless, they have
been illustrated in this case study and may be generalized to whatever problems and policies one might wish to contemplate. Here are some of the
more important ones.

I. There are no "new" social problems, nor are there any truly new
responses. However, there are reinterpretations and new labels attached to
old or familiar phenomena—all variations on themes. So don't ignore history and don't be distracted by the flashy new packaging. But *do* take time

to understand the significance of the latest incarnations. What forces are directing us to frame the problem, here and now, using the words and metaphors we do?

2. How we frame the problem is directly correlated to how we respond to it. Look for the relationship and understand the *pas de deux*. Ask two separate questions: Is that the way the problem *should* be framed? And is that the way the solution *should* be delivered? As social advocates, consider your strategic choices: do you want to attack either, neither, or both?

3. Legislation arguably marks the maturity of the way a public problem is temporarily defined in public discourse, but consider carefully what came before and what happens after. New legislation tethers a social problem's definition in time and historical space, but ask of the antecedent forces that shaped it: what are the values, prejudices, and assumptions that came attached to this formulation? Furthermore, once these are locked in place, think critically of the incremental adjustments that modify the design afterward. Should we stay anchored where we are? Or should we cut loose and try again?

4. Similarly, the impacts of our policy choices are never fully realized until they become institutionalized. As other systems adjust their operations and as individuals adjust their behaviors to accommodate new additions, the overall service structure is modified. These adjustments can take decades to become engrained patterns of behavior or established relationships. So while the initial public response to a social problem seems obvious (i.e., providing crisis shelter to runaway youth), the secondary and tertiary consequences may generate complications. (For example, how many homeless youth bounce between shelter and street rather than shelter to home? Or how many missing foster care teenagers are surviving using homeless youth shelters?)

5. Don't be fooled into thinking that any social problem, or the discussion of it, sits exclusively within the confines of the domains we set. Domains of policy and areas of study are socially created; they have permeable boundaries. Juvenile justice spills over into child welfare and mental health and public education. Popular culture infuses itself into serious political debate. To excise the parts is to lose the richness and complexity of the whole.

6. Equally important, however, is that the socially constructed domains have real implications for real people. These implications are played out during implementation, administration, and delivery of services. So while

the boundaries may not be "real," the impact that flows from them are. It matters mightily whether we slot a "runaway youth" into the juvenile justice system or into the child welfare system.

7. Listen to the underdogs, the outsiders, and the marginal and marginalized voices. The messenger may appear strange (perhaps he has purple hair, calls herself Pink, or has multiple body piercings). The mainstream may dismiss the messenger, and with it the message, as irrelevant, but it rarely is. Insights come from the outside. The marginal can and does move inward. Oddballs often have the really good ideas. Look for them. Listen to them. Give them serious thought.

8. The media matter. Think critically and read carefully. Watch, read, and consume the news not just for its content but also for its construction. Don't toss aside the newspaper without pausing to consider the verbs used in the headlines or the photograph(s) selected to illustrate the story. What other words or photographs might have been chosen? How might these selections seep, almost unnoticed and unchallenged, into our subconscious understanding of the world?

9. When social problems become "typified" in the media, we can predict that "typical" spokespersons will emerge and be called upon to give voice for an entire population. This has implications for the crossover between media construction of, say, "typical" runaways and those individual children anointed to speak on behalf of the entire population at legislative hearings or in other public forums. There are direct relationships between conceptualizing the typical, locating a "typical" individual, and giving him or her public voice to represent the population. Don't forget to ask who was silenced as atypical in the process.

10. When we systematically exclude the voice of one group of players who should be at the negotiation table on any social problem or political issue (say, parents in the runaway debate), watch for them to organize and return. Be attentive and aware of who is being excluded in public debate in any historic moment because they will not stay excluded forever. Wonder, or even predict, how they will resurface and intervene later on.

11. Look for the stable "reality" of a social problem. It is the eye of the storm. What are its core features? They are the ones that defy the rhetoric and values that spin as debris around them. How does the spin change over time? How does that influence the way the public reacts?

12. All the "myths" (or spin) about any social problem are probably true to some extent, so be careful how you choose which one(s) to invest your time and energy in believing. Runaways, for example, include kids who sit and mope at the end of the family driveway until dinnertime. They also include kids who stay at a friend's house for a weekend to take a break from home, kids who are driven away from home by severe sexual or physical abuse, and kids who have been locked out of the house by an adult caretaker. They include kids who die on the street, but I know firsthand that they also include those who graduate from Berkeley, Columbia, and the University of Michigan or Alabama. All the myths are true—the little adventurer, the little girl prostitute, the defiant child, the fleeing child, and perhaps even the poetic wanderer. However, the image we associate with the label—and then use as shorthand for the problem—has consequences.

13. Demographic trends matter, not just because they paint a portrait of who we are at any given moment but also because they indicate where we are going. Be assured that the constellation of policy and programs on one side of any demographic blip is likely to look very different than the constellation on the other side of that demographic blip. What are the implications for policy, problem construction, service delivery, and the very social fabric of our world? The future isn't a complete mystery. We can plan based on what we know. In a world that thinks in increasingly shorter political life cycles and time frames, fight the urge to engage in this myopic vision. Think longitudinally.

14. Worry about who funds our social welfare systems. What does reliance on that funding stream say about service delivery? Federal funding, with its accountability, can stifle radical creativity, but nonetheless its predictability provides security and stability that the private sector may not enjoy. Private-sector providers may be able to compose compelling cases about needy children which are easily sold in funding-raising newsletters. But what if the cause, the issue, or the specific population is less palatable to public taste and thus less easily marketed? People will open their checkbooks to help a runaway child driven out of utter desperation to survival sex, but are less inclined to do so for a crack-addicted, streetwise, teenage hustler. What if both descriptions are of the very same kid? Where do fiscal and moral responsibilities for the public's well-being intersect? Where is the proper balance of public and private responsibility?

15. Be aware of the ever-shifting balance of power between children, their parents, and the state. There is a triangle of rights and responsibility. When we protect children's legal rights in that triumvirate of power, we are necessarily decreasing the rights of parents or state. When we increase the police power or social control of the state, we decrease that of parents and youth. Where should the balance rest in a free society?

16. Consider the price of freedom. What are we willing to pay? What are we willing to sacrifice? Protecting children's liberty interests will contribute to the untimely death of some young street prostitutes. It is a cost of freedom. Failing to protect their liberty interests may cost all of us even more basic freedoms. What can we live with in the life-liberty trade-off?

Finally, there is one last lesson I try to convey. As an educator who faces classrooms filled with very bright, determined, socially conscious, and dedicated students, year after year, it is perhaps the most important one of all: individual actors matter and individual actions matter. Not just those we might agree to characterize at the time as historically significant—such as the presidents we elect and the wars they start; the justices that sit on the Supreme Court and the decisions they render; the cultural icons we worship or we vilify—but *everyone*. It may not seem like our actions and efforts will shake history to its roots, but we each contribute in significant and frequently unappreciated ways in shaping the world around us. None of these actions is inconsequential to the whole. As the Diggers would argue, it takes each of us creating the condition we describe to shape and change our world.

The final lesson I learned from the Diggers—but also from exploring the lives and ideas of so many diverse and interesting people during my journey with this material. Consider the unlikely association of the following cast of characters: J. Anthony Lukas, Nathaniel Sheppard, Selwyn Raab, Stephen A.O. Golden, Herbert Huncke, Neal Cassady, Jack Kerouac, Senator Birch Bayh, Gregory Corso, Reverends Larry Beggs and Bruce Ritter, Peter Coyote, William Treanor, Brian Slattery, policemen Capt. Francis Daly and Officer Warren McGinniss, Judge Stanley Gartenstein, Esther Gesicki, Dean Siering, Veronica Brunson, Linda Fitzpatrick, Dominic Tucci, and Dean Allen Corll. Together they comprise murder victims and murderers; politicians and journalists; jurists and radical youth leaders; police officers and poets; grassroots community organizers and drug-addicted street hustlers. I have come to appreciate that each made contributions to this story in ways that were beyond the scope of the actor's original intentions. So this final lesson involves appreciating that individual acts and actions are likely to reverberate beyond our limited ability to make meaning of them. That's not a bad lesson for social work students and advocates to take with them on the road.

Appendix 1
Runaway Youth Act
Senate Bill S. 2829

(Bayh/Cook Bill)

A BILL To strengthen interstate reporting and interstate services for parents of runaway children; to conduct research on the size of the runaway youth population; for the establishment, maintenance, and operation of temporary housing and counseling services for transient youth, and for other purposes

Be it enacted by the Senate and House of Representatives of the United States of American in Congress assembled, That this Act may be cited as the "Runaway Youth Act".

FINDINGS AND DECLARATION OF POLICY

Sec. 2. The Congress hereby finds that—

(1) the number of juveniles who leave and remain away from home without parental permission has increased to alarming proportions, creating a substantial law enforcement problem for the communities inundated, and significantly endangering the young people who are without resources and live on the street;

(2) that the exact nature of the problem is not well defined because national statistics on the size and profile of the runaway youth population are not tabulated;

(3) that many of these young people, because of their age and situation, are urgently in need of temporary shelter and counseling services;

(4) *that the anxieties and fears of parents whose children have run away from home can best be alleviated by effective interstate reporting services and the earliest possible contact with their children;*[1]

(5) that the problem of locating, detaining, and returning runaway children should not be the responsibility of already overburdened police departments and juvenile justice authorities; and

(6) that in view of the interstate nature of the problem, it is the responsibility of the Federal Government to develop accurate reporting of the problem nationally and to develop an effective system of temporary care outside the law enforcement structure.

TITLE I

SEC. 101. The Secretary of Health, Education, and Welfare is authorized to make grants and to provide technical assistance to localities and nonprofit private agencies in accordance with the provisions of this title beginning July 1, 1972, and ending June 30, 1975. Grants under this title should be made for the purpose of developing local facilities to deal primarily with the immediate needs of runaways in a manner which, wherever possible, is outside the law enforcement structure and juvenile justice system. The size of such grants should be determined by the number of runaway children in the community and the existing availability of services. Among applicants priority should be given to private organizations or institutions who have had past experience in dealing with runaways.

---

1. Deleted in final version of the Runaway Youth Act (P.L. 93–415).

SEC. 102. (a) To be eligible for assistance under this title, an applicant must propose to establish, strengthen, or fund an existing or proposed runaway house, a locally controlled facility providing temporary shelter, and counseling services to juveniles who have left home without the specific permission of their parents or guardians.

(b) In order to qualify, an applicant must submit a plan to the Secretary of Health, Education, and Welfare meeting the following requirements and including the following information. Each house—

(1) shall be located in an area which is demonstrably frequented by or easily reachable by runaway children;

(2) shall have a maximum capacity of no more than twenty children, with a ratio of staff to children of sufficient proportion to insure adequate supervision and treatment;

(3) shall develop an adequate plan for contacting the child's parents and insuring his safe return according to the best interests of the child;[2]

(4) shall develop an adequate plan for insuring proper relations with law enforcement personnel, and the return of runaway from correctional institutions;

(5) shall develop an adequate plan for aftercare counseling involving runaway *children* and their parents within *a twenty-five mile radius of the house*;[3]

2. The final version of the Runaway Youth Act (P.L. 93–415) reads: "shall develop adequate plans for contacting the child's parents or relatives (*if such action is required by State law*) and assuring the safe return of the child according to the best interests of the child, *for contacting local government officials pursuant to informal arrangements established with such officials by the runaway house, and for providing for other appropriate alternative living arrangements*. (Italicized text indicates subsequent change in wording.)

3. Italics above indicate passage deleted in final version of the Runaway Youth Act (P.L. 93–415) and changed to read: "shall develop an adequate plan for aftercare counseling involving runaway *youth* and their parents within *the State in which the runaway house is located and for assuring, as possible, that after case services will be provided to those children who are returned beyond the State in which the runaway house is located* ." (Italicized text indicates subsequent change in wording.)

(6) shall keep adequate statistical records profiling the children and parents which it serves:[4]

(7) shall submit annual reports to the Secretary of Health, Education, and Welfare detailing how the house has been able to meet the goals of its plans and reporting the statistical summaries required in section 102(b)(6);

(8) shall demonstrate its ability to operate under accounting procedures and fiscal control devices as required by the Secretary of Health, Education, and Welfare; and

(9) shall supply such other information as the Secretary of Health, Education, and Welfare deems necessary.[5]

SEC. 103. An application by a State, locality, or nonprofit private agency for a grant under this title may be approved by the Secretary only if it is consistent with the applicable provisions of this title and meets the requirements set forth in section 102.

SEC. 104. Nothing in this title shall be construed to deny grants to nonprofit private agencies which are fully controlled by private boards or persons but which in other ways meet the requirements of this title and agree to be legally responsible for the operation of the runaway house. Nothing in this title shall give the Federal Government *and its agencies* control over the staffing and personnel decisions of facilities receiving Federal funds, *except as the staffs of such facilities must meet the standards under this title.*[6]

---

4. The final version of the Runaway Youth Act (P.L. 93–415) reads: "shall keep adequate statistical records profiling the children and parents which it serves, *except that records maintained on individual runaway youths shall not be disclosed without parental consent to anyone other than another agency compiling statistical records or a government agency involved in the disposition of criminal charges against an individual runaway youth, and reports or other documents based on such statistical records shall not disclose the identity of individual runaway youths.* (Italicized text indicates subsequent change in wording.)

5. Added to final version of P.L. 93–415 is: "(9) shall submit a budget estimate with respect to the plan submitted by such house under this subsection."

6. Italicized text deleted from the final version of the Runaway Youth Act (P.L. 93–415).

SEC. 105. The Secretary of Health, Education, and Welfare shall annually report to Congress on the status and accomplishments of the runaway houses which were funded with particular attention to—

(1) their effectiveness in alleviating the problems of runaway youth;

(2) *their effectiveness in insuring an early return to the children's homes and in encouraging* the resolution of intrafamily problems through counseling and other services;[7]

(3) *their effectiveness in reducing drug abuse and undesirable conditions existing in areas which runaway youth frequent;*[8] and

(4) their effectiveness in strengthening family relationships and encouraging stable living situations for children.[9]

SEC. 106. As used in this title, the term "State" shall include Puerto Rico, the District of Columbia, Guam, and the Virgin Islands.

SEC. 107. (a) *The Federal share for the construction of new facilities under this title shall be no more than 50 per centum.*[10] The Federal share for the acquisition and renovation of existing structures, the provision of counseling services, staff training, and the general costs of operations of such facility's budget for any fiscal year shall be 90 per centum.[11]

7. Italicized text deleted from final version of the Runaway Youth Act (P.L. 93–413). The final version of P.L. 93–415 reads: "their ability to reunite children with their families and to encourage the resolution of intrafamily problems through counseling and other services"

8. Italicized text deleted from the final Runaway Youth Act (P.L. 93–415).

9. Added to the final version of P.L. 93–415 is "their effectiveness in helping youth decide upon a future course of action" and "shall supply such other information as the Secretary reasonably deems necessary."

10. Italicized text deleted in final version of P.L. 93–415.

11. Added to the final version of P.L. 93–415 is: "The non-Federal share may be in cash or in kind, fairly evaluated by the Secretary, including plant equipment, or services."

(b) The Secretary of Health, Education, and Welfare shall pay to each applicant which has an application approved 90 per centum of the cost of such applications.[12]

(c) Payments under this section may be made in installments, in advance, or by way of reimbursement, with necessary adjustments on account of overpayments or underpayments.

(d) *There is authorized to be appropriated for each of the fiscal years 1973, 1974, and 1975 not to exceed $10,000,000 to carry out this title.*[13]

TITLE II

SEC. 201. The Secretary of Health, Education, and Welfare shall gather information and carry out a comprehensive statistical survey defining the major characteristics of the runaway youth population and determining the areas of the country most affected. Such survey shall include, but not be limited to, the age, sex, socioeconomic background of runaway children, the places from which and to which children run, and the relationship between running away and other illegal behavior. The Secretary shall report to Congress not later than June 30, 1973.

SEC. 202. There is authorized to be appropriated a sum not to exceed $500,000 to carry out this title.

---

12. Italicized text deleted from the final version of P.L. 93–415.
13. Italicized text deleted from the final version of P.L. 93–415.

Appendix 2
Runaway Youth Act
House Bill H.R. 9298

March 1974

A BILL To strengthen interstate reporting and interstate services for parents of runaway children; to conduct research on the size of the runaway youth population; for the establishment, maintenance, and operation of temporary housing and counseling services for transient youth, and for other purposes

Be it enacted by the Senate and House of Representatives of the United States of America in Congress assembled, That this Act may be cited as the "Runaway Youth Act."

FINDINGS AND DECLARATION OF POLICY

Sec. 2. The Congress hereby finds that—

(1) the number of juveniles who leave and remain away from home without parental permission has increased to alarming proportions, creating a substantial law enforcement problem for the communities inundated, and significantly endangering the young people who are without resources and live on the street;

(2) the exact nature of the problem is not well defined because national statistics on the size and profile of the runaway youth population are not tabulated;

(3) many of these young people, because of their age and situation, are urgently in need of temporary shelter and counseling services;

(4) the problem of locating, detaining, and returning runaway children should not be the responsibility of already overburdened police departments and juvenile justice authorities; and

(5) in view of the interstate nature of the problem, it is the responsibility of the Federal Government to develop accurate reporting of the problem nationally and to develop an effective system of temporary care outside the law enforcement structure.

TITLE I

SEC. 101. (a) The Secretary of Health, Education, and Welfare is authorized to make grants and to provide technical assistance to localities and nonprofit private agencies in accordance with the provisions of this title. Grants under this title should be made for the purpose of developing local facilities to deal primarily with the immediate needs of runaways in a manner which[1] is outside the law enforcement structure and juvenile justice system. The size of such grants should be determined by the number of runaway children in the community and the existing availability of services. Among applicants priority should be given to private organizations or institutions who have had past experience in dealing with runaways:

(b) The Secretary may promulgate and enforce any rules, regulations, standards, and procedures which he may deem necessary and appropriate to fulfill the purposes of this Act.[2]

---

1. The Bayh bill had "wherever possible" inserted here.
2. This section is not in the Bayh version.

SEC. 102. (a) To be eligible for assistance under this title, an applicant must propose to establish, strengthen, or fund an existing or proposed runaway house, a locally controlled facility providing temporary shelter, and counseling services to juveniles who have left home without the permission of their parents or guardians.

(b) In order to qualify, an applicant must submit a plan to the Secretary of Health, Education, and Welfare meeting the following requirements and including the following information. Each house—

(1) shall be located in an area which is demonstrably frequented by or easily reachable by runaway children;

(2) shall have a maximum capacity of no more than twenty children, with a ratio of staff to children of sufficient proportion to insure adequate supervision and treatment;

(3) shall develop an adequate plan for contacting the child's parents *or relatives in accordance with the law of the State in which the runaway house is established*[3] and insuring his safe return according to the best interests of the child;

(4) shall develop an adequate plan for insuring proper relations with law enforcement personnel, and the return of runaways from correctional institutions;

(5) shall develop an adequate plan for aftercare counseling involving runaway children and their parents within *the State in which the runaway house is located and assuring, as possible, that aftercare services will be provided to those children who are returned beyond the State in which the runaway house is located.*[4]

---

3. Italics not in original Bayh version.

4. Italics not in original version. This differs considerably from the Bayh version, which mandated aftercare for children within "a twenty-five mile radius of the house."

(6) shall keep adequate statistical records profiling the children and parents which it serves: Provided, however, that records maintained on individual runaways shall not be disclosed without parental consent to anyone other than another agency compiling statistical records or a government agency involved in the disposition of criminal charges against an individual runaway: Provided, furthur, that reports or other documents based on such statistical records shall not disclose the identity of individual runaways;

(7) shall submit annual reports to the Secretary of Health, Education, and Welfare detailing how the house has been able to meet the goals of its plans and reporting the statistical summaries required in section 102(b)(6);

(8) shall demonstrate its ability to operate under accounting procedures and fiscal control devices as required by the Secretary of Health, Education, and Welfare; and

(9) shall supply such other information as the Secretary of Health, Education, and Welfare reasonably deems necessary.

SEC. 103. An application by a State, locality, or nonprofit private agency for a grant under this title may be approved by the Secretary only if it is consistent with the applicable provisions of this title and meets the requirements set forth in section 102. *Priority shall be given to grants smaller than $50,000.*[5]

SEC. 104. Nothing in this title shall be construed to deny grants to nonprofit private agencies which are fully controlled by private boards or persons but which in other ways meet the requirements of this title and agree to be legally responsible for the operation of the runaway house. Nothing in this title shall give the Federal Government and its agencies control over the staffing and personnel decisions of facilities receiving Federal funds, except as the staffs of such facilities must meet the standards under this title.

---

5. Italics not in original Bayh bill.

Appendix 2

SEC. 105. The Secretary of Health, Education, and Welfare shall annually report to Congress on the status and accomplishments of runaway houses which were funded with particular attention to—

(1) their effectiveness in alleviating the problems of runaway youth;

(2) their ability *to reunite children with their families*[6] and to encourage the resolution of intrafamily problems through counseling and other services; and

(3) their effectiveness in strengthening family relationships and encouraging stable living situations for children.[7]

SEC. 106. As used in this title, the term "State" shall include Puerto Rico, the District of Columbia, Guam, and the Virgin Islands.

SEC. 107. (a) The Federal share for the construction of new facilities under this title shall be no more than 50 per centum. The Federal share for the acquisition and renovation of existing structures, the provision of counseling services, staff training, and the general costs of operations of such facility's budget for any fiscal year shall be 90 per centum. *The non-Federal share may be in cash or in kind, fairly evaluated, including plant equipment, or services.*[8]

(b) Payments under this section may be made in installments, in advance, or by way of reimbursement, with necessary adjustments on account of overpayments or underpayments.

(c) For the purposes of carrying out this title there is authorized to be appropriated for each of the fiscal years 1974, 1975, and 1976 the sum of $10,000,000.[9]

---

6. The Bayh bill requires reporting "their effectiveness in insuring an early return to the children's homes and in encouraging the resolution of intrafamily problems through counseling and other services."

7. Deleted from the Bayh version is: "(3) their effectiveness in reducing drug abuse and undesirable conditions existing in areas which runaway youth frequent."

8. The italicized section was not in the original Bayh bill.

9. In the Bayh bill this is a maximum amount. In the house bill it is a flat sum.

TITLE II

SEC. 201. The Secretary of Health, Education, and Welfare shall gather information and carry out a comprehensive statistical survey defining the major characteristics of the runaway youth population and determining the areas of the country most affected. Such survey shall include, but not be limited to, the age, sex, socioeconomic background of runaway children, the places from which and to which children run, and the relationship between running away and other illegal behavior. The Secretary shall report to Congress not later than June 30, 1974.

SEC. 202. Records containing the identity of individual runaways gathered for statistical purposes pursuant to section 201 may under no circumstances be disclosed or transferred to any individual or other agency, public or private.[10]

SEC. 203. For the purpose of carrying out this title there is authorized to be appropriated the sum of $500,000.[11]

10. This confidentially provision did not appear in the Bayh bill.
11. In the Bayh bill this is a maximum amount. In the house bill it is a flat sum.

Appendix 3
Title III of the Juvenile Justice and Delinquency Prevention Act

Runaway Youth Act

Public Law 93–415

September 7, 1974

Short Title

SEC. 301. This title may be cited as the "Runaway Youth Act."

FINDINGS

SEC. 302. The Congress hereby finds that—

(1) the number of juveniles who leave and remain away from home without parental permission has increased to alarming proportions, creating a substantial law enforcement problem for the communities inundated, and significantly endangering the young people who are without resources and live on the street;

(2) the exact nature of the problem is not well defined because national statistics on the size and profile of the runaway youth population are not tabulated;

(3) many such young people, because of their age and situation, are urgently in need of temporary shelter and counseling services;

(4) the problem of locating, detaining, and returning runaway children should not be the responsibility of already overburdened police departments and juvenile justice authorities;[1] and

(5) in view of the interstate nature of the problem, it is the responsibility of the Federal Government to develop accurate reporting of the problem nationally and to develop an effective system of temporary care outside the law enforcement structure.

RULES

SEC. 303. The Secretary of Health, Education, and Welfare (hereafter referred to as the "Secretary") may prescribe such rules as he considers necessary or appropriate to carry out the purposes of this title.

PART A—GRANTS PROGRAM

PURPOSE OF GRANT PROGRAM

SEC. 311. The Secretary is authorized to make grants and to provide technical assistance to localities and nonprofit private agencies in accordance with the provisions of this part. Grants under this part shall be made for the purpose of developing local facilities to deal primarily with the immediate needs of runaway youth in a manner which is outside the law enforcement structure and juvenile justice system. The size of such grant shall be determined by the number of runaway youth in the community and the existing availability of services. Among applicants priority shall be given to private organizations or institutions which have had past experience in dealing with runaway youth.

---

1. The section of findings referring to parents in the original Bayh bill (S. 2829) is deleted in the final version. It read: "that the anxieties and fears of parents whose children have run away from home can best be alleviated by effective interstate reporting services and the earliest possible contact with their children."

ELIGIBILITY

SEC. 312. (a) To be eligible for assistance under this part, an applicant shall propose to establish, strengthen, or fund an existing or proposed runaway house, a locally controlled facility providing temporary shelter, and counseling services to juveniles who have left home without permission of their parents or guardians.

(b) In order to qualify for assistance under this part, an applicant shall submit a plan to the Secretary meeting the following requirements and including the following information. Each house—

(1) shall be located in an area which is demonstrably frequented by or easily reachable by runaway youth;

(2) shall have a maximum capacity of no more than twenty children, with a ratio of staff to children of sufficient portion to assure adequate supervision and treatment;

(3) shall develop adequate plans for contacting the child's parents or relatives (*if such action is required by State law*) and assuring the safe return of the child according to the best interests of the child, *for contacting local government officials pursuant to informal arrangements established with such officials by the runaway house, and for providing for other appropriate alternative living arrangements;*[2]

(4) shall develop an adequate plan for assuring proper relations with law enforcement personnel, and the return of runaway youths from correctional institutions;

(5) shall develop an adequate plan for aftercare counseling involving runaway youth and their parents *within the State in which the runaway house is located and for assuring, as possible, that after case services will be provided to those children who are returned beyond the State in which the runaway house is located;*[3]

2. Italicized text does not appear in Bayh (S. 2829) or House version (H.R. 9298) of the bill.

3. Italicized text replaces "within a twenty-five mile radius of the house" in Bayh version (S. 2829). The House bill (H.R. 9298) reflects this final language.

(6) shall keep adequate statistical records profiling the children and parents which it serves, *except that records maintained on individual runaway youths shall not be disclosed without parental consent to anyone other than another agency compiling statistical records or a government agency involved in the disposition of criminal charges against an individual runaway youth, and reports or other documents based on such statistical records shall not disclose the identity of individual runaway youths;*[4]

(7) shall submit annual reports to the Secretary detailing how the house has been able to meet the goals of its plans and reporting the statistical summaries required by paragraph (6);

(8) shall demonstrate its ability to operate under accounting procedures and fiscal control devises as required by the Secretary;

(9) *shall submit a budget estimate with respect to the plan submitted by such house under this subsection;*[5] *and*

(10) *shall supply such other information as the Secretary reasonably deems necessary.*[6]

APPROVAL BY SECRETARY

SEC. 313. An application by a State, locality, or nonprofit private agency for a grant under this part may be approved by the Secretary only if it is consistent with the applicable provisions of this part and meets the requirements set forth in section 312. Priority shall be given to grants smaller than $75,000. In considering grant applications under this part, priority shall be given to any applicant whose program budget is smaller than $100,000.

---

4. The confidentiality section was not in the original Bayh (S. 2829) but was in the House bill (H.R. 9298).

5. Italicized text not included in the Bayh/House bills (S. 2829/H.R. 9298).

6. Italicized text not included in the Bayh bill (S. 2829).

GRANTS TO PRIVATE AGENCIES, STAFFING

SEC. 314. Nothing in this part shall be construed to deny grants to nonprofit private agencies which are fully controlled by private boards or persons but which in other respects meet the requirements of this part and agree to be legally responsible for the operation of the runaway house. Nothing in this part shall give the Federal Government control over the staffing and personnel decisions of facilities receiving Federal funds.[7]

REPORTS

SEC. 315. The Secretary shall annually report to the Congress on the status and accomplishments of the runaway houses which are funded under this part, with particular attention to—

(1) their effectiveness in alleviating the problems of runaway youth;

(2) their ability to reunite children with their families and to encourage the resolution of intrafamily problems through counseling and other services;[8]

(3) their effectiveness in strengthening family relationships and encouraging stable living conditions for children; and

(4) *their effectiveness in helping youth decide upon a future course of action.*[9]

FEDERAL SHARE

SEC. 316. (a) The Federal share for the acquisition[10] and renovation of existing structures, the provision of counseling services, staff training, and the general

7. Deleted from the Bayh/House version is the provision that "staffs of such facilities must meet the standards under this title" (S. 2829/H.R. 9298).

8. The Bayh bill reads: "their effectiveness in insuring an early return to the children's homes and in encouraging the resolution of intrafamily problems through counseling and other services."

9. Not included in the Bayh/House bills (S. 2829/H.R. 9298).

10. This version deletes "construction for new facilities" language from the Bayh/House versions (S. 2829/H.R. 9298).

costs of operations of such facility's budget for any fiscal year shall be 90 per centum. *The non-Federal share may be in cash or in kind, fairly evaluated by the Secretary, including plant, equipment, or services.*[11]

(b) Payments under this section may be made in installments, in advance, or by way of reimbursement, with necessary adjustments on account of overpayments or underpayments.

PART B—STATISTICAL SURVEY

SURVEY; REPORT

SEC. 321. The Secretary shall gather information and carry out a comprehensive statistical survey defining the major characteristics of the runaway youth population and determining the areas of the Nation most affected. Such survey shall include the age, sex, and socioeconomic background of runaway youth, the places from which and to which children run, and the relationship between running away and other illegal behavior. The Secretary shall report the results of such information gathering and survey to the Congress not later than June 30, 1975.

RECORDS

SEC. 322. Records containing the identity of individual runaway youths gathered for statistical purposes pursuant to section 321 may under no circumstances be disclosed or transferred to any individual or to any public or private agency.

PART C—AUTHORIZING OF APPROPRIATIONS

SEC. 331 (a) To carry out the purpose of part A of this title there is authorized to be appropriated for each of the fiscal years ending June 30, 1975, 1976, 1977, the sum of $10,000,000.

(b) To carry out the purposes of part B of this title there is authorized to be appropriated the sum of $500,000.

---

11. Italicized text not included in Bayh bill (S. 2829) but added in the House version (H.R. 9298).

Notes

Foreword: A Personal Journey to Some Research Questions

1. The Faith Community was a group of devout, religious-based individuals who agreed to work for Covenant House for at least one year for a weekly stipend of $12. They lived in a Covenant House–owned building, prayed regularly, and received room, board, and insurance.

2. In stark comparison, in 1990 the *New York Times* reported that the National Network of Runaway and Youth Services estimated "the federal government spent about $29 million on similar programs" (R. Blumenthal, S. Daley, and M. A. Farber [1990, Feb. 6], "Image of Covenant House Is Eroded by Sex Charges," *New York Times*, A1, B4). In short, Covenant House's budget dwarfed total federal expenditures on runaway shelters.

3. In 1990 these included Anchorage, Alaska; Los Angeles, Calif., Fort Lauderdale, Fla., New Orleans, La., Houston, Tex., and outreach programs in New Jersey.

4. These included programs in Guatemala, Honduras, Mexico, and Panama.

5. Blumenthal, Daley, and Farber, "Image of Covenant House Is Eroded by Sex Charges," *New York Times*, A1, B4.

6. In 1980, Covenant House had 250 employees and an operating budget of $8 million. By 1989, Covenant House had grown to fifteen cities, six countries, had approximately 1,700 employees, and an annual budget of $85 million. Cravath, Swaine & Moore, and Kroll Associates (1990, Aug. 3), *Statement of the Oversight Committee of Covenant House* and *A Report to the Board of Directors and the Oversight Committee of Covenant House*, 7.

7. R. Redmond and M. Redmond (1990), The paradoxes of Covenant House—Mythmaking and lifesaving, *Commonweal* 117.10 (May 18): 311–16; 313.

8. Cravath, Swaine & Moore, and Kroll (1990), 7.

9. Redmond and Redmond (1990), 313.

10. B. Lambert (1987, Dec. 1), "Hiring Burglars and 'Stealing' Buildings: Tales of Father Ritter," *New York Times*, B3.

11. S. H. Verhovek (1987, Sept. 23), "Koch and Priest Trade Barbs in Battle for Chelsea Building," *New York Times*, B3.

12. E. Kolbert (1987, Oct. 27), "Koch Drops His Fight with Priest Over a Building," *New York Times*, B3.

13. R. D. McFadden (1984, Jan. 27), "'Heroes for the '80's' Seek to Share Their Spotlight," *New York Times*, A10.

14. "Youth Shelter Wins Praise from Reagan" (1984, Jan. 26), *New York Times*, B9.

15. "Mrs. Reagan Visits Home for Runaway Youths" (1985, June 19), *New York Times*, B1.

16. "The Thing Thing" (1989, June 28), editorial, *New York Times*, A22.

17. To understand the significance of this story one must place oneself in the historic mind-set that existed before the church scandal of the early twenty-first century. For most of the public the allegations against Ritter were scandalous and seemed to come from out of the blue (although rumors had circulated among law enforcement circles and some of the agency's critics for some time).

18. R. Sullivan (1989, Dec. 14), "Covenant House Under Scrutiny," *New York Times*, B5.

19. R. Sullivan (1989, Dec. 15), "Ritter Denies Sex Allegations on Covenant House," *New York Times*, B2.

20. Ibid.

21. M. A. Farber (1989, Dec. 21), "Priest Accuser Is Called a Liar by His Father," *New York Times*. B3.

22. M. A. Farber (1990, Mar. 7), "Ritter Drew $140,000 from Youth Trust," *New York Times*, B1, B4.

23. Blumenthal, Daley, and Farber, "Image of Covenant House Is Eroded by Sex Charges," *New York Times*, A1, B4.

24. R. Blumenthal (1990, Mar. 6), "A $1 Million Fund Tapped by Ritter to Make 4 Loans," *New York Times*, A1, B4.

25. M. A. Farber (1990, Mar. 10), "O'Connor Is Moving to Clear Up 'Mess' at Covenant House," *New York Times*, A1, A30; and J. Barbanel (1990, Apr. 28), "Reeling from Its Crisis, Covenant House Scales Back," *New York Times*, A1.

26. Barbanel, "Reeling from Its Crisis, Covenant House Scales Back," *New York Times*, A1.

27. Ritter predicted that there would be other allegations, which he dismissed as "copy cats" (Blumenthal, Daley, and Farber, "Image of Covenant House Is Eroded by Sex Charges," *New York Times*, A1, B4). On January 24 the *Village Voice* published an extensive article alleging Ritter had maintained a long-term sexual relationship with former resident John Melican. Shortly thereafter, Darryl Bassile, a former Covenant House resident, made similar allegations that were ultimately investigated by the Franciscan order. There was documented evidence that Mr. Bassile had made his allegations to a therapist long before Kite's charges became public. Although the names Kite, Melican, and Bassile were the most public, in the end Kroll Associates investigated over fourteen separate allegations of inappropriate sexual misconduct and, while affirming that "none of the allegations, when viewed individually, can be proved beyond any question," noted that the "cumulative evidence" was "extensive" and would have led, at the very least, to Ritter's forced resignation (Cravath, Swaine & Moore, and Kroll [1990], 16–17).

28. In the first week of March, Covenant House acknowledged that Ritter had maintained a $1 million trust fund since 1983, ostensibly for the benefit of runaway youth. The fund had tax-exempt status, but annual reports had not been filed with the IRS; it was not registered with the New York State Attorney General's charities bureau; and it had been created without the knowledge of the Franciscan order (although the declaration of purpose reported the trust was formed by the order with Ritter as authorized agent). Furthermore, although the fund had not yet been used for the benefit of any youth, it had been used to extend personal loans to Ritter, his family, friends, and business associates. Cravath, Swaine & Moore, and Kroll (1990), 19–26. See also Blumenthal, "A $1 Million Fund Tapped by Ritter to Make 4 Loans," *New York Times*, A1, B4; Farber, "Ritter Drew $140,000 from Youth Trust," *New York Times*, B1, B4; R. Blumenthal (1990, Mar. 9), "I.R.S. Says It's Turned Up No Reports on Ritter Trust," *New York Times*, B3; Farber, "O'Connor Is Moving to Clear Up 'Mess' at Covenant House," *New York Times*, A1, A30.

29. This included the transformation of allegations by Covenant House levied against Kevin Kite that he had obtained false identity papers by appropriating the identity of a deceased boy after reading an obituary, and to an acknowledgment that a Covenant House lawyer and a priest had provided the

papers to Kite after falsifying documents and appropriating a name without family permission. Cravath, Swaine & Moore, and Kroll (1990), 31–32; M. A. Farber and R. Blumenthal (1990, Feb. 15), "How Covenant House Gave Drifter a False I.D.," *New York Times*, B1, B4; J. Barron (1990, Mar. 30), "Franciscans Stripping Ritter of Special Status as Inquiry Ends," *New York Times*, B1, B4.

30. Manhattan District Attorney Robert Morgenthau closed the original criminal investigation on February 28, 1990, and in a prepared statement said that there was insufficient evidence to warrant criminal charges (M. A. Farber [1990, Mar. 1], "No Charges Against Ritter on Finances," *New York Times*, B1, B6). In addition, New York State Attorney General Robert Abrams opened a preliminary investigation in December 1989 which was closed in early February 1990 (D. Hevesi (1990, Feb. 8), "Macchiarola Steps into Job with Covenant House," *New York Times*, B5). However, in early March, Abrams opened another seemingly more serious investigation on the legality of the "Franciscan Charitable Trust" and personal loans made from it to personal friends and colleagues of Ritter (M. A. Farber [1990, Mar. 2], "Abrams to Investigate Covenant House Loans," *New York Times*, B1, B4; Farber, "Ritter Drew $140,000 from Youth Trust," *New York Times*, B1, B4). This investigation was eventually closed, with "Covenant House cleared of any criminal charges" in "handling of charitable contribution" in September 1990. However Abrams's office recommended a number of actions, which Covenant House took, including "severing of all ties with Father Ritter" (M. A. Farber [1990, Sept. 28], "Covenant House Cleared in Abrams Inquiry," *New York Times*, B4).

31. In January 1990 the Franciscan order began investigating Darryl Bassile's case. On February 6 the order directed Father Bruce to take a "leave of absence" pending full investigation of the allegations of sexual misconduct (M. A. Farber [1990, Feb. 7], "Founder of Covenant House Steps Aside in Church Inquiry," *New York Times*, A1, B2). Upon the completion of this investigation on March 30, Ritter was directed to return to the friary and nineteen days later he permanently resigned his position at Covenant House (J. Barron [1990, Feb. 28], "Ritter and Successor Quit Covenant House Posts," *New York Times*, A1).

32. Investigations opened and closed with regularity. Manhattan District Attorney Robert Morgenthau's investigation into financial wrongdoings first announced in December was eventually closed the day after Ritter resigned. On March 1, Morgenthau announced that in spite of evidence of some "some questionable financial transactions," no criminal charges would be filed against Ritter and that in spite of the fact that Covenant House acted improperly in sup-

plying Mr. Kite with false identity papers he, in consultation with the boy's family, had decided not to file criminal charges.

But also on March 1, NYS Attorney General Robert Abrams announced that his office was opening an investigation into the legality of personal loans made from the trust fund (done without the knowledge of the corporate board) (Farber, "Abrams to Investigate Covenant House Loans," *New York Times*, B1, B4).

33. During Father Bruce's forced leave of absence in March, former New York City School Chancellor Frank Macchiarola headed the agency in a short-lived stint (Hevesi, "Macchiarola Steps into Job with Covenant House," *New York Times*, B5). When Ritter resigned permanently on March 30, he did so apparently in conjunction with a request that the board replace the opinionated Macchiarola with Covenant House's chief operating officer (and long-time Ritter associate and friend), Jim Harnett. When Harnett came under some scrutiny for having negotiated loans for the Charitable Trust fund, the board requested help from John Cardinal O'Connor in finding both a new interim president and a permanent replacement for Ritter (A. L. Goldman [1990, Mar. 19], "Cardinal Acts to Replace Ritter's Aides," *New York Times*, B1, B5). On March 26 the board approved two of Cardinal O'Connor's recommendations for temporary replacement: Msgr. William J. Toohy became acting president and chief executive, and Msgr. Timothy A. McDonnell was made acting deputy president (W. G. Saxon [1990, Mar. 26], "Cardinal's Choice to Fill in as Covenant House Leader," *New York Times*, B3).

34. M. A. Farber (1990, May 1), "Ritter Inquiry Leading Many to Quit Board," *New York Times*, B1.

35. The Oversight Committee included William Ellinghaus (former president of AT&T), Reverend Theodore M. Hesburgh (former president of Notre Dame University), Rabbi Marc Tanenbaum, Cyrus Vance (former Secretary of State) and Paul Volcker (former chairman of the Federal Reserve). Kroll Associates and the law firm of Cravath, Swaine & Moore submitted a final report on the investigation to the Oversight Committee and to the Covenant House Board of Directors on August 3, 1990.

36. Farber, "Abrams to Investigate Covenant House Loans," *New York Times*, B1, B4; Blumenthal, "A $1 Million Fund Tapped by Ritter to Make 4 Loans," *New York Times*, A1, B4.

37. Farber, "Ritter Inquiry Leading Many to Quit Board," *New York Times*, B1; Cravath, Swaine & Moore, and Kroll (1990).

38. Cravath, Swaine & Moore, and Kroll (1990), i.

39. Blumenthal, Daley, and Farber, "Image of Covenant House Is Eroded by Sex Charges," *New York Times*, A1, B4.

40. A. M. Rosenthal (1990, Jan. 11), "Passage from Ezekiel," *New York Times*, A23.

41. A. Stanley (1990, June 6), "Covenant House to Cut Programs and Employees," *New York Times*, B3.

42. In preparing this foreword I ventured into an old dusty file box from my days at Covenant House. Among the papers I found a handwritten note from one of my staff attorneys, Jay Sullivan, dated April 21, 1990. He references an April 20 meeting in which my department was informed that the agency would undergo a 50 percent cut and that the legal department would be "impacted." Jay, whose salary was funded through a Skadden, Arps Pro Bono Fellowship, offers to take a substantial salary cut if the savings could be parlayed into fending off other legal department layoffs. The self-sacrificing kindness of the offer speaks to the commitment, loyalty, and intimacy of the staff.

43. M. A. Farber (1990, July 12), "Nun Is Named Covenant House President," *New York Times*, B1.

44. A more recently added question is what role did pedophile priests play in the runaway shelter movement? It turns out that Ritter is not the only priest involved with the early runaway shelter movement who has been accused of sexual improprieties.

45. E. H. Carr (1969), *What is history?* (New York: Knopf), 26.

46. Ibid.

1. Testing Freedom: On the Road to a Runaway Problem

1. S. Raab (1977, Oct. 3), "Veronica's Short, Sad Life—Prostitution at 11, Death at 12," *New York Times*, 1, 36.

2. R. R. Silver (1960, Apr. 12), "Boy Talks Way 1,500 Miles on $25," *New York Times*, 1, 27.

3. Under the current version of the Runaway and Homeless Youth Act, a *street youth* is defined as, "a juvenile who spends a significant amount of time on the street or in other areas of exposure to encounters that may lead to sexual abuse." 42 USC Sec. 5712 (d)(d)(2).

4. Under current federal definitions of a *runaway*, an *episode* is defined as when

- A child leaves home without permission and stays away overnight; or
- A child 14 years old or younger (or older and mentally incompetent) who is away from home chooses not to come home when expected to and stays away overnight; or
- A child 15 years old or older who is away from home chooses not to come home and stays away two nights. (H. Hammer, D. Finkelhor, and A. J. Sedlak [October 2002], *Runaway/thrownaway children: National estimates and characteristics*, 2.

The government attempts to factor in age, parental awareness, child competence, child choice, and duration away from home as determinants of a runaway episode.

5. Silver, "Boy Talks Way 1,500 Miles on $25," *New York Times*, 1, 27; "L.I. Boy Flies Home After Free Journey" (1960, Apr. 13), *New York Times*, 78.

6. There is one earlier "runaway, girl" entry from 1875 but none for the next forty-five years. The 1919 entry marks the first of regularly appearing entries in the *New York Times Index*.

7. For example, the New York City Children's Court published a pamphlet in 1887 entitled *Institutions to which children are committed by the Children's Court of the City of New York together with the conditions governing their admission and other important information*. Some of these institutions accepted only children who were committed by "police magistrates and courts of law" for "being disorderly, vagrant, or criminal" (Kellogg 1887:114), but the vast majority of entries were for private charities which accepted youth who were committed by their parents or came on their own. The pamphlet lists and describes 84 institutions grouped according to religious denomination (Roman Catholic, Protestant, Jewish and nonsectarian). These institutions covered care of boys, girls, blind, crippled, defective, destitute, orphans, deaf mutes, friendless, unmarried mothers, truants, juvenile delinquents, and one for "epileptics and other feeble-minded persons, exclusive of insane epileptics" (Kellogg 1887).

8. For further discussion see Stephen O'Connor (2001), *Orphan trains: The story of Charles Loring Brace and the children he saved and failed* (New York: Houghton Mifflin); Marilyn Irvin Holt (1992), *The orphan trains: Placing out in America* (Lincoln: University of Nebraska Press).

9. In his historic study of London's poor (*London Labour and the London Poor* [1860]; rpt., New York: Dover, 1968), Henry Mayhew described the breadth of income-generating activities available to youth. He meticulously computed sta-

tistics on the investment and projected earnings of child street vendors and identified no less than 48 items, grouped under five major headings, sold by them,
including metal products (such as cutlery, needles, gilt watches, dog-collars, tin-
ware); crockery and glass, textiles (such as cottons, lace, table covers, belts, waist-
coats); chemicals (such as black-lead, French polish, grease-removing composi-
tion, razor paste, cigar-lights, fly papers, rat poison); and miscellaneous (such as
walking sticks, whips, tobacco, sponges, eye-glasses, dolls, spice, and roulette
boxes). Although no such exhaustive documentary study was conducted of New
York City's street traders, it is reasonable to assume that youth had a number of
similar opportunities available to them in urban areas of the United States. For
a historic account of urban street youth in the United States during the Progressive Era, see David Nasaw (1985), *Children of the city: At work and at play* (New
York: Oxford University Press).

10. See Nasaw, *Children of the city.*

11. Ibid., 75.

12. 1st Annual Report, Children's Aid Society (1854), 10–11.

13. Ibid., 11.

14. Ibid.

15. 10th Annual Report, Children's Aid Society (1863), 10–18.

16. Ibid.

17. Ibid.

18. Ibid.

19. Ibid.

20. Ibid.

21. Annual Report, Children's Aid Society (1941), 19.

22. National Research Council/Institute of Medicine (2001), *Juvenile crime:
Juvenile justice* (Washington, D.C.: National Academy Press), 157.

23. A. Kahn (1953), *A court for children* (New York: Columbia University
Press), 19.

24. National Research Council/Institute of Medicine (2001), *Juvenile crime:
Juvenile justice,* 157.

25. *Mens rea* is defined as "an element of criminal responsibility: a guilty
mind; a guilty or wrongful purpose; a criminal intent." Henry Campbell Black
(1990), *Black's Law Dictionary,* 6th ed. (St. Paul, Minn: West), 985.

26. Wayward Minor Act, N.Y. Code Crim. Proc. §913 et seq.

27. Laws of New York, 146th Session, 1923, V I–II; Albany, NY: J B Lyon Co.,
State Printers, Ch. 868; pp. 1687–1688.

28. Laws of New York, 148th Session, 1925, V I–II; Albany, NY: J B Lyon Co., State Printers, Ch. 389; pp. 711–12.

29. Children's Court Act of the State of New York, as amended in 1930 (Laws of New York, 153rd Session, 1930, V. I, Albany, NY: J B Lyon Co., State Printers, Ch. 393, §2 par. 2 [d]), p. 829.

30. Children's Court Act, § 2 (2) (d).

31. Early Children's Court reports show that while delinquency cases were brought against boys, in much larger numbers than girls, boys were more likely to be charged with disorderly conduct, while girls were more likely to be charged with waywardness and desertion of their homes.

32. Nasaw cites a 1913 study by the People's Institute on juvenile arrests in Irish and German neighborhoods on the West Side of New York City which found that "more than 50 percent of the arrests made in the district were for non-crimes" including "begging, bonfires, fighting, gambling, jumping on street cars, kicking the garbage can, loitering, playing football on the streets, pitching pennies, playing ball, playing shinney, playing water pistol, putting out lights, selling papers, shooting craps, snowballing, subway disturbances and throwing stones" (Nasaw, *Children of the city*, 23).

33. Family Court Act, Laws of New York, 1962, ch. 686.

34. All states have a variation of this "in need of supervision" statute, although they are called different names such as Juveniles in Need of Supervision (JINS), Children in Need of Supervision (CHINS), and Families in Need of Supervisions (FINS).

35. Runaway Youth Act, § 302 (2). (See appendix 3.)

36. R. Baker (1972, Feb. 3), "Observer: The Nomadic Big New People," *New York Times*, 33.

37. Baker, "The Nomadic Big New People," 33.

38. Ibid.

39. In 1946 every birth indicator in the United States leaped dramatically. Between 1945 and 1946 the fertility rate of the United States jumped from 85.9 to 101.9 (per 1,000 women aged 15–44 years); the birthrate increased from 20.4 to 24.1 per thousand; and live births increased from 2,858,000 to 3,411,000, a 19 percent increase from the previous year (see USDHHS, Natality, 1980). The average fertility rate for the preceding twenty years had been 85.3, and the last year the fertility rate had climbed above 100/1000 was in 1926; the average birthrate for the twenty years before that had been 20.5. The 1946 increases signaled the beginning of the Baby Boom. The fertility rate increase continued to

remain above the 100/1000 level for nearly twenty years before it fell to 96.3 in 1965, continuing a steady decline which had started in 1962. The birthrate averages 24.2 for the next twenty years, beginning a slow decline in 1959 but not falling below 20/1000 until 1965. Live births remain above 4,000,000 for the decade between 1954 and 1964 but begin a slow decline in 1962. Therefore, the start of the Baby Boomer cohort is clearly 1946. The years between 1959 and 1965 signal its end.

40. R. Baker (1966, May 26), "Observer: Congress, Beer, and Flexible Youth," *New York Times*, 46.

41. Baker, "Observer: Congress, Beer, and Flexible Youth," *New York Times*, 46.

42. Typical legal disabilities include incapacity to enter contracts for goods and services, to hold property, to keep wages if their parent lay claim to them, and their limited freedom of independent movement imposed upon them through regulations like age-based curfews, truancy rules, or through assumptions (e.g., that their domicile is derived through their parents and may not be independently established). See H. W. Beaser (1975, Apr.), *Runaway youth from what to where: The legal status of runaway children*, Final Report, Educational Systems Corp. (Washington, D.C.: USDHEW).

43. Although arguments for lowering the voting age had long been made, the final trek toward the Twenty-sixth Amendment began on June 22, 1970, when the Voting Rights Act (P.L. 91–285) setting the minimum voting age at 18 for federal, state, and local elections was signed into law by President Nixon under a cloud of constitutional uncertainty. Nixon expressed his own reservations at the same time and urged Congress to continue consideration of a constitutional amendment. The constitutional debate focused on whether congressional power extended to imposing minimum-age voting requirements on state and local elections. The complex issue was settled by a deeply divided U.S. Supreme Court in *Oregon v. Mitchell*, 400 U.S. 112, 91 S. Ct. 260, 27 L.Ed.2d 272 (1970). The court found a constitutional basis in the time, place, and manner clause (art. 1, sec. 4, cl. 1) to sustain the age adjustment with respect to electing representatives and senators and, by logical extension, the president, but found no constitutional support for extending the power to proscribe voter qualifications for state and local elections.

Congress found this notion of "dual age voting" for federal and state officials unpalatable, not only because the arguments in favor of an adjusted voting age were arguably stronger, not weaker, at the state and local levels but also because

of the logistical problems and costs associated with creating a bifurcated registration and voting system within the states. Those arguing in favor of the
amendment noted that younger voters would constitute nearly 10 percent of the
state's voting population in most states. Congress moved ahead with the Voting
Rights Amendment, which was ratified by three-fourths of the states and certi-
fied on July 5, 1971. The amendment reads: "The right of citizens of the United
States, who are eighteen years of age or older, to vote shall not be denied or
abridged by the United States or by any State on account of age."

44. Beaser, *Runaway youth from what to where*, 43.

45. "Adults at 18 in California" (1972, Mar. 5), *New York Times*, 57.

46. Ibid.

47. There are many examples of state action attempting to accommodate the
lower age of majority. One of the most dramatic may be California's Emanci-
pated Minors statute, enacted in 1978 (just a legislative heartbeat after the state
lowered its age of majority in 1972). This law permits children as young as 13 to
initiate emancipation proceedings (essentially seeking the right to become
adults early). Of course, California never got into the business of routinely
emancipating its youngsters. The statute nonetheless illustrates the conceptual
problem faced by state lawmakers trying to make adolescent policy frameworks
logically consistent with a lower age of majority.

48. Free (aka Abbie Hoffman) (1968), *Revolution for the hell of it* (New York:
Dial), 26.

2. Media Myth Spinning: From Runaway Adventurers to
Street Survivors (1960–1978)

1. Evidence for this chapter comes from articles published in the *New York
Times* over the entire 18-year study period. The *New York Times* was selected for
four reasons. First, it is a nationally and internationally recognized paper of
record. Second, because it had (and has) separate sections for its national and
local news, it is a rich source of information on the interaction of national, state,
and local events. Third, because it is a daily paper, it provided the maximum possible data sources. Fourth, it is well indexed and its archives are readily available.

Although the *New York Times*'s archives are now accessible online and can be
retrieved through electronic searches, this research was conducted before that
conversion. Thus the method of retrieval required for this project necessitated

consulting hardcopies of the annual index, and then locating articles on microfiche. While this process was extremely time-consuming and cumbersome, I am not convinced that electronic search engines provide a better method of systematically locating articles for the purpose of studying social problem construction. Electronic word searches, while democratic in their retrieval based on words, aren't subject to the same conceptual organizational scrutiny of article content that is required for indexing. To some extent, understanding that organizational structure and its evolution was central to this study (indeed, the index itself was useful evidence of problem construction). Further discussion on the sample-selection process and method of analysis are reported in K. Staller (1999), Runaway youth: Contending cultural voices and policy responses, 1960–1978 (unpublished dissertation).

2. P. Ehrlich (1961, June 30), "A Runaway Is a Child with Woes," *New York Times*, 16.

3. E. Perlmutter (1964, Mar. 15), "To the Runaways, the Fair Is a Lure," *New York Times*, 72.

4. For example, Inspector Joseph Max, who headed the Juvenile Aid Division of the Philadelphia Police Department, says, "Most kids come back—and fast," and Capt. John C. Clancy of the Youth Investigation Division of the NYPD is reported commenting, "I'd say 99 and 44–100th *plus*," in E. S. Ringold (1964, May 10), "Why They Run Away from Home," *New York Times Magazine*, 63.

5. Ringold, "Why They Run Away from Home," *New York Times Magazine*, 63.

6. Perlmutter, "To the Runaways, the Fair Is a Lure," *New York Times*, 72.

7. Ibid.

8. P. Benjamin (1964, May 18), "Where's Dominic Been 9 Days? 12-Year-Old Lived at the Fair," *New York Times*, 1, 32.

9. Benjamin, "Where's Dominic Been 9 Days?" *New York Times*, 1, 32.

10. Ibid.

11. Ibid., 32.

12. R. R. Silver (1960, Apr. 12), "Boy Talks Way 1,500 Miles on $25," *New York Times*, 1, 27.

13. Silver, "Boy Talks Way 1,500 Miles on $25," *New York Times*, 1, 27; and "L.I. Boy Flies Home After Free Journey (1960, Apr. 13), *New York Times*, 78.

14. "L.I. Boy Flies Home After Free Journey," *New York Times*, 78.

15. B. Weinraub (1966, Aug. 17), "Runaway Girls Increasing Here," *New York Times*, 41.

16. S. A. O. Golden (1966, Dec. 18), "Rising Number of Missing Teen-Agers, Mostly Girls, Reported to Police," *New York Times,* 66.

17. In September 1966, Weinraub authored another article of interest. In it he reports on the NYPD Vice Squad's efforts to clean up midtown Manhattan, which resulted in the greatest number of prostitution arrests in ten years. His police informant observed that arrestees appeared to be "new ones in the trade who don't have records" and expressed surprise that "for some reason many seem to be coming from out of town" (B. Weinraub [1966, Sept. 17], "City-Vice Squads in Midtown Drive," *New York Times,* 19). Weinraub does not link these prostitution trends to the increasing number of runaway girls. With Veronica Brunson's tragic 1977 front-page child prostitution tale, coupled with a flurry of stories about the "Minnesota Pipeline," it is worth pondering whether the raw material to tell the same story was available to Weinraub in 1966 had the public been receptive to hearing it.

18. Weinraub, "Runaway Girls Increasing Here," *New York Times,* 41.

19. In hindsight, these data raise a provocative but unanswerable question as to whether there was an increase in runaway *behavior* in girls or whether there was simply an increase in reporting.

20. Quoted in Golden, "Rising Number of Missing Teen-Agers," *New York Times,* 66.

21. The ethnicity of the other girl was not specified. Runaway articles of this period rarely make note of race or ethnicity. Given the lack of attention to this detail in reporting runaway stories, my assumption is that the journalists were mostly dealing with middle-class Caucasian youth. Golden may have reported the Puerto Rican identity, in part, because he observes and reports the contents of a chart on the wall of Joseph Lynch, captain of the Missing Persons Unit. The final of five reasons cited for children to run away is the "effort by foreign-born [*sic*] parents to instill a European mode of living in their American-born children." The other four motivations included "distaste for school," "disagreeable home surroundings," "a spirit of adventure," and "excessive greed of the parents for the child's earnings."

22. Golden, "Rising Number of Missing Teen-Agers," 66.

23. See, for example, M. Arnold (1967, May 5), "Organized Hippies Emerge on Coast," *New York Times,* 41, 42; H. S. Thompson (1967, May 14), "The 'Hashbury' Is the Capital of the Hippies," *New York Times Magazine,* 29; A. O. Golden (1967, Aug. 7), "200 Hippies Stage an 8th St. 'Be-Out,'" *New York Times,* 26; S. A. O. Golden (1967, Aug. 19), "A Challenging Period of Adjustment Has Set

in Among Hippies in San Francisco: Hippie Regulars on Haight Want Part-Timers to Take a Trip," *New York Times*, 27; P. Hofmann (1967, June 5), "Hippies Hangout Draws Tourists," *New York Times*, 63.

24. Thompson, "The 'Hashbury' Is the Capital of the Hippies," *New York Times Magazine*, 123.

25. For example, Hunter S. Thompson provided a generic description of an ever-changing group of street performers in front of Haight-Ashbury's Drog Store: "There will always be at least one man with long hair and sunglasses playing a wooden pipe of some kind. He will be wearing either a Dracula cape, a long Buddhist robe, or a Sioux Indian costume. There will also be a hairy blond fellow wearing a Black Bart cowboy hat and a spangled jacket that originally belonged to a drum major in the 1949 Rose Bowl parade. He will be playing the bongo drums. Next to the drummer will be a dazed-looking girl wearing a blouse (but no bra) and a plastic mini-skirt, slapping her thighs to the rhythm of it all. . . . Backing them up will be an all-star cast of freaks, every one of them stoned." Thompson, "The 'Hashbury' Is the Capital of the Hippies," 120.

26. For example:

• "He wears a large gold earring and, around his head, a light blue cloth band. It holds in place on his forehead a stuffed parakeet—the tail of which curls along the ridge of his nose. He calls himself "Bird" and is somewhat typical of the Haight-Ashbury hippies." (Arnold, "Organized Hippies Emerge on Coast," *New York Times*, 40)

• "Many wear ponchos. Bells and beads and even seeds around their necks are common." (Arnold, "Organized Hippies Emerge on Coast," 42)

• ". . . two long-haired youths, one with a Hindu bead collar dangling over his bare chest." (P. Hofmann, "Hippies Hangout Draws Tourists," *New York Times*, 63)

• "One boy wore his blond hair in a pigtail that reached the bright yellow and green and red Mexican serape over his shoulders. He wore brown corduroy pants and no shoes. She had on red bell-bottom pants and sandals." (Golden, "A Challenging Period of Admustment Has Set In," *New York Times*, 27).

27. Arnold, "Organized Hippies Emerge on Coast," 42.

28. Ibid.

29. M. Arnold (1967, Nov. 3), "State G.O.P. Chief's Daughter, 16, Sought in East Village," *New York Times*, 42.

30. The girl was eventually located nineteen days later.

31. Quoted in Arnold, "State G.O.P. Chief's Daughter, 16, Sought in East Village," *New York Times*, 42.

32. Quoted in Arnold, "State G.O.P. Chief's Daughter, 16, Sought," 42.

33. Ibid.

34. S. A. O. Golden (1967, Aug. 20), "An 'A' Student Joins the Hippies to Study Herself," *New York Times*, 70.

35. E. Shorris (1967, Oct. 29), "Love Is Dead," *New York Times Magazine*, 27.

36. See J. A. Lukas (1967, Oct. 16), "The Two Worlds of Linda Fitzpatrick," *New York Times*, 1, 33; J. A. Lukas (1967, Oct. 17), "Police Inquiry in Hippie Killings Leaves Family of Girl 'Puzzled': Full Story Sought," *New York Times*, 1, 40; J. A. Lukas (1967, Oct. 18), "Police Hopeful of Easing Hippie Problem Here," *New York Times*, 1, 36; J. A. Lukas (1967, Oct. 19), "The Case of a Runaway Flower Child," *New York Times*, 1.

37. E. Perlmutter (1967, Oct. 9), "Girl, Youth Slain in 'Village' Cellar," *New York Times*, 1, 43.

38. Ibid., 1.

39. M. Arnold (1967, Oct. 20), "Homicides Swell 'Missing' Reports," *New York Times*, 36.

40. Quoted in J. Cook (1967, Aug. 18), "The Runaway: 'It Can't Happen to Me,' Parents Say, But It Does," *New York Times*, 22.

41. Schrage, quoted in Cook, "The Runaway," 22.

42. Ibid.

43. J. P. Sterba (1973, Aug. 14), "Texas Toll of Boys Rises to 27 in Nation's Biggest Slaying Case," *New York Times*, 1, 18.

44. T. Morgan (1975, Nov. 16), "Little Ladies of the Night," *New York Times Magazine*, 34.

45. N. Sheppard (1977, Nov. 5), "Recruiting of Teen-Age Prostitutes Is Increasing in Minneapolis Area," *New York Times*, 8; S. Raab (1977, Nov. 8), "An Appeal to Girls on 'Minnesota Strip,'" *New York Times*, 33; S. Raab (1977, Nov. 10), "Prostitutes from Midwest Vanish from 8th Avenue During Hunt by Visiting Police," *New York Times*, B2; N. Sheppard (1977, Nov. 14), "Teen-Age Runaways Turn to Prostitution as Rebellion," *New York Times*, 20; "Midwest Teen-Agers Tell of Forced Vice" (1977, Nov. 15), *New York Times*, 29; N. Sheppard (1977, Nov. 25), "Money, Not New York, Lures Minnesota Prostitutes," *New York Times*, 18; J. Cummings (1977, Dec. 10), "Priest's Shelter Tries to Salvage Times Sq. Youths," *New York Times*, 25; S. Raab (1977, Dec. 29), "2 Visiting Policemen Assail Counterparts," *New York Times*, 23.

46. Mayor Beame, whose tenure ended in 1977, had made the Times Square cleanup a high priority on his political agenda. He was accused of merely mimicking the plan of previous mayor John Lindsay. Mayor-elect Koch, who took office in January 1978, followed suit and vowed to continue the fight to clean up the area.

47. S. Raab (1977, Oct. 3), "Veronica's Short, Sad Life—Prostitution at 11, Death at 12," *New York Times*, 1, 36.

48. Raab, "An Appeal to Girls on 'Minnesota Strip,'" *New York Times*, 33.

49. Raab, "2 Visiting Policemen Assail Counterparts," *New York Times*, B3.

50. S. Raab (1977, Oct. 30), "Pimps Establish Recruiting Link to the Midwest," *New York Times*, 1, 21; and Sheppard, "Recruiting of Teen-Age Prostitutes Is Increasing in Minneapolis Area," *New York Times*, 8.

51. Sheppard, "Teen-Age Runaways Turn to Prostitution as Rebellion," *New York Times*, 20.

52. Ibid.

53. R. D. McFadden (1975, Mar. 1), "8 Weeks Here a Lifetime for a Runaway Girl of 15," *New York Times*, 1, 30.

54. Raab, "Veronica's Short, Sad Life," 1, 36.

55. McFadden, "8 Weeks Here a Lifetime for a Runaway Girl of 15," *New York Times*, 1.

56. McFadden, "8 Weeks Here a Lifetime," 30.

57. Ibid.

58. Ibid.

59. Raab, "Veronica's Short, Sad Life," 36.

60. McFadden, "8 Weeks Here a Lifetime," 1, 30.

61. Ibid., 30.

62. Ibid.

63. Raab, "Veronica's Short, Sad Life," 1.

64. Ibid.

3. Spinning Myths from Runaway Lives:
A Hip Beat Version of Dropping Out

1. Senate Committee on the Judiciary, *Legislative Hearings on S. 2829, the Runaway Youth Act: Hearings before the Subcommittee to Investigate Juvenile Delin-*

quency, 92d Cong., 1st sess., January 13 and 14, 1972 (Washington, D.C.: GPO), 6.

2. J. Kerouac (1957; rpt., 1976), *On the Road* (New York: Penguin).

3. "How can the counterculture be evaluated?" asks sixties historian Terry Anderson. "Reliable surveys and statistics on this amorphous blob do not exist, so it is difficult to judge. Subsequently, most assessments have been personal and emotional" (Anderson 1995:289). Furthermore the kinds of public records that are available to study the Establishment or mainstream voices (such as the *New York Times,* court records, legislative history, and testimony used as evidence in other parts of this book) often do a disservice to the youth voice and youth perspective. This is particularly true when studying marginalized groups associated with the counterculture. Terry H. Anderson (1995), *The movement and the sixties: Protests in America from Greensboro to Wounded Knee* (New York: Oxford University Press).

Accordingly, this study relies on eclectic, but interrelated, sources to examine the runaway discourse among American youth. Evidence comes from four primary sources. They are:

- the literary output of young, influential spokesmen for the generation. This includes poets and writers (i.e., the Beats, including Jack Kerouac and Gregory Corso), whose work influenced those coming of age in the sixties, as well as contemporary youth spokesmen and lyricists (i.e., Bob Dylan, Jefferson Airplane, Grateful Dead, and Country Joe and the Fish).

- the autobiographical accounts of key figures of the counterculture or those closely associated with the movement, including the Beats (Herbert Huncke, Neal Cassady), the San Francisco Diggers (Emmett Grogan, Peter Coyote, Chester Anderson, Peter Berg, etc.), and the East Village counterculture (Abbie Hoffman, Paul Krassner, Jerry Rubin). Some of these accounts are contemporaneous, others nearly contemporaneous, and others represent later reflective narratives (careful attention is paid to the difference).

- the contemporaneous underground publications associated with the counterculture (including underground newspapers, Digger papers, broadsides, and other community notices).

- information from sympathetic "inside-outsiders." These include service providers who acted as a bridge between traditional services and the counterculture communities (Larry Beggs, David Smith, Bruce Ritter) and social scientists who studied the counterculture by immersing themselves in it (Delbert Earisman, Lewis Yablonsky, Ned Polsky, Henry Miller).

By necessity, data analysis from these rich and diverse sources of material could not be approached as systematically as other texts. However, every attempt has been made to read widely, focus only on primary not secondary documents and materials, to seek to triangulate data from multiple independent sources, and to assess the credibility of each source given its author and the context and circumstances of its production.

4. M. W. Doyle (2002), Staging the revolution: Guerrilla theatre as a counterculture practice, 1965–68, in P. Braunstein and M. W. Doyle, eds. (2002), *Imagine nation: The American counterculture of the 1960s and '70s*, 80 (New York: Routledge).

5. M. Arnold (1967, May 5), "Organized Hippies Emerge on Coast," *New York Times*, 41, 42.

6. T. Parkinson (1961), *A casebook on the Beats* (New York: Crowell), 83–88; 85.

7. E. Grogan (1972), *Ringolevio: A life played for keeps* (Boston: Little Brown), 239–40. For a reprint of the poem in its entirety, see G. Corso's "Power," in Parkinson, *A casebook on the Beats*, 83–88. Of primary importance is the line, "Standing on a street corner waiting for no one is Power" (85).

8. Etan Ben-Ami (1989, Jan. 12), Oral history interview with Peter Coyote (Mill Valley, Calif.); the Digger Archives (www.diggers.org/oralhistory/peter_interview.html) (accessed July 30, 2002). Also see the Official Peter Coyote Web page (www.petercoyote.com/print.html) (accessed September 30, 2005).

9. Grogan, *Ringolevio*, 458.

10. J. Rubin (1970), *Do it* (New York: Simon and Schuster), 232–33.

11. Excerpted: See G. Corso's "Variations on a Generation," in Parkinson, *A casebook on the Beats*, 88–97; also reprinted in A. Charters, ed., (1992), *The portable beat reader*, 182–83 (New York: Penguin).

12. See Charters, ed., *The portable beat reader*; S. Watson (1995), *The birth of the beat generation: Visionaries, rebels, and hipsters, 1944–1960* (New York: Pantheon); B. Cook (1971), *The beat generation* (New York: Scribner's).

13. This East Coast cluster cross-pollinates with a group of San Francisco Renaissance poets (including Kenneth Rexroth, Lawrence Ferlinghetti, Michael McClure, Gary Snyder, Philip Whalen, Philip Lamantia, Lew Welch, Bob Kauf-

man) who are sometimes included as "Beats" in textbooks and anthologies. The original Beats spent time on both coasts. Ginsberg flirted with a graduate program in English at Berkeley in 1955 but dropped out. Cassady and his wife Carolyn had a home outside San Francisco which became a West Coast destination for East Coast Beats.

14. Watson, *Birth of the beat generation*, 71.

15. Ibid., 72.

16. Burroughs, "Foreword" to B. G. Schafer, ed. (1997), *The Herbert Huncke reader* (New York: Morrow), ix.

17. Watson, *Birth of the beat generation*, 72. For further discussion of Hunke, Cassady, and Carl Solomon as "Beat icons," see ibid., 71–94.

18. Huncke in such important works as Kerouac's *The Town and the City*, *On the Road*, and *Book of Dreams*; in Burroughs's *Junkie*; in Holmes's *Go*; and in one of Ginsberg's most famous poems, *Howl*. Cassady appeared in Kerouac's *On the Road*, *The Dharma Bums*, *Desolation Angels*, *Big Sur*, and *Book of Dreams*.

19. *Go*'s title is derived from "one of Cassady's favorite expressions." Neal Cassady, a man who was in perpetual motion, is a central character in the book (Charters, ed., *The portable beat reader*, xx).

20. J. C. Holmes (1952, Nov. 16), "This Is the Beat Generation," *New York Times Magazine*, 10.

21. See Charters, ed., *The portable beat reader*, xx.

22. Ibid., xviii.

23. See J. Kerouac's "The Origins of the Beat Generation," in Parkinson, *A casebook on the Beats*, 73

24. R. Thomas (1996, Aug. 9), "Herbert Huncke, the Hipster Who Defined 'Beat,' Dies at 81," *New York Times*, B7.

25. Ibid.

26. On a personal note, I spent the better part of a day searching for this autobiography, which Columbia University's computerized system insisted was available at several different libraries. I finally found it—no bigger than a large postage stamp—dwarfed and all but lost among the towering volumes surrounding it. It is, I think, an adequate metaphor for Huncke's life, which was overshadowed by the literary icon he became in the hands of the Beats. H. Huncke (1987), *Guilty of everything* (New York: Hanuman). Huncke's autobiography has since been published as part of an anthology edited by Benjamin G. Schafer (*The Herbert Huncke reader*: part 3, "Guilty of Everything," 227–302).

27. Thomas, "Herbert Huncke" (obituary), *New York Times*.

28. Huncke relied on sympathetic benefactors (or hustled them, depending on one's viewpoint) for his whole life. The *Times*'s obituary notes that even though Huncke's "books did not make much money" his "friends contributed willingly" to his upkeep and that Huncke "seemed proud that he had no talent for regular work." According to the *Times*, one of Huncke's "most generous benefactors" was "a man who had never met him: Jerry Garcia of the Grateful Dead," who reportedly paid Huncke's rent for the last few years of his life. The *Times* concluded that this is "a reflection of his continued standing" among "counter-culturists." Thomas, "Herbert Huncke" (obituary).

29. H. Huncke, excerpts from "Guilty of Everything," in Schafer, 228. Page numbers for subsequent references to this edition are cited in the main text.

30. Reprinted in Schafer, *The Herbert Huncke reader* : "Dear Dad," 310–12.

31. Ibid., 311–12.

32. Ibid., 311.

33. H. Huncke, "In the Park," in *Huncke's Journal* and reprinted in Schafer, *The Herbert Huncke reader*, 60.

34. Ibid.

35. Ibid., 60–63.

36. Thomas, "Herbert Huncke" (obituary).

37. Herbert Huncke (1987), *Guilty of everything* (Madras and New York: Hanuman Books), 69.

38. Thomas, "Herbert Huncke" (obituary).

39. Charters, ed., *The portable beat reader*, xviii.

40. Ibid.

41. Watson, *Birth of the beat generation*, 73.

42. Kerouac's notion of "spontaneous prose" (see J. Kerouac's "Essentials of Spontaneous Prose," in Parkinson, *A casebook on the Beats*, 65–76) was derived from "Cassady's belief that writing should be read as 'a continuous chain of undisciplined thought' which was "communicated in hundreds of letters to Kerouac" (Charters, ed., *The portable beat reader*, 189). Kerouac called Cassady's construction "kickwriting," which he defined as writing "only what kicks you and keeps you overtime awake from sheer mad joy" (Charters, ed., 189). Writing from "sheer mad joy" was entirely consistent with Cassady's character.

43. Grogan, *Ringolevio*, 311

44. Ibid.

45. Cassady worked as a brakeman on the South Pacific railroad until he had to serve time on a marijuana conviction.

46. For the sake of historical fairness, Cassady's adventures occurred before the introduction of highway speed limits and before public awareness campaigns against drunk driving. In the early 1970s, Congress enticed the states to establish the 55 mph speed limit by using federal highway fund incentives as a conservation measure during the era's oil crisis. Serious public awareness campaigns against drunk driving can be linked to the birth of MADD (Mothers Against Drunk Driving) in 1980.

47. G. Ball, ed. (1995), *Allen Ginsberg: Journals Mid-Fifties, 1954–1958* (New York: HarperCollins), 59.

48. Watson, *Birth of the beat generation*, 289.

49. Burroughs's disdain for Cassady should, perhaps, be understood through the filter of his lust for Allen Ginsberg, who was smitten by Cassady.

50. Burroughs to Ginsberg, letter dated 1/30/49, printed in O. Harris, ed. (1993), *The Letters of William S. Burroughs, 1945–1959* (New York: Viking), 37.

51. Ibid., 80.

52. Although John Clellon Holmes, an admirer of Cassady, once said, "I have thought of Neal as being a psychopath for quite some time." Watson, *Birth of the beat generation*, 80.

53. S. Turner (1996), *Angelheaded Hipster: A Life of Jack Kerouac* (New York: Viking), 102.

54. Neal Cassady (1971; rpt., 1977), *The First Third and Other Writing* (San Francisco: City Lights), 4.

55. Cassady (1977), *The First Third*, 1. Page numbers for subsequent references to this edition are cited in the main text.

56. Burroughs to Kerouac, letter dated 3/15/49, in Harris, ed., *Letters of William S. Burroughs*, 42.

57. Cassady (1977), *The First Third*, 3. Page numbers for subsequent references to this edition are cited in the main text.

58. Cassady described witnessing his older half-brothers regularly "pound" his beloved father's face "bloody" (Cassady, *The First Third*, 3) and reports of their method, "one would knock him down, then stand him up for the other to smash to the floor" (44). These "brain-blinding rages" ended only when "exhaustion" set in (3).

59. Cassady reports his brothers' "sadisms" included "a generous amount of hatred for animals," including "flushing kittens down the toilet" and "sharp

shooting" stray cats, which one would swing "by the tail to gain full velocity, while the other shot it full of holes before it fell to earth" (ibid., 25).

60. Letter to Kerouac dated July 3, 1949, in Charters, ed., *The portable beat reader*, 193.

61. Ibid.

62. Watson, *Birth of the beat generation*, 80.

63. Earlier, Cassady had spent time locked up in a "juvenile jail"—following his father's arrest for public drunkenness—among boys with "serious anti-social behavior" and who seemed to young Cassady like "regular convicts; like the real bigtime criminals" (Cassady, *The First Third*, 66). At the time, there was no prohibition on jailing status offenders with juvenile delinquents.

64. Charters, ed., *The portable beat reader*, 193.

65. The Pranksters are probably best known for their "acid test" graduations, a series of events that mixed psychedelic drugs (most notably LSD) with the music of the resident Prankster band, the Grateful Dead. Ken Babbs describes traveling to one such event: "The great bus, Further, hurtles north through the night heading for the Portland Acid Test. At the wheel, Neal Cassady, narrowing the 1/30th lag between perception and action to 1/49th of a second. Aboard, preparing themselves for the task ahead, the Pranksters and the Grateful Dead. At the front, Cassady rapping. In the middle, the Pranksters tootling and bon-going. In the back there is singing." Paul Perry (1990; rpt., 1996), *On the bus: The complete guide to the legendary trip of Ken Kesey and the Merry Pranksters and the birth of the counterculture* (New York: Thunder's Mouth Press), xvi.

It was a psychedelic road show both inside and outside the bus.

66. Turner, *Angelheaded Hipster*, 195.

67. The trip's purpose is difficult to ascribe because "there were so many dif-fering agendas going into the bus trip" (Perry, *On the bus*, 43). Underground press editor and satirist Paul Krassner said the Pranksters "were truly followers of the American pioneer spirit but without killing any Indians" (Perry, *On the bus*, xxii). A variation of Krassner's description comes from Kesey himself, who called the Pranksters "the unsettlers of 1964 going backwards across the Great Plains" (Perry, *On the bus*, 52). It was a runaway road show and American adventure.

During the trip, the Pranksters had a disappointing encounter with the "ill," "ill at ease," and alcoholic Jack Kerouac—who had removed himself from the second-generation counterculture scene but joined the Pranksters one evening in order to see Cassady (Ginsberg interview in Perry [1990], *On the bus*, 87–88).

Kerouac will later complain that Kesey "ruined" Cassady (Turner, *Angelheaded Hipster*, 205).

68. Perry, *On the bus*, 102.

69. Cited in Charters, ed, *The portable beat reader*, xxx.

4. Digger Free: Power in Autonomy, Independence in a Free City Network (1966–1968)

1. In 1964 the *Los Angeles Free Press* became the first underground paper. By 1969 at least five hundred such tabloids were being published. By 1967, editors of the underground papers banned together to form the Underground Press Syndicate (UPS), which "helped share stories" and defend against "an increasing number of legal assaults" (Peck 1985:xvi). In the August edition of the *East Village Other*, thirty-four papers from eleven states, Canada, and Great Britain are listed as affiliates (see *EVO* [1967, Aug. 1–14], 2.17). In addition to an alternative perspective on local and national news, the underground papers provided a nationwide network of information of interest to radical and counterculture communities. For a complete treatment of the history of the underground press, see Abe Peck (1985), *Uncovering the sixties: The life and times of the underground press* (New York: Citadel).

2. For further studies of Diggers and their place in the 1960s counterculture, see M. W. Doyle, Staging the revolution: Guerrilla theatre as a counterculture practice, 1965–68, in P. Braunstein and M. W. Doyle, eds. (2002), *Imagine nation: The American counterculture of the 1960s and '70s*, 71–97 (New York: Routledge); and D. Cavallo, "It's Free because It's Yours": The Diggers and the San Francisco scene, 1964–1969, in Cavallo (1999), *A fiction of the past: The sixties in American history*, 97–144 (New York: St. Martin's). For a complete study of the Haight-Ashbury Diggers in the context of American utopian movements, see Michael William Doyle (1997, Aug.), The Haight-Ashbury Diggers and the cultural politics of utopia, 196568 (Ph.D. diss., Cornell University). See also K. M. Staller (1999), Runaway youth: Contending cultural voices and policy responses, 1960–1978 (Ph.D. diss., Columbia University).

3. In the East Village, flamboyant public spokesmen such as Abbie Hoffman, Jim Fouratt, Paul Krassner, and Ronald ("Galahad") Johnson briefly called themselves Diggers.

4. C. Anderson (folder: 1967, Apr.), "Uncle Tim'$ Children" (4/17/67), University of California at Berkeley, Bancroft Library (hereafter, BANC) (MSS92/839c; 1:4 Communication Company [hereafter, Com/co]).

5. Doyle, Staging the revolution, 74.

6. The Haight-Ashbury Diggers took their name from the short-lived English Digger Movement of 1649–50. This communistic group (sometimes called the "first utopian socialists") temporarily flourished alongside the longer-lived, better-established Levellers (Sabine 1941:2). Both initiatives were set against the backdrop of dire economic conditions in England, failed harvests, starvation of the poor, economic disruption of a civil war, and heavy taxation of the common people. A. Hopton, ed. (1989), *Digger tracts, 1649–50* (London: Aporia Press); and G. H. Sabine (1941), *The works of Gerrard Winstanley: With an appendix of documents relating to the Digger Movement* (Ithaca: Cornell University Press).

The Digger Movement was spearheaded by the mystic experience of Gerrard Winstanley (1609–1676), who "received in a trance" the command to 'work together; eat bread together.'" Winstanley insisted on "freedom for the poor" and, for him, "the meaning of freedom lies in the unrestricted right to use the earth" (Winstanley, quoted in Hopton 1989:5). So in April 1649, "some half dozen poor men . . . appeared upon the common land at St. George's Hill and began to dig the ground and prepare it for sowing parsnips, carrots, and beans" (Sabine 1941:11). It was a "design to cultivate the common land for the support of the needy" (Sabine 1941:11).

According to Sabine, Winstanley tried to "visualize a social system of a different sort" in which he tried to "frame for himself a different idea of property and a different idea of the relationship between property and government" (Sabine 1941:5). Under Winstanley's vision of society there "should be no beggars," and the "utilization of available land for social purposes" was the "solution of the problem of poverty and unemployment" (Sabine 1941:14).

The Haight-Ashbury Diggers appropriately appropriated the Digger name. The seekers of the 1960s also rejected traditional institutions of the dominant culture and sought to visualize a different social system, to redefine the relationships with property and with government, and to feed the poor using common property. Furthermore, both movements were founded in notions of love. In the seventeenth century, *The Digger Song* rejected "lawyers, clergy, gentrye, cavaleers" and urged "noble Diggers all, stand up now." The final stanza concluded with a mission of love:

To Conquer them by love, come in now, come in now,

To conquer them by love, come in now;

To conquer them by love, as itt does you behove,

For hee is King above, noe power is like to love.

Glory here Diggers all.

7. For more detailed discussion of the relationship between Diggers and the San Francisco Mime Troupe, see Doyle, Staging the revolution, and Cavallo, "It's Free because It's Yours."

8. This idea (and others) was picked up, and arguably corrupted, by self-proclaimed East Coast Diggers Abbie Hoffman and Jerry Rubin. Hoffman wrote, "The key to the puzzle lies in theater. We are theater in the streets: total and committed" (Free [aka Hoffman] 1968:27), and Rubin declared, "Life is theater and we are the guerrillas attacking the shrines of authority, from the priest, to the holy dollar, to the two-party system, zapping people's minds and putting them through changes in actions in which everyone is emotionally involved" (Rubin 1970:250). Free (aka Hoffman) (1968), *Revolution for the hell of it* (New York: Dial); Rubin (1970), *Do it* (New York: Simon and Schuster).

There was considerable tension between the West Coast and East Coast Diggers. For further discussion, see Staller, Runaway youth.

9. Peter Berg, "Trip Without a Ticket" (first distributed Oct. 1966), California Historical Society's San Francisco MSS Collection, hereafter CHS (Haight Street Diggers, MS3159/1, folder 1). Originally published by the Diggers circa winter 1966–67, reprinted by the Communication Company (2d ed., June 28, 1967, San Francisco). For online version (Aug. 1968), see *The Digger Papers* (www.diggers.org/digger_papers.html).

10. Braunstein and Doyle, eds., *Imagine nation*, 80.

11. Ibid., 95n28.

12. Anderson (folder: 1967, Jan.), "If you're not a digger you're property" (1/28/67), BANC (MSS92/839c; 1:1) (Com/co).

13. Given the fact the Diggers were a leaderless group, it is problematical to put too much credence in any single source. Certainly there are writers and spokespersons who have emerged as the historians of the movement. Although Emmett Grogan's mostly autobiographical work, *Ringolevio: A life played for keeps*, has been criticized for some of its more fanciful elements, it contains considerable information that is possible to corroborate with other sources.

Ringolevio was first published in 1972 (Boston: Little, Brown), which makes it fairly contemporaneous. Peter Coyote has written a series of essays that have been published in a book (1998), *Sleeping where I fall* (Washington, D.C.: Counterpoint). These essays first appeared in draft and are still available on the Digger Archives Web page (see note 31). The archives continue to be a wonderful source of information. Originally, Com/co broadsides were available in historical archives. The most complete collection is held by Berkeley's Bancroft Library. Finally, second-generation historians such as Michael Doyle and Dominick Cavallo have also studied and written about the Digger movement.

14. Anderson (folder: 1967, Jan.), "Be Free" (undated), BANC (MSS92/839c; 1:1) (Com/co).

15. Braunstein and Doyle, eds., *Imagine nation*, 78–79.

16. The dispute turned angry with the publication of Abbie Hoffman's pamphlet, *Fuck the System* (reprinted in Free [aka Hoffman], *Revolution for the hell of it*, 220–27). Hoffman's book was derived from ideas originally articulated and distributed as part of the free flow of information by West Coast Diggers. Hoffman is accused of "stealing" and marketing these "free ideas" and is labeled a traitor. Writes Grogan of the "theft":

> It was that pile of papers which supplied Abbot Hoffman with all the superficial information and hipster phrases that enabled him to act like he was one of the died-in-the-wool originals. The Hun's [Peter Berg] pieces were particularly valuable to Hoffman because they gave him the key to explaining how everything he did was theater—brilliant, guerrilla theater in the streets." (Grogan, *Ringolevio*, 458–59)

A heated debate ensued between the Haight-Ashbury and East Village Digger factions over whether free ideas could, in fact, be stolen. Grogan contends Hoffman could "steal 'free'" because "he made believe that he was what they represented" while "the people who wrote them worked at [them] all the time" (Grogan, *Ringolevio*, 459). Hoffman, in Grogan's eyes, was a charlatan. Peter Coyote provides a clearer explanation in his account of the confrontation between Hoffman and Peter Berg over the same issue:

> One morning he [Hoffman] woke up Peter Berg by pounding on the door and shouting in his pronounced New England twang, "Petah, Petah, I bet

you think I stole everything from ya, doncha?" This was indisputably true. Berg stumbled to the door, regarded the cheerful hairball before him as if he were sucking a lemon, then responded sleepily, "No, Abbie. I feel like I gave a good tool to an idiot." Coyote (1998), "Emmett: A Life Played for Keeps," in Coyote, *Sleeping Where I Fall*, 71.

The debate is informative for several reasons. For West Coast Diggers, ideas were recorded, and distributed, as an integral part of action. They were the "tools," the blueprints and the communication structure in the real work of creating a free communal existence. They were *not* a declaration of organizing principles. Hoffman cut his teeth as a SNCC organizer (Student Nonviolent Coordinating Committee) and cites Marshall McLuhan's *Understanding Media* as a major influence on his work. Although Hoffman professes, at times, to be a community organizer, his primary focus was always on bigger social agendas and wider audiences.

17. Todd Gitlin (1987), *The sixties: Years of hope, days of rage* (New York: Bantam).

18. Doyle attributed the Digger maxim, "Do your [own] thing," to Emmett Grogan, who used "Do your thing / Do it for FREE," in a Digger broadside in 1966 (Doyle, The Haight-Ashbury Diggers, 106*n*101).

19. Grogan, *Ringolevio*, 302. Although hippies were accused of avoiding work, core members of the Digger community worked extremely hard (albeit not in traditional jobs or for traditional compensation). Coyote observes that "survival takes work" and pointed to spending "half a day in a junkyard dismantling an old truck for parts" (P. Coyote, The free fall chronicles: Crossing the free frame of reference [*see* www.diggers.org/freefall/freefram.html]; Coyote, *Sleeping where I fall*).

And Grogan writes of providing Free Food every day: "Cooking two or three twenty-gallon milk cans full of stew for two hundred people can be a goof, if you do it once a year, but try doing it for two or three days in a row, for two or three weeks, for two or three months. And not get paid—not make any money from it at all. It's a bitch" (Grogan, *Ringolevio*, 264).

20. Grogan, *Ringolevio*, 236–37.

21. It is too simplistic to characterize the Digger system as a barter economy. Bartering implies both ownership interests in the property being exchanged as well as some negotiable value. The Diggers rejected both notions. Goods and

services were produced because they met the needs of the producer and not necessarily the consumer. Thus production was not driven by market demand but by the whims of producers. Exchanging goods occurred as part of theater, not as negotiated transactions.

22. Quoted in J. C. Albert and S. E. Albert (1984), *The sixties papers: Documents of a rebellious decade* (New York: Praeger), 408.

23. Grogan, *Ringolevio*, 245–49.

24. Berg (1966), "Trip Without a Ticket."

25. Allen Ginsberg (1967, July), "Dialectics of Liberation," NBR/CHS (Haight Street Diggers, MS3159/1; folder 1), *The Digger Papers*.

26. Berg (1966), "Trip Without a Ticket."

27. Doyle, The Haight-Ashbury Diggers, 208–209.

28. Berg (1966), "Trip Without a Ticket."

29. In addition to the "game," a Com/co broadside was distributed entitled "Public Nuisance New Sence [sic] Nonsense," which was a call to the community for plaintiffs for a lawsuit to challenge California's Public Nuisance law (Penal Code 370, 372). It sought "statements from people who have been arrested under these statutes to be included in a legal brief [sic] before the Federal Court of Appeals" and provided the phone number and address of attorney Richard Weinstein. The statutes, according to the broadside, covered "blocking sidewalks, failure to disperse, obstructing the right of way, maintaining a public nuisance, and other such bullshit charges." Anderson (folder: 1967, Apr.), "Public Nuisance New Sence [sic] Nonsense" (undated), BANC (MSS92/839c; 1:4) (Com/co).

In short, the Digger theater which involved claiming the streets also spilled over into a legal challenge of the public law targeted primarily at street behavior.

30. Etan Ben-Ami (1989, Jan. 12), Oral history interview with Peter Coyote (Mill Valley, Calif.), The Digger Archives (www. diggers.org/oral history/peter_interview.html) (accessed July 30, 2002). Also see the official Peter Coyote Web site (www.petercoyote.com/annt_html) (accessed September 30, 2005).

31. H. S. Thompson (1967, May 14), "The 'Hashbury' Is the Capital of the Hippies," *New York Times Magazine*, 120. Illicit drug use caused a dilemma for journalists and researchers interested in the counterculture. Thompson observed that "the only way to write honestly about the scene is to be part of it . . . yet to write from experience is an admission of felonious guilt" (ibid., 120, 122).

Social scientist Lewis Yablonsky (1968), who studied hippies extensively in 1967, included a chapter detailing his decision to take one LSD trip as a critical component of his research. Lewis Yablonsky (1968), "Red, white, and blue," in *The hippie trip* (New York: Pegasus), 224–37.

32. Grogan, *Ringolevio*, 233.

33. Gitlin, *The sixties*, 201.

34. P. Perry (1990; rpt., 1996), *On the bus: The complete guide to the legendary trip of Ken Kesey and the Merry Pranksters and the birth of the counterculture* (New York: Thunder's Mouth Press), xxii.

35. Ben-Ami, Oral history interview with Peter Coyote.

36. The Stock Exchange event, orchestrated by Abbie Hoffman and Jim Fouratt in August 1967, involved dropping dollar bills from the visitor's gallery overlooking the trading floor of the NYSE. The headline in the *New York Times* read "Hippies Shower $1 Bills on Stock Exchange Floor." The *Times* described the reaction: "Stockbrokers, clerks and runners turned and stared at the visitor's gallery. A few smiled and blew kisses, but most jeered, shouted, pointed fingers and shook their fists. Some clerks ran to pick up the bills until security guards hustled the hippies out, to cheers and applause from the floor" (Kifner, [1967, Aug. 25], 23).

Hoffman's account of the event was a tad more dramatic: "The sacred electronic ticker tape, the heartbeat of the Western world, stopped cold. Stock brokers scrambled over the floor like worried mice, scurrying after the money. Greed had burst through the business-as-usual" (A. Hoffman [1980], *Soon to be a major motion picture* [New York: Putnam], 101).

After their eviction, the group gathered on Broad Street and "joined hands and skipped in a circle on the crowded sidewalk chanting, 'Free, free,' with Hoffman standing in the center setting a $5.00 bill on fire," resulting in "an outraged exchange runner [charging] into the middle of the circle shouting 'you're disgusting' and, grabbing the flaming bill, stamped on it" (J. Kifner, "Hippies Shower $1 Bills on Stock Exchange Floor," *New York Times*, 23).

Although West Coast Diggers had little patience for Hoffman's self-promotion through the media, the event illustrates Digger theater at its best. It evoked a series of responses from the "life-players" which were carefully recorded and disseminated by the *Times*, which itself became a player in the event. Recalled Hoffman later, "The press didn't yet realize that these images were disruptive to society" (Hoffman 1980:108). He believed that those sympathetically inclined, particularly American youth, would understand the event no matter how it was reported. He wrote: "A spark had been ignited. The system cracked a little . . . with that gesture, an image war had begun. In the minds of millions of teenagers the stock market had just crashed" (Hoffman 1980:102).

The event clearly embodied Digger sentiments about capitalism. Hoffman likened the event to the "TV-version of driving money changers from the temple," noting that the ideas "just keep getting recycled" (Hoffman 1980:102).

37. Braunstein and Doyle, eds., *Imagine nation*, 80.

38. Doyle noted that "other projects inspired or directed by the Diggers included the establishment of free medical clinics, community switchboards, free stores, rural communes . . . free crash pads, and the like. These models for an alternative society were initiated in the Bay area in 1967 and were replicated in numerous locations throughout the country thereafter" (Doyle, The Haight-Ashbury Diggers, 136).

39. Grogan, *Ringolevio*, 259.

40. Ibid., 302.

41. Berg (1966), "Trip Without a Ticket" (see also www.diggers.org/digger_papers.htm). See also Grogan, *Ringolevio*, 302.

42. Ben-Ami, Oral history interview with Peter Coyote.

43. Cavallo, "It's Free because It's Yours," 141.

44. *The Digger Papers* (1968, Aug.), "The Post-Competitive, Comparative Game of Free City," 15 (www.diggers.org/digger_papers68/postcomp.html).

45. Grogan, *Ringolevio*, 246–47.

46. Coyote, "Emmett: A Life Played for Keeps," in *Sleeping where I fall*, 71.

47. Grogan, *Ringolevio*, 248.

48. Grogan, *Ringolevio*, 247; Thompson, "The 'Hashbury' Is the Capital of the Hippies."

49. Rubin, *Do it*, 236.

50. Thompson, "The 'Hashbury' Is the Capital of the Hippies," 29, 121; Claude Hayward memo (1967, May 23), NBR/CHS (Haight Street Diggers, MS3159/1, folder 1), *The Digger Papers*.

51. The East Village Free Store was organized by Abbie Hoffman and Jim Fouratt. As usual, Hoffman both parroted and pirated core Digger ideas, managing to attract media attention in the process. Hoffman wrote, "We saw ourselves as visionaries in the Mean Streets" and argued dramatically that "a utopia would rise out of the garbage." Unlike Grogan, Hoffman likened the Free Store to "a Salvation Army depot minus the price tags"; it was, he said, "less a store than a philosophical experience" and it "stood as the symbol

of a new kind of economic exchange" (Hoffman, *Soon to be a major motion picture*, 97).

52. Grogan, *Ringolevio*, 266.

53. Berg (1966), "Trip Without a Ticket."

54. Grogan, *Ringolevio*, 297–98.

55. Yablonsky, *The hippie trip*, 201.

56. Grogan, *Ringolevio*, 286.

57. Ben-Ami, Oral history interview with Peter Coyote.

58. EVO 1967; Delbert L. Earisman (1968), *Hippies in our midst* (Philadelphia: Fortress Press).

59. Ben-Ami, Oral history interview with Peter Coyote.

60. Cited in Yablonsky, *The hippie trip*. Leary's famous slogan is cited in Martin A. Lee and Bruce Shlain (1985), *Acid dreams—The complete social history of LSD: The CIA, the sixties, and beyond* (New York: Grove Weidenfeld), 89.

61. Ben-Ami, Oral history interview with Peter Coyote.

62. Anderson (folder: 1967, Apr.), "Oh Dear, Oh My" (4/17/67), BANC (MSS92/839c; 1:4) (Com/co).

63. Anderson, (folder: 1967, Apr.), "Survival School" (undated), BANC (MSS92/839c; 1:4) (Com/co).

64. Ibid.

65. Anderson (folder: 1967, Feb.), "Busted" (undated), BANC (MSS92/839c; 1:2) (Com/co).

66. Anderson (folder: 1967, Mar.), "The Rules of the Game if Busted" (undated), BANC (MSS92/839c; 1:3) (Com/co).

67. Anderson (folder: 1967, Mar.), "Beat the Heat" (undated), BANC (MSS92/839c; 1:3) (Com/co).

68. Doyle described the Haight Digger nucleus as a group of NYC expatriates and "free spirits who were following Jack Kerouac's road west to the Beat poets' city of internal exile [San Francisco]" (Doyle, The Haight-Ashbury Diggers, 94).

69. Grogan, *Ringolevio*, 286.

70. Claude Hayward memo (1967, May 23), *The Digger Papers*.

71. Grogan, *Ringolevio*, 276.

72. Anderson (folder: 1967, Apr.), "Gurus, Wizards, Teachers" (4/17/67), BANC (MSS92/839c; 1:4) (Com/co).

73. Brilliant makes direct reference to runaways in several other songs. One, sung to the melody of "America the Beautiful," has an opening stanza:

> O beautiful for hairy beard,
> For psychedelic smiles
> For lava-lamps and costumes weird
> And run-away juveniles

In a song called "The Singing Hippie," Brilliant urged leaving home to become hip and promised the community will love the kids the world rejects:

> If a truly hip hippie
> Is what you really want to be
> Just take a tip from me
> Leave your mother and your dad
> Move into a hippie pad
> In the great Haight-Ashbury
>
> We love kids the world rejects
> We approve of every sex

74. Anderson (folder: 1967, Apr.), "Uncle Tim'$ Children" (4/17/67), BANC (MSS92/839c; 1:4) (Com/co).

75. Ibid.

76. Anderson (folder: 1967, Apr.), "Oh Dear, Oh My" (4/17/67), BANC (MSS92/839c; 1:4) (Com/co).

77. She was Phyllis Wilner (*see* Coyote, The free fall chronicles, at www.diggers.org/freefall/freefram.html). According to Coyote, she had "fled New York and the chaos of life with a schizophrenic mother at fourteen years old, opting for the safer unpredictability of life on the streets."

78. Richard Goldstein (1967, Mar. 16), "In Search of George Metesky," *Village Voice* 12.32: 6; Grogan, *Ringolevio*, 266.

79. Grogan, *Ringolevio*, 266.

80. Ben-Ami, Oral history interview with Peter Coyote.

81. Hoffman, *Soon to be a major motion picture*, 88.

82. Ibid.

83. Anderson (folder: 1967, June), "We Should Cherish Every Chance for Laughter That We Get (6/8/67), BANC (MSS92/839c; 1:6) (Com/co).

84. In some instances, minors had trouble hawking underground newspapers. The *East Village Other* reported that the Ottawa police "seized about 100

copies of *The Ottawa Free Press*, a member of UPS" and "arrested two teenagers" for "possessing an obscene publication" (*EVO*, "Poor Paranoid's" [1967, Aug. 1–4] 2.17, 7). By the fall of 1967, hawking newspapers in the Haight became more difficult for minors because publishers held identification cards for those who obtained papers on consignment. Minors without IDs faced added complications if they were stopped by police because they could be detained based on lack of identification establishing age.

85. Free (aka Hoffman), *Revolution for the hell of it*; Yablonsky, *The hippie trip*.

86. Grogan, *Ringolevio*, 293.

87. Ibid., 276.

88. Ibid., 363.

89. Ben-Ami, Oral history interview with Peter Coyote.

90. Grogan, *Ringolevio*, 286. In New York City, Digger Galahad's (Ronald Johnson) East Village crash pad was raided so many times his case was taken up by the ACLU and he declared (for public consumption only) that house rules prohibited his commune from having "anything to do with a girl under 18 years old." Hoffman had little tolerance for Galahad, whom he described as both racist and as a "harem lord" (Hoffman, *Soon to be a major motion picture*, 99).

91. Grogan, *Ringolevio*, 286–87.

92. Earisman, *Hippies in our midst*; John Kifner (1967, Oct. 11), "The East Village: A Changing Scene for Hippies," *New York Times*, 32.

93. Free (aka Hoffman), *Revolution for the hell of it*, 74.

94. Ibid., 74–75.

95. *The Digger Papers* (1968, Aug.), "The Post-Competitive, Comparative Game of Free City" (www.diggers.org/digger_papers68/postcomp.html).

96. Anderson (folder: 1967, Mar.), "To Our Straight Friends" (3/19/67), BANC (MSS92/839c; 1:3) (Com/co).

97. Doyle, The Haight-Ashbury Diggers, 187–88.

98. Grogan, *Ringolevio*, 288.

99. Ibid., 289.

100. Ibid.

5. The Grassroots Rise of Alternative Runaway Services (1967–1974)

1. R. Rodriquez (2003, June 25), "At Odds With Ourselves" (oral essay), "The NewsHour with Jim Lehrer" (Public Broadcasting Service).

2. As documented in chapter 1, youth shelters are not without historical precedent. In the late nineteenth century Charles Loring Brace, the founder of the Children's Aid Society, established a network of lodging houses in New York City. This system of services looked much like the current runaway shelter system. Huckleberry House is probably the first of the 1960s generation of such services.

3. G. Flanigan (1974, May 2), written statement. House Committee on Education and Labor, *Juvenile Justice and Delinquency Prevention and Runaway Youth: Hearings before the Subcommittee on Equal Opportunities*, H.R. 9298, 93rd Cong., 2d sess., Mar. 29 (Los Angeles), Apr. 24, May 1, 2, 8, and 21, 1974 (Washington, D.C.: GPO), 308.

4. The emergence of the runaway shelter movement follows a similar path as that documented by the battered women's shelter movement during roughly the same historical period. For a study of the battered woman's movement see S. Schechter (1982), *Women and male violence: The visions and struggles of the battered women's movement* (Boston: South End Press).

5. B. C. McQuaker (1994, May 2). House Committee on Education and Labor, *Juvenile Justice and Delinquency Prevention and Runaway Youth: Hearings before the Subcommittee on Equal Opportunities*, 93rd Cong., 2d sess., Mar. 29, Apr. 24, May 1, 2, 8, and 21, 1974 (Washington, D.C.: GPO), 301.

6. A. Hoffman (1968), *Fuck the system* (reprinted in Free [aka Hoffman], *Revolution for the hell of it* [New York: Dial], 220–27).

7. Larry Beggs (1969), *Huckleberry's for runaways* (New York: Ballantine), 8.

8. Beggs, *Huckleberry's for runaways*, 8.

9. Ibid., 9.

10. Although Huckleberry House was established in response to the Summer of Love crisis, Beggs argued that people were naive to believe the runaway problem would disappear with the start of the school year because "runaways are the results of family conflict" (Beggs, *Huckleberry's for runaways*, 15). Thus the founders of Huckleberry's were well aware that they were not dealing with a temporary social issue. However, they were certainly capitalizing on the social crisis in developing and marketing the service structure.

11. Miller, quoted in "Two Houses Run by Church Offer Runaways Haven in Fairfield" (1976, May 9), *New York Times*, 37.

12. B. Ritter (1987), *Covenant House: Lifeline to the street* (New York: Doubleday), 1.

13. Ibid., 2.

14. Credible allegations of Ritter's sexual misconduct with youth who sought shelter date back to this period.

15. Bruce Ritter (1981, Nov. 5), written statement ("Exploitation of Children"), Senate Judiciary Committee, *Hearings before the Subcommittee on Juvenile Justice*, (Washington, D.C.: GPO), 34.

16. "C-4," undated, Ozone House Collection, box 5; folder: Ozone House Peoples' Handbook, c. 1970s (Bentley Historical Library, University of Michigan, Ann Arbor).

17. Although Looking Glass was located in a house, it never provided shelter directly for youth. Instead it was designed to refer youth to foster homes when necessary. G. Flanigan (1974, May 2), written statement. House Committee, *Juvenile Justice and Delinquency Prevention*, 317.

18. Ibid.

19. Ibid.

20. Anne E. Fortune and William J. Reid (1972, Sept.), *Images in Looking Glass: A study of a counseling center for runaways* (Chicago: Travelers Aid Society of Metropolitan Chicago, supported by Illinois Law Enforcement Commission Grant 5653466 in cooperation with Cook County Commission on Crime and Criminal Justice and Department of Human Resources of the City of Chicago), 8–9.

21. Fortune and Reid, *Images in Looking Glass*, 11.

22. Ibid.

23. B. C. McQuaker (1974, May 2), House Committee, *Juvenile Justice and Delinquency Prevention*, 302.

24. At hearings for the Runaway Youth Act in 1972, Huckleberry House's director Brian Slattery argued that research supported the notion that "the runaway crisis offers a unique opportunity to give assistance to families when they most want it, and to wait at all may be to wait too long. Their recommendation was that communities set up around the clock, on the spot, emergency aid services for teenagers and their families." B. Slattery (1972, Jan. 13), Senate Committee on the Judiciary, *Runaway Youth Act Hearings before the Subcommittee to Investigate Juvenile Delinquency*, 92d Cong., 1st sess., January 13 and 14, 1972 (Washington, D.C.: GPO), 32.

25. G. Flanigan (1974, May 2), written statement. House Committee, *Juvenile Justice and Delinquency Prevention*, 305.

26. At Congressional hearings on the Runaway Youth Act in 1972, William Treanor described the agreement his staff at Runaway House (founded in 1968 in Washington, D.C.) made with its youth: "We will trust you as much as we are

able; we will not exploit you in any way; we will not contact your parents, the police or anyone else without your knowledge and consent; you can stay at Runaway House as long as you observe the rules and are actively working on your problems. . . . We provide a warm, trusting environment where young people can decide for themselves what to do about their family situations. For many, it's the fist time in their lives that they have been able to make an important decision themselves. The runaway has the opportunity to talk over family problems with the counselors and the other runaways. We try to help the young person realize how realistic his or her plans are." W. Treanor (1972, Jan. 13), Senate Committee on the Judiciary, *Runaway Youth Act Hearings before the Subcommittee to Investigate Juvenile Delinquency*, 92d Cong., 1st sess., Jan. 13 and 14, 1972 (Washington, D.C.: GPO), 18.

27. Huckleberry House Web page (www.huckleberryyough.org). In 1972, codirector of Huckleberry House, Brian Slattery, argues to a congressional subcommittee on the Runaway Youth Act that "the decision-making of young people can be trusted, and when their decision-making power is trusted, young people usually involve their energies in constructive and responsible ways, rather than in undermining the system which suppresses their decision-making, whether that system be family, school, or government." Slattery (1972, Jan. 13), Senate Committee, *Runaway Youth Act Hearings before the Subcommittee to Investigate Juvenile Delinquency*, 37.

28. Board of Directors meeting (minutes for Nov. 29, 1972), Ozone House Collection, box 1; folder: Board of Director Minutes, 1972–1982 (Bentley Historical Library, University of Michigan, Ann Arbor).

29. Fortune and Reid, *Images in Looking Glass*, 25.

30. Ozone House Peoples' Handbook, dated Dec. 1976, Ozone House Collection, box 5; folder: Ozone House Peoples' Handbook (Bentley Historical Library, University of Michigan, Ann Arbor), 2.

31. Fortune and Reid, *Images in Looking Glass*, 16.

32. Ibid.

33. Ibid., 5–6.

34. Ibid., 4.

35. As the agencies evolved, so too did the complexity of the confidentiality arguments. For example, the stated purpose of Covenant House's confidentiality policy was "to protect the privacy and sanctuary of residents" and "to encourage youth to accept services and build a relationship of trust based upon the assurance of confidentiality" (CH Confidentiality Manual). The agency drew

from a variety of sources to justify its confidentiality policy, including New York State's Runaway and Homeless Youth Act (1978), the federal Runaway and Homeless Youth Act (1974), the drug treatment provisions, social services law, state civil procedure law, professional privileges of social workers, attorneys, physicians, priests, and psychologists, and the U.S. Constitution. The manual included separate sections for dealing with parents, police and the press.

36. Emmett Grogan (1972), *Ringolevio: A life played for keeps* (Boston: Little Brown), 288–89.

37. Fortune and Reid, *Images in Looking Glass*, 15.

38. Ibid., 3.

39. Beggs, *Huckleberry's for runaways*, 119. By 1972 the codirector of Huckleberry House, Brain Slattery, testified at a congressional hearing that about 15 percent of its clients wanted housing but couldn't, or wouldn't, get consent from parents, bringing the percentage more in line with that reported at Looking Glass. When asked by Indiana senator Birch Bayh what happened to these youth, Slattery reported that they were "informed as accurately as we can of the consequences of living on the street, some of the alternatives, survival techniques for living on the street, but he is certainly in no way obstructed from returning to the street." Slattery (1972, Jan. 13), Senate Committee, *Runaway Youth Act Hearings before the Subcommittee to Investigate Juvenile Delinquency*, 34–35.

40. Board of Directors Meeting, dated June 3, 1975, Ozone House Collection, box 1; folder: Board of Director Minutes, 1972–1982 (Bentley Historical Library, University of Michigan, Ann Arbor).

41. Grogan, *Ringolevio*, 288–89.

42. Michigan Compiled Laws, § 722.15.

43. Beggs, *Huckleberry's for runaways*, 9.

44. Ibid., 45–59.

45. Letter to Board of Directors from Barbara Nesbitt (Publicity-Fundraising Coordinated), dated May 29, 1973, Ozone House Collection, box 5; folder: Board of Directors Newsletters, 1973–82 (Bentley Historical Library, University of Michigan, Ann Arbor).

46. Ozone House Peoples' Handbook (Dec. 1976), Ozone House Collection, 12.

47. Ibid.

48. Ibid., 15.

49. Letter to Board of Directors from Barbara Nesbitt (Publicity-Fundraising Coordinated), dated May 29, 1973, Ozone House Collection.

50. Mole Homes, dated Dec. 1976, Ozone House Collection, box 5; folder: Ozone House Peoples' Handbook (Bentley Historical Library, University of Michigan, Ann Arbor), 15.

51. Mole Homes, loose undated page, Ozone House Collection.

52. Board of Directors Meeting (minutes for Nov. 29, 1972), Ozone House Collection.

53. Mole Homes (Dec. 1976), Ozone House Collection, 13.

54. R. Blumenthal (1968, July 29), "Hippie Finds a Free Pad at Y.M.C.A," *New York Times*, 33.

55. D. Janson (1971, July 18), "Philadelphia Minister Aids Runaways," *New York Times*, 41.

56. "Phone-a-Home Program Gives Runaways a Place to Run To" (1972, Nov. 25), *New York Times*, 18.

57. "Two Houses Run by Church Offer Runaways Haven in Fairfield," *New York Times*, 37.

58. J. Klemesrud (1972, May 1), "Where Runaways Can Find a Haven," *New York Times*, 38.

59. J. Cummings (1977, Dec. 10), "Priest's Shelter Tries to Salvage Times Sq. Youths," *New York Times*, 29.

60. "Two Houses Run by Church Offer Runaways Haven in Fairfield," 37.

61. E. J. Dionne (1977, Apr. 2), "An Oasis for Runaway Teen-Agers Appears in a Pornographic Desert," *New York Times*, 33.

62. "Phone-a-Home Program Gives Runaways a Place to Run To," *New York Times*, 18.

63. "Two Houses Run by Church Offer Runaways Haven in Fairfield," 37.

64. Janson, "Philadelphia Minister Aids Runaways," *New York Times*, 41.

65. Dionne, "An Oasis for Runaway Teen-Agers Appears in a Pornographic Desert," 33.

66. Klemesrud, "Where Runaways Can Find a Haven," 38.

67. J. P. Sterba (1973, Aug. 11), "Texas Police Find Four More Bodies; The Total Is Now 23," *New York Times*, 1, 17.

68. J. P. Sterba (1973, Aug. 14), "Texas Toll of Boys Rises to 27 in Nation's Biggest Slaying Case," *New York Times*, 1, 18.

69. Sterba, "Texas Police Find Four More Bodies; The Total Is Now 23," *New York Times*, 1.

70. Sterba, "Texas Toll of Boys Rises to 27," *New York Times*, 1.

71. "4,000 Runaways Aided by Hotline: Volunteers in Houston Help Young-sters Nationwide" (1974, Oct. 21), *New York Times*, 28.

72. J. P. Sterba (1975, July 13), "Phone Services for Runaways," *New York Times*, 38. In 1972, Operation Peace of Mind was joined by a second national runaway hotline, the National Runaway Switchboard, based in Chicago. In 1974, Operation Peace of Mind lost out to a Chicago-based hotline in competi-tion for federal funding. In 1979, Operation Peace of Mind changed its name to Runaway Hotline, and even later to Texas Runaway Hotline. By the early 1980s the hotline had abandoned its national reach and focused primarily on provid-ing service within the state of Texas. The National Runaway Switchboard is still in operation.

73. Ibid.

74. Sterba, "Texas Toll of Boys Rises to 27," 1, 18.

75. R. Flaste, (1975, May 16), "May and June, Runaway Months: What Should Parents Do?" *New York Times*, 43.

76. Sterba, "Phone Services for Runaways," 38.

77. Ibid. See also "4,000 Runaways Aided by Hotline," *New York Times*, 28.

78. Board of Directors Meeting, dated May 14, 1974, Ozone House Collec-tion, box 1; folder: Board of Director Minutes, 1972–1982 (Bentley Historical Library, University of Michigan, Ann Arbor).

79. Board of Directors Meeting, dated Oct. 14, 1975, Ozone House Collec-tion, box 1; folder: Board of Director Minutes, 1972–1982 (Bentley Historical Library, University of Michigan, Ann Arbor).

80. Board of Directors Meeting, dated May 14, 1974, Ozone House Collec-tion.

81. Board of Directors Meeting, dated Oct. 14, 1975, Ozone House Collection.

82. Ibid.

83. Looking Glass closed its program in 1973 largely because it could not solve its funding problems. Ms. Flanigan attributed the program's financial problems in part to the unwillingness of funders to provide ongoing support, after initial seed grants for experimental program development, and partly because staff at Looking House lacked the expertise in writing for grants or other related skills necessary to keep the program alive and competitive. G. Flanigan (1974, May 2), written statement. House Committee, *Juvenile Justice and Delinquency Preven-tion*, 313–14.

6. Shifting Institutional Structures: From Moral Guidance to Autonomous Denizens (1960–1978)

1. The court case samples used for this chapter included twenty-two decisions on wayward minors written between 1930 and 1972. Of these cases, six decisions were rendered by the New York Court of Appeals, four by the Appellate Division, and the remaining fourteen were trial court cases. The PINS sample was obtained by doing a Lexis search, which originally produced 284 cases decided between 1962 and 1978. Of these, 160 were eliminated as being off-subject, and of the remaining cases 124 were retained for analysis. Of these, twelve are decisions by the New York Court of Appeals, sixty-six are from the Appellate Division, and forty-six trial court decisions. For further discussion on the method of analysis, see K. M. Staller (1999), Runaway youth: Contending cultural voices and policy responses, 1960–1978 (Ph.D. diss., Columbia University).

2. Family Court Act, Laws of New York, 1962, ch. 686 .

3. A *juvenile delinquent* was defined as a "person over seven and less than sixteen years of age who does any act which, if done by an adult, would constitute a crime" (FCA, § 712 [a]).

4. Other states enacted status offenses or "in need of supervision" statutes called CHINS, JINS, MINS, FINS, etc., targeted at children, juveniles, minors, and families in need of supervision, respectively.

5. PINS was defined as "a male less than sixteen years of age and a female less than 18 years of age who is an habitual truant or who is incorrigible, ungovernable or habitually disobedient and beyond the lawful control of parent or other lawful authority" (FCA, § 712 [b]).

6. *Gesicki v. Oswald*, (1971) 336 F. Supp. 371, affirmed 92 S.Ct. 1773, 406 U.S. 913, 32 L.Ed. 2d 113; *Gesicki v. Oswald*, (1971, SDNY) 336 F. Supp. 365.

7. *Gesicki v. Oswald*, (1971) 336 F. Supp. 371; 375 (fn. 5).

8. *Gesicki v. Oswald*, (1971) 336 F. Supp. 371; 375 (fn. 5).

9. *Gesicki v. Oswald*, (1971) 336 F. Supp. 371; 375 (fn. 5).

10. *Gesicki v. Oswald*, (1971, SDNY) 336 F. Supp. 365, 369.

11. *Gesicki v. Oswald*, (1971) 336 F. Supp. 371, 374.

12. Laws of the State of New York, 185th sess., 1962, V III, Albany, NY, ch. 686; art. 7, § 712 (b).

13. *Patricia A. v. City of New York*, (1972) 31 NY2d 83.

14. The court found that the "argument that discrimination against females on the basis of age is justified because of the obvious danger of pregnancy in an

immature girl and because of out-of-wedlock births which add to the welfare relief burdens for the State and city is without merit." Furthermore, the court went on to say that "the conclusion seems inescapable that lurking behind the discrimination is the imputation that females who engage in misconduct, sexual or otherwise, ought more to be censured, and their conduct subject to greater control and regulation than males." (*Patricia A. v. City of New York*, [1972] 31 NY2d 83, 89).

15. *In the Matter of Neil M. v. Gregory M.*, (1972) 71 Misc. 2d 396, 399–400.

16. *In the Matter of Neil M. v. Gregory M.*, (1972) 71 Misc. 2d 396, 397.

17. *In the Matter of Neil M. v. Gregory M.*, (1972) 71 Misc. 2d 396, 401.

18. The New York State legislature amended the PINS statute in 2003 to raise the age to 18. However, between 1972 and 2003 the maximum age remained 16.

19. The New York State legislature attempted to address the deficiency in 1972 by amending the definition of delinquent to include violations, but the bill was vetoed by the governor.

20. *In the Matter of Rooney*, (1965) 48 Misc. 2d 890, 893.

21. *In the Matter of Rooney*, (1965) 48 Misc. 2d 890, 891.

22. *In the Matter of Rooney*, (1965) 48 Misc. 2d 890, 893.

23. See *Carter v. Family Court of New York*, (1964, Second Dept.) 22 AD2d 888; *In re David W.*, (1970, Fourth Dept.) 34 AD2d 1100; *In re Anna "AA,"* (1971, Third Dept.) 36 AD2d 1001.

24. *Bordone v. Allen*, (1969, Fourth Dept.) 33 AD2d 890; *In re Mark V.*, (1970, Fourth Dept.) 34 AD2d 1101; *In re Richard K.*, (1970, First Dept.) 35 AD2d 716; *In re Anna "AA,"* (1971, Third Dept.) 36 AD2d 1001.

25. *In the Matter of David W. v. Zolla D.*, (1971) 28 NY2d 589.

26. See *In re Richard W.*, (1968, Second Dept.) 29 AD2d 873; *In re Robert F.*, (1968, Fourth Dept.) 30 AD2d 933, Sept. 27, 1968; *In re Paul H.*, (1975, Second Dept.) 47 AD2d 853.

27. *In re Zelma B.*, (1972, Second Dept.) 39 AD2d 573; *In re James K.*, (1975, Second Dept.) 47 AD2d 946; *In re Theodore F.*, (1975, Second Dept.) 47 AD2d 945.

28. See *In re Gary C.*, (1973, Second Dept.) 42 AD2d 704.

29. See *In re Joseph G.*, (1976, Second Dept.) 52AD 2d 924.

30. *In the Matter of Rooney*, (1965) 48 Misc. 2d 890; *In the Matter of Charles Le Bruno*, (1966) 49 Misc 2d 505.

31. See *In re Adele W.*, (1972, Second Dept) 39 AD2d 543; *In re Michael S.*, (1972, First Dept.) 40 AD2d 633; *In re Daisy H.*, (1972, First Dept) 40 AD2d 775.

32. *In the Matter of Iris R.*, (1974) 33 NY2d 987.

33. *Fish v. Horn*, (1964) 14 NY2d 905; *Fish v. Horn*, (1964, First Dept.) 20 AD2d 395.

34. *Fish v. Horn*, (1964, First Dept.) 20 AD2d 395, 398.

35. K. Teltsch (1968, Aug. 25) "Agencies Unable to Aid Children: Facilities for Youths in Need of Supervision Inadequate," *New York Times*, 13.

36. Laws of New York (L. 1964, ch. 518; L. 1965, ch. 126; L. 1966, ch. 705).

37. *In re Lloyd*, (1970, First Dept.) 33 AD2d 385, 386.

38. Ibid.

39. *In re Lloyd*, (1970, First Dept) 33 AD2d 385, 387.

40. R. E. Tomasson (1970, Mar. 11), "Youth, 15, Poses Dilemma to Court: 2d Hearing Ordered in Hope of Finding Place for Him," *New York Times*, 32.

41. *In re Lloyd*, (1970, First Dept) 33 AD2d 385, 386–87.

42. *In re Lloyd*, (1970, First Dept) 33 AD2d 385, 387.

43. *In re Jeannette P.*, (1970, Second Dept.) 34 AD2d 661; *In re Arlene H.*, (1971, Second Dept.) 38 AD2d 570); *In re Stanley M.*, (1972, Second Dept.) 39 AD2d 746); *In re Jeanette M.*, (1972, Second Dept.) 40 AD2d 977, and finally, *Ellery C.* (1972).

44. *In re Jeannette P.*, (1970, Second Dept.) 34 AD2d 661.

45. *In re Arlene H.*, (1971, Second Dept.) 38 AD2d 570, 571.

46. Ibid.

47. *In re Stanley M.*, (1972, Second Dept.) 39 AD2d 746.

48. *In re Jeanette M.*, (1972, Second Dept.) 40 AD2d 977, 978.

49. *In the Matter of Ellery C. v. Redlich*, (1973) 32 NY2nd 588.

50. Ibid.

51. Ibid.

52. Ibid.

53. *In the Matter of Ellery C. v. Redlich*, (1973) 32 NY2nd 588, 592.

54. *In the Matter of Ellery C. v. Redlich*, (1973) 32 NY2nd 588, 591.

55. *In the Matter of Ellery C.*, (1972, Second Dept.) 40 AD2d 862, 865.

56. P. Kihss (1973, Dec. 6), "Court May Have Freed Slaying Suspect, 16," *New York Times*, 1, 39.

57. *Certo v. State of New York*, Claim No. 58212, (1976, Third Dept.) 53 AD2d 971.

58. *Certo v. State of New York*, Claim No. 58212, (1976, Third Dept.) 53 AD2d 971, 972.

59. *In re Lavette M.*, (1974, First Dept.) 44 AD2d 666.

60. *In re Maurice C.*, (1974, Second Dept.) 44 AD2d 114, 115.

61. *In re Maurice C.*, (1974, Second Dept.) 44 AD2d 114, 116.

62. *In re Maurice C.*, (1974, Second Dept.) 44 AD2d 114, 115.

63. *In re Maurice C.*, (1974, Second Dept.) 44 AD2d 114, 116.

64. Ibid.

65. *In the Matter of Lavette M. v. Corporation Counsel of the City of New York and Maurice C. v. Corporation Counsel of the City of New York*, (1974) 35 NY2d 136.

66. *In the Matter of Lavette M. v. Corporation Counsel of the City of New York and Maurice C. v. Corporation Counsel of the City of New York*, (1974) 35 NY2d 136, 142.

67. Ibid.

68. Ibid.

69. *In the matter of Cecilia R.*, (1975) 36 NY2d 317.

70. *In the matter of Cecilia R.*, (1975) 36 NY2d 317, 323.

71. *In the matter of Cecilia R.*, (1975) 36 NY2d 317, 321 (fn. 4).

72. *In the Matter of Felix R.*, (1978) 96 Misc. 2d 221, 223.

73. S. Raab (1977, Nov. 2), "City Plans New Strategy to Deal with Prostitutes Under Age of 16," *New York Times*, 27.

74. Raab, "City Plans New Strategy to Deal with Prostitutes Under Age of 16," *New York Times*, 27.

75. J. Cummings (1977, Dec. 10), "Priest's Shelter Tries to Salvage Times Sq. Youths," *New York Times*, 29.

76. The bill was unanimously affirmed by both the Senate (52–0 with four members excused) on July 18, 1978, and the Assembly (45–0) on June 22, 1978. It had first been introduced in both the Senate (S. 13006) and Assembly (A. 10346) on May 25. Gov. Hugh Carey signed the bill into law on August 7, 1978. Thus, from bill to law took about ten weeks, during summer months. Its effective date was January 1, 1979. The initial bill appropriated $2 million of state funds to provide a 50 percent match to localities. Participation was optional. Appropriations for FY 78–79 were $750,000, and the full program level for FY79–80 was estimated at from $1.5 to $2 million. Counties receiving approval of a runaway plan before January 1, 1980, received a 75 percent reimbursement for the first year, 75 percent for the second year, 60 percent for the third year, and 50 percent thereafter (Division of Budget Recommendations Memo).

77. State agency support came from Commissioner Barbara B. Blum, New York State Department of Social Services; Margot Thomas, State Division of Probation; Mario Cuomo, New York State, Department of State; Anthony P. De Bello, New York State, Board of Social Welfare; Eleanor Levinson, Assistent

Director, Suffolk County Conference on Juvenile and Criminal Justice; James D. Griffin, Mayor of Buffalo; Edwin L. Crawford, Executive Director, New York State Association of Counties; and Joseph S. Dominelli, Executive Secretary, Chairman Legislative Committee, New York State Legislative Committee, New York State Association of Chiefs of Police, Inc.

78. Letters of Support for the Runaway and Homeless Youth Act from private agencies included Charles J. Tobin, New York State Catholic Conference (Albany); Gus Potter, Region 2 Representative, National Network of Runaway and Youth Services, Inc. (region Hempstead) (program office, Washington, D.C.); Noel Rubinton, Jewish Child Care Association of New York (NYC); Berkeley D. Johnson, Jr., Federation of Protestant Welfare Agencies (NYC); Dan M. Potter, Executive Director, Council of Churches of the City of New York; Carol R. Lubin, Director, Policy Research and Social Issues, United Neighborhood Houses of New York, Inc.; Gwen Ingram, Director Youth Center, National Council on Crime and Delinquency (NJ); Joseph Garvin, Executive Director, New York State Council of Voluntary Child Care Agencies; Victor Remer, Executive Director, Children's Aid Society.

79. From memorandum (microfilm version) on the original draft of the bill for the New York State Runaway and Homeless Youth Act of 1978 (S. 10346 and A. 13006); original in the Governor's Bill Jacket Collection, New York State Archives, State Education Department, Cultural Education Center, Albany, N.Y.

80. J. W. Polier, Chairman, Committee on Mental Health Services inside and outside the Family Court in the City of New York (1972), *Juvenile justice confounded: Pretentions and realities of treatment services* (Paramus, N.J.: National Council on Crime and Delinquency), 4.

7. Legitimization Through Legislation—The Runaway Youth Act: National Attention to the Runaway Problem (1971–1974)

1. G. Flanigan (1974, May 2), written statement, House Committee on Education and Labor, *Juvenile Justice and Delinquency Prevention and Runaway Youth: Hearings before the Subcommittee on Equal Opportunities,* H.R. 9298, 93rd Cong., 2d sess., Mar. 29 (Los Angeles), Apr. 24, May 1, 2, 8, and 21, 1974 (Washington, D.C.: GPO), 308.

2. L. Siegel and J. Senna (2000), *Juvenile delinquency: Theory, practice, and law,* 7th ed. (Belmont, Calif.: Wadsworth/Thomson Learning), 464.

3. See *Kent v. US*, (1966) 383 US 541; *In re Gault*, (1967) 387 US 1; In re Winship, (1970) 397 US 359; *McKeiver v. Pennsylvania*, (1971) 403 US 528; *Tinker v. Des Moines*, (1972) 404 US 1042.

4. Findings and Declaration of Policy, S. 2829, sec. 2 (1).

5. Findings and Declaration of Policy, S. 2829, sec. 2 (2). The legislation rested on the notion that there was an "alarming" increase in runaways, yet in the next breath Congress noted that little was known about runaways because of the lack of statistics. Social problem constructionists frequently take note of "the numbers game" in creating and forwarding social issues (see J. Best [1990], *Threatened children: Rhetoric and concern about child-victims* [Chicago: University of Chicago Press]). One commonly cited indicator of the increasing runaway problem was the FBI's arrest statistics, which showed growth in runaway arrests between 1964 and 1971, followed by a brief decline immediately preceding legislative enactment. These data are misleading, however, because runaway arrests were not added as a separate statistical category until 1964. In itself, this is evidence of the nascence of running away as a publicly defined problem in the 1960s. However, and more to the point, the dramatic increases reported are attributable, in part, to the creation of a new statistical category as well as being partially demographically driven. Furthermore, runaway youth were historically arrested on a number of related charges, including vagrancy, disorderly conduct, waywardness, loitering, prostitution, and curfew violations. Under the best of circumstances, runaway arrests are an imperfect proxy for the size of the problem, even within the realm of law enforcement statistics. An estimate of the overall size of the runaway population that was often repeated in the literature between 1974 and the early 1980s is over one million. B. Bayh (1974, Apr. 24), House Committee on Education and Labor, *Juvenile Justice and Delinquency Prevention and Runaway Youth: Hearing before the Subcommittee on Equal Opportunities*, 93rd Cong., 2d sess., March 29 (Los Angeles), April 24, May 1, 2, 8, and 21 (Washington, D.C.: GPO), 159. See also Opinion Research Corporation (1976), *National statistical survey on runaway youth* (prepared for the HEW, Office of Human Development, Office of Youth Development (Princeton: Opinion Research Corp.), 26; A. R. Roberts (1982), Stress and coping patterns among adolescent runaways, *Journal of Social Services Research* 5.1&2: 15–27 ; A. Moses (1978), The Runaway Youth Act: Paradoxes of reform, *Social Services Review* 52.2: 227–43.

There was no attempt to discern what percentage of the increase was attributable either to newly created statistical categories or to the general demographic situation created by the large number of Baby Boomers. Since baseline statistics were not kept (another indicator of the nascence of running away as a public problem), it is impossible to know if there was an actual increase in the relative numbers of children who were running away. The only real source of information for the "alarming" increase in runaways came from anecdotal claims in the media.

6. Findings and Declaration of Policy, S. 2829, sec. 2 (3).

7. Findings and Declaration of Policy, S. 2829, sec. 2 (4).

8. Findings and Declaration of Policy, S. 2829, sec. 2 (5).

9. Findings and Declaration of Policy, S. 2829, sec. 2 (6).

10. S. 2829, sec. 102 (a).

11. S. 2829, sec. 101.

12. Runaway Youth Act (S. 645).

13. Juvenile Justice and Delinquency Prevention Act of 1974 (P.L. 93–415).

14. Hearings were held by the subcommittee to investigate juvenile delinquency on the Runaway Youth Act on January 13 and 14, 1972, and the bill was unanimously passed by the Senate on July 31, 1972. Senator Bayh reintroduced RYA as S. 645 on January 31, 1973, which was unanimously passed by the Senate on June 8, 1973. On July 16, 1973, the RYA was introduced in the House as H.R. 9298 and was incorporated into H.R. 15276 and S. 831 (JJDPA) and sent to President Gerald Ford on August 21, 1974. President Ford signed JJDPA of 1974 (P.L. 93–415), including Title III, the Runaway Youth Act, on September 7, 1974.

15. See N. Sheppard (1973, Aug. 14), "Police in Houston Explain Procedure on Runaways," *New York Times*, 18; N. Sheppard (1973, Aug. 16), "With 20,000 Runaways in City, Police Are Confident That Chances for a Mass Tragedy Are Slight," *New York Times*, 17.

16. Daly, quoted in Sheppard, "With 20,000 Runaways in City, Police Are Confident That Chances for a Mass Tragedy Are Slight," *New York Times*, 17.

17. Short, quoted in Sheppard, "Police in Houston Explain Procedure," 18.

18. Ibid.

19. In 1972, New York had attempted to solve some of these problems by creating a special NYPD squad of six officers that focused on juvenile runaways. Public announcement of the NYPD's Runaway Squad was made in June 1972 ("Police Unit to Seek Runaways" [1972, June 21], *New York Times*, 47). The police commissioner said the squad's goal was to intercept runaways "before they become victims of crime or engage in delinquent behavior." The Runaway Squad was charged with the responsibility of filing persons in need of supervi-

sion (PINS) petitions in family court. Thus, this specialized police unit—standing in the place of parents who might normally be expected to file the PINS petition—took affirmative legal action to start proceedings in cases where no outstanding warrant existed. Of course, to be effective, the youth in question had to fall within reach of New York State's statute. The fact that the PINS jurisdiction only covered youth below the age of 16 was problematic. Police could do nothing with someone who was 16 or older.

20. Sheppard, "With 20,000 Runaways in City, Police Are Confident," *New York Times*, 17. It is important to remember that the age of majority was still set at 21 years in many states in 1972. The Twenty-sixth Amendment, which lowered the voting age from 21 to 18, was ratified in 1972. States thereafter began lowering the age of majority to 18.

21. Ibid.

22. B. Bayh (1974, Apr. 24), Senate Committee, *Juvenile Justice and Delinquency Prevention*, 159.

23. A. F. Hawkins (1974, May 2), House Committee, *Juvenile Justice and Delinquency Prevention*, 260.

24. William Treanor (director, Runaway House, Washington, D.C.); Brian Slattery (codirector, Huckleberry House, San Francisco): John Wedemeyer (director, The Bridge, San Diego); Gerda Flanigan (the Looking Glass, Chicago); and Ray Ben David (Focus Runaway House, Las Vegas).

25. Law enforcement was represented by a group from New York City's NYPD, including Capt. Francis J. Daly (Youth Aid Division); Sgt. James Greenwald and Officer Warren McGinnis (Runaway Unit) and Det. James Williams (Missing Persons Unit). In addition to the New York City officers, there was Maj. John A. Bechtel, head of the Investigations and Services Division of the Montgomery County Police Department and Jerry Wilson, chief of police in Washington, D.C.

26. Private service providers included individuals from the YWCA and the Travelers Aid Society.

27. A. Hoffman (1968) "Runaways: The slave revolt," in Free (aka Hoffman), *Revolution for the hell of it* (New York: Dial), 73–76.

28. W. Treanor (1972, Jan. 13), Senate Committee on the Judiciary, *Runaway Youth Act Hearings before the Subcommittee to Investigate Juvenile Delinquency*, 92d Cong., 1st sess., Jan. 13 and 14, 1972 (Washington, D.C.: GPO), 8.

29. Dr. R. M. Arter (1972, Jan. 14), Senate Committee, *Runaway Youth Act Hearings before the Subcommittee to Investigate Juvenile Delinquency*, 153.

30. A. F. Hawkins (1974, May 2), House Committee, *Juvenile Justice and Delinquency Prevention*, 259.

31. Capt. F. J. Daly (1974, May 2), House Committee, *Juvenile Justice and Delinquency Prevention*, 291.

32. B. Bayh (1972, Jan. 13), Senate Committee, *Runaway Youth Act Hearings before the Subcommittee to Investigate Juvenile Delinquency*, 5.

33. Capt. F. J. Daly (1974, May 2), written statement, House Committee, *Juvenile Justice and Delinquency Prevention*, 294.

34. Capt. F. J. Daly (1974, May 2), House Committee, *Juvenile Justice and Delinquency Prevention*, 295.

35. Ibid.

36. A. F. Hawkins (1974, May 2), House Committee, *Juvenile Justice and Delinquency Prevention*, 260.

37. B. Slattery (1972, Jan. 13), Senate Committee, *Runaway Youth Act Hearings before the Subcommittee to Investigate Juvenile Delinquency*, 36.

38. Ibid.

39. J. Wedemeyer (1972, Jan. 14), Senate Committee, *Runaway Youth Act Hearings before the Subcommittee to Investigate Juvenile Delinquency*, 95.

40. J. A. Bechtel (1972, Jan. 13), *Runaway Youth Act Hearings before the Subcommittee to Investigate Juvenile Delinquency*, 48.

41. Ibid.

42. Ibid., 52.

43. Capt. F. J. Daly (1974, May 2), written statement, House Committee, *Juvenile Justice and Delinquency Prevention*, 291.

44. Ibid., 291.

45. Ibid., 294.

46. Ibid., 292.

47. Ibid.

48. Ibid.

49. A. F. Hawkins (1974, May 2), House Committee, *Juvenile Justice and Delinquency Prevention*, 296.

50. W. McGinnis (1974, May 2), House Committee, *Juvenile Justice and Delinquency Prevention*, 296.

51. Officer McGinniss made a more convincing case to reporter Ted Morgan, who did a (Sunday) *New York Times Magazine* story on the NYPD's Runaway Unit. McGinniss described the process to the reporter while on the street: "We observe them; we see if they're walking aimlessly, if they're wearing unseason-

able dress, if they've got makeshift luggage; we look at the degree of filthiness; we listen for out-of-town accents. See those two girls with the duffel bags? They're clean and neat and walking directly to where they're going. They're also laughing and talking. If they were runaways they'd look more somber." Ted Morgan (1975, Nov. 16), "Little Ladies of the Night: Today's Runaway Is No Norman Rockwell Tyke," *New York Times Magazine*, 44.

52. G. Flanigan (1974, May 2), written statement, House Committee, *Juvenile Justice and Delinquency Prevention*, 307.

53. W. Treanor (1972, Jan. 13), Senate Committee, *Runaway Youth Act Hearings before the Subcommittee to Investigate Juvenile Delinquency*, 8.

54. R. B. David (1974, May 2), House Committee, *Juvenile Justice and Delinquency Prevention*, 272.

55. J. V. Wilson (letter) (1972, Jan. 19), Senate Committee, *Runaway Youth Act Hearings before the Subcommittee to Investigate Juvenile Delinquency*, 77–78.

56. Capt. F. J. Daly (1974, May 2), written statement, House Committee, *Juvenile Justice and Delinquency Prevention*, 292.

57. Ibid., 294.

58. M. Gold (1974, May 2), House Committee, *Juvenile Justice and Delinquency Prevention*, 286.

59. P. Rutledge (1972, Jan. 13), Senate Committee, *Runaway Youth Act Hearings before the Subcommittee to Investigate Juvenile Delinquency*, 24.

60. Dr. R. Arter (1972, Jan. 14), Senate Committee, *Runaway Youth Act Hearings before the Subcommittee to Investigate Juvenile Delinquency*, 155.

61. Findings and Declaration of Policy, S. 2829, sec. 2 (4).

62. S. 2829, sec. 102 (b)(3).

63. The Runaway Youth Act of 1974, P. L. 93–415, § 312 (b)(3) (see also appendix 3).

64. Ibid.

65. R. B. David (1974, May 2), House Committee, *Juvenile Justice and Delinquency Prevention*, 268.

66. B. Slattery (1972, Jan. 13), Senate Committee, *Runaway Youth Act Hearings before the Subcommittee to Investigate Juvenile Delinquency*, 34–35.

67. J. A. Bechtel (1972, Jan. 13), Senate Committee, *Runaway Youth Act Hearings before the Subcommittee to Investigate Juvenile Delinquency*, 52–53.

68. Capt. F. J. Daly (1974, May 2), House Committee, *Juvenile Justice and Delinquency Prevention*, 295. The agency to which Daly refers is most likely Covenant House's Under 21/New York. In general, Covenant House main-

tained a chilly relationship with the NYPD for the decades during Ritter's reign.

69. The congressional findings, on which the RYA is based, concludes that running away has the result of "significantly endangering the young people who are without resources and live on the street" (42 USC 5701 § 302 [1]) and that "young people, because of their age and situation, are urgently in need of temporary shelter" (42 USC 5701 § 302 [3]) (see also appendix 3).

70. Congressional findings, on which the RYA are based, conclude that runaways are "creating a substantial law enforcement problem for the communities inundated" (42 USC 5701 § 302 [1]) and that "the problem of locating, detaining and returning runaway children should not be the responsibility of already overburdened police departments and juvenile justice authorities" (42 USC 5701 § 302 [4]). Grant eligibility requires developing "an adequate plan for assuring proper relations with law enforcement personnel, and the return of runaway youths from correctional institutions" (42 USC 5712 § 312 [b][4]). However, the goal of the RYA is to assist public or nonprofit private agencies develop "local facilities to deal primarily with the immediate needs of runaway youth in a manner which is outside the law enforcement structure and juvenile justice system" (42 USC 5701, § 311). (See also appendix 3.)

71. The law reads "in view of the interstate nature of the problem, it is the responsibility of the Federal Government to develop accurate reporting of the problem nationally and to develop an effective system of temporary care outside the law enforcement structure": 42 USC 5701 § 302 (4). (See also appendix 3.)

8. Natural Extensions—Problem, Services, and Policy (1974–)

1. Scott McKenzie's pop hit "If You're Going to San Francisco" was released in June 1967 and peaked at number four on *Billboard*'s charts.

2. For an interesting discussion on the emergence of the "missing child" phenomenon in the early 1980s, see Joel Best (1990), *Threatened children: Rhetoric and concern about child-victims* (Chicago: University of Chicago Press), ch. 2: "Rhetoric in claims about missing children," 22–44. See also N. J. Fritz and D. L. Altheide (1987), The mass media and the social construction of the missing child problem, *Sociological Quarterly* 28.4: 473–92.

3. There are two prongs to the definition of "missing" children. The first includes those who "may have been removed by another from the control of

such individual's legal custodian" without consent (42 USC 5772 (1) (A). The definition seems to exclude runaways. However the second prong includes those where the "circumstances of the case strongly indicate that such individual is likely to be abused or sexually exploited." (42 USC 5772 (1)(B). This could well include runaway children who were thought to be at-risk.

4. 42 USC 5773 (b) (1) (A) (i).

5. D. Canedy (2002, May 1), "Miami 5-Year-Old Missing for a Year Before Fact Noted," *New York Times*, 16; D. Canedy (2002, May 3), "Case of Lost Miami Girl Puts Focus on Agency," *New York Times*, 19; and "Florida's Little Girl Lost (2002, May 13), *Time* 159.19, 55.

6. "Agency Has Lost Track of 302 Kids" (2002, Aug. 30), *Ann Arbor News*, B5.

7. Ibid.

8. I once worked as an assistant for a prominent researcher who studied the movement of children through the foster care system by using large administrative data sets. A small number of case records (relative to the overall number of children in the system) were labeled closed because the child was "AWOL." Out of necessity, since it was impossible to trace the outcome of these cases, these data were simply omitted from the study analysis. I understood the logic of the omission; nonetheless, from a child advocate's perspective those AWOL cases represented real children. On more than a few occasions in my work at Covenant House, youth who were AWOL from foster care ended up on the shelter's doorstep. One national study found that 38 percent of the children arriving at runaway shelters had prior histories in the foster care system. D. Bass (1992), *Helping vulnerable youths: Runaway and homeless adolescents in the United States* (Washington, D.C.: NASW Press).

9. NBC Evening News with Tom Brokaw (2002, Nov. 27), "In depth: Foster care kids, simply missing."

10. Lisa Myers, NBC News, Los Angeles (2002, Nov. 26), "A tragic case study in foster care."

11. Lisa Myers, NBC News, Los Angeles (2002, Nov. 26), ibid.

12. Ibid.

13. Ibid.

14. Juvenile Justice Amendments of 1977 (P.L. 95–115).

15. Juvenile Justice Amendments of 1980 (P.L. 96–509).

16. Juvenile Justice Amendments of 1994 (P.L. 103–322); Runaway and Homeless Youth Act, § 5712d(d)(2).

17. RHYA 42 USC § 5701 (9).

18. Juvenile Justice Amendments of 2003 (P.L. 108–96).

19. Juvenile Justice Amendments of 2003 (P.L. 108–96).

20. P.L. 93–415 Runaway Youth Act § 302 (4) (5). (See appendix 3.)

21. RHYA 42 USC § 5711 (a).

22. RHYA 42 USC § 5701 (6) (7).

23. In FY 2003, 345 Basic Centers received funding.

24. See the work of Shanna Thompson and David Pollio: D. E. Pollio, S. J. Thompson, and C. S. North (2000), Agency-based tracking of difficult-to-follow populations: Runaway and homeless youth programs in St. Louis, MO., *Community Mental Health Journal* 36.3: 247–58; S. J. Thompson, D. E. Pollio, and L. Bitner (2000), Outcomes for adolescents using runaway and homeless youth services, *Journal of Human Behavior and the Social Environment* 3.1: 79–87; S. J. Thompson, D. E. Pollio, J. Constantine, D. Reid, and V. Nebbitt (2002), Short-term outcomes for youth receiving runaway and homeless shelter services, *Research on Social Work Practice* 12.5: 589–603; and S. J. Thompson, A. Safyer, and D. E. Pollio (2001), Differences and predictors of family reunification among subgroups of runaway youths using shelter services, *Social Work Research* 25.3: 163–72.

25. H. Hammer, D. Finkelhor, and A. J. Sedlak (2002) have conducted an extensive second-wave research project called the National Incidence Studies of Missing, Abducted, Runaway, and Thrownaway Children (NISMART-2) for the Office of Juvenile Justice and Delinquency Prevention (OJJDP: www.ojjdp .ncjrs.org/pubs/missing). These data were drawn from three sources: household surveys of adult caretakers, household surveys of youth, and a study of juvenile facilities. It is the most comprehensive examination to date of the scope of the runaway and homeless youth problem although there are obvious limitations to what parents and/or youth might report in a survey. Hammer and his colleagues determined that 1,682,900 youth had experienced a runaway/thrownaway incident in 1999 and 71 percent of those were endangered during the incident.

26. L. Kaufman (2004, Sept. 15), "Finding a Future for a Troubled Girl with a Past: Is the Answer to the Growing Problem of Child Prostitution Forced Counseling or Incarceration?" *New York Times*, 27, 28.

27. Ibid., 27.

28. E. J. Dionne (1977, Apr. 2), "An Oasis for Runaway Teen-Agers Appears in a Pornographic Desert," *New York Times*, 33.

29. Kaufman, "Finding a Future for a Troubled Girl," *New York Times*, 27.

30. Ibid.

31. See, for example, P. Jenkins (1998), *Moral panic: Changing concepts of the child molesterer in modern America* (New Haven: Yale University Press).

32. Kaufman, "Finding a Future for a Troubled Girl," *New York Times*, 27.Page numbers for subsequent references to this *New York Times* article will be cited in the main text.

33. *In the matter of Cecilia R.* (1975), 36 NY2d 317, 323.

34. J. A. Riis (1971, reprinted from 1892 edition), *How the other half lives* (New York: Dover), 153.

35. Kaufman, "Finding a Future for a Troubled Girl," 28.

Selected Bibliography

Baron, S. W. and T. F. Hartnagel. (1997). Attributions, affect, and crime: Street youths' reactions to unemployment. *Criminology* 35.3: 409–34.

Baron, S. W. and T. F. Hartnagel. (1998). Street youth and criminal violence. *Journal of Research in Crime and Delinquency* 3.2: 166–92.

Bass, D. (1992). Helping homeless youths: Runaway and homeless adolescents in the United States. Washington, D.C.: NASW Press.

Brennan, T., D. Huizinga, and E. Elliot. (1978). *The social psychology of runaways.* Lexington, Mass.: Lexington Books.

Cochran, B. N., A. J. Stewart, J. A. Ginzler, and A. M. Cauce. (2002). Challenges faced by homeless sexual minorities: Comparison of gay, lesbian, bisexual, and transgender homeless adolescents with their heterosexual counterparts. *American Journal of Public Health* 92.5: 773–77.

Council on Scientific Affairs. (1989). Health care needs of homeless and runaway youths. *Journal of the American Medical Association* 262.10: 1358–61.

Dachner, N. and V. Tarasuk. (2002). Homeless "squeegee kids": Food insecurity and daily survival. *Social Science and Medicine* 54: 1039–49.

DeRosa, C. J., S. B. Montgomery, J. Hyde, E. Iverson, and M. D. Kipke. (2001). HIV risk behavior and HIV testing: A comparison of rates and associated factors among homeless and runaway adolescents in two cities. *AIDS Education and Prevention* 13.2: 131–48.

Ensign, J. (1998). Health issues of homeless youth. *Journal of social distress and the homeless* 7.3: 159–74.

Ensign, J. and J. Gittelsohn. (1998). Health access to care: Perspectives of homeless youth in Baltimore City, U.S.A. *Social Science and Medicine* 47.12: 2087–99.

Finkelhor, D., G. Hotaling, and A. Sedlak. (May 1990). Missing, abducted, runaway, and throwaway children in America: First report—Numbers and characteristics national incidence studies/Executive summary. Washington, D.C.: Office of Juvenile Justice and Delinquency Prevention *and* Westat. #87–MC–CX–K069.

Finley, S. and M. Finley. (1999). Sp'ange: A research story. *Qualitative Inquiry* 5.3: 313–37.

Forst, M. L. (1994). Sexual risk profiles of delinquent and homeless youths. *Journal of Community Health* 19: 101–14.

Gaetz, S. and B. O'Grady, B. (2002). Making money: Exploring the economy of youth homeless workers. *Work, Employment, and Society* 16.3: 433–56.

Government Accountability Office. (1989). *Homelessness: Homeless and runaway youth receiving services at federally funded shelters.* Washington, D.C.: GAO/HRD–90–45.

Greene, J. M. and C. L. Ringwalt. (1998). Pregnancy among three national samples of runaway and homeless youth. *Journal of Adolescent Health* 23: 370–77.

Greene, J. M., S. T. Ennett, and C. L. Ringwalt. (1997). Substance use among runaway and homeless youth in three national samples. *American Journal of Public Health* 87.2: 229–35.

Greene, J. M., S. T. Ennett, and C. L. Ringwalt. (1999). Prevalence and correlates of survival sex among runway and homeless youths. *American Journal of Public Health* 89.9: 1406–1409.

Hagan, J. and B. McCarthy. (1997). *Mean street: Youth crime and homelessness.* Cambridge: Cambridge University Press.

Hammer, H., D. Finkelhor, and A. J. Sedlak. (Oct. 2002). NISMART (National Incidence Studies of Missing, Abducted, Runaway, and Thrownaway Children), *Runaway/Thrownaway children: National estimates and characteristics.* Washington, D.C.: Office of Juvenile Justice and Delinquency Prevention (OJJDP). Grant Number 95–MC–CX–K004.

Hoyt, D. R., K. D. Ryan, and A. M. Cauce. (1999). Personal victimization in a high-risk environment: Homeless and runaway adolescents. *Journal of Research in Crime and Delinquency* 36.4: 371–92.

Kaufman, J. G. and C. S. Widom. (1999). Childhood victimization, running away, and delinquency. *Journal of Research in Crime and Delinquency* 36.4: 347–70.

Kipke, M., S. Montgomery, and R. MacKenzie. (1997). Homeless youth: Drug use patterns and HIV risk profiles according to peer group affiliation. *AIDS and Behavior* 1: 247–59.

Koopman, C., M. Rosario, and M. Rothman-Borus. (1994). Alcohol and drug use and sexual behaviors placing runaways at risk for HIV infection. *Addictive Behaviors* 19: 95–103.

Kruks, G. (1991). Gay and lesbian homeless/street youth: Special issues and concerns. *Journal of Adolescent Health* 12.7: 515–18.

Kurtz, P. D., S. V. Jarvis, and G. L. Kurtz. (1991). Problems of homeless youths: Empirical findings and human services issues. *Social Work* 36.4: 309–14.

Kurtz, P. D., E. W. Lindsey, S. Jarvis, and L. Nackerud. (2000). How runaway and homeless youth navigate troubled waters: The role of formal and informal Helpers. *Child and Adolescent Social Work Journal* 17.5: 381–402.

Leslie, M. B., J. A. Stein, and M. J. Rotheram-Borus. (2002). Sex-specific predictors of suicidality among runaway youth. *Journal of Clinical Child and Adolescent Psychology* 31.1: 27–40.

Lindsey, E. W., P. D. Kurtz, S. Jarvis, N. R. Williams, and L. Nackerud. (2000). How runaway and homeless youth navigate troubled waters: Personal strengths and resources. *Child and Adolescent Social Work Journal* 17.2: 115–40.

Luna, G. C. (1991). Street youth: Adaptation and survival in the AIDS decade. *Journal of Adolescent Health* 12.7: 511–14.

MacKellar, D. A., L. A. Valleroy, J. P. Hoffmann, D. Glebatis, M. LaLota, W. McFarland, J. Westerholm, and R. S. Janssen. (2000). Gender differences in sexual behaviors and factors associated with nonuse of condoms among homeless and runaway youth. *AIDS Education and Prevention* 12.6: 477–91.

McCarthy, B. and J. Hagan. (1995). Getting into street crime: The structure and process of criminal embeddedness, *Social Science Research* 24: 63–95.

Miller, H. (1991). *On the fringe: The dispossessed in America*. Lanham, Md.: Lexington Books.

Mundy, P., M. Robertson, J. Robertson, and M. Greenblatt. (1990). The prevalence of psychotic symptoms in homeless adolescents. *Journal of American Academy of Child and Adolescent Psychiatry* 29.5: 724–31.

Office of Juvenile Justice and Delinquency Prevention (OJJDP). (1989). *Annual report on missing children*. Washington, D.C.: U.S. Department of Justice, Office of Justice Programs.

Pennbridge, J. N., T. E. Freese, and R. G. MacKenzie. (1992). High-risk behaviors among male street youth in Hollywood, California. *AIDS Education and Prevention* (Fall Supplement): 24–33.

Pollio, D. E., S. J. Thompson, and C. S. North. (2000). Agency-based tracking of difficult-to-follow populations: Runaway and homeless youth programs in St. Louis, Mo. *Community Mental Health Journal* 36.3: 247–58.

Rotheram-Borus, M. J. (1993). Suicidal behavior and risk factors among runaway youths. *American Journal of Psychiatry* 150.1: 103–107.

Rotheram-Borus, M. J. and C. Koopman. (1991). Sexual risk behaviors, AIDS knowledge, and beliefs about AIDS among runaways. *American Journal of Public Health* 81.2: 208–10.

Rotheram-Borus, M. J., H. F. L. Meyer-Bahlburg, C. Koopman, M. Rosario, T. M. Exner, R. Henderson, M. Mattieu, and R. S. Gruen. (1992). Lifetime sexual behaviors among runaway males and females. *Journal of Sex Research* 29.1: 15–29.

Rotheram-Borus, M. J., J. Song, M. Gwadz, M. Lee, R. Van Rossem, and C. Koopman. (2003). Reductions in HIV risk among runway youth. *Prevention Science* 4.3: 173–87.

Rothman, J. (1991). *Runaway and homeless youth: Strengthening services to families and children*. White Plains, N.Y.: Longman.

Shane, P. G. (1991). An invisible health and social policy issue: Homeless/runaway youth. *Journal of Health and Social Policy* 2.4: 3–14.

Sickmund, M. (Nov., 1990). Runaways in juvenile courts. *OJJDP update on statistics*. Washington, D.C.: OJJDP.

Simons, R. L. and L. B. Whitbeck. (1991). Running away during adolescence as a precursor to adult homelessness. *Social Service Review* 65: 224–47.

Staller, K. M. (2004). Runaway youth system dynamics: A theoretical framework for analyzing runaway and homeless youth policy. *Families in Society* 85.3: 379–491.

Stricof, R. L., J. T. Kennedy, T. C. Nattell, I. B. Weisfuse, and L. F. Novick. (1991). HIV seroprevalence in a facility for runaway and homeless adolescents. *American Journal of Public Health* 81 (Supp.): 50–53.

Sweet, R. W. (Nov.–Dec. 1990). "Missing children": Found facts. *OJJDP: Juvenile Justice Bulletin*. Reprinted from *NIJ Reports*, no. 224.

Teare, J. F., K. Authier, and R. Peterson. (1994). Differential patterns of post-shelter placement as a function of problem type and severity. *Journal of Child and Family Studies* 3.1: 7–22.

Thompson, S. J., D. E. Pollio, and L. Bitner (2000). Outcomes for adolescents using runaway and homeless youth services. *Journal of Human Behavior and the Social Environment* 3.1: 79–87.

Thompson, S. J., D. E. Pollio, J. Constantine, D. Reid, and V. Nebbitt. (2002). Short-term outcomes for youth receiving runaway and homeless shelter services. *Research on Social Work Practice* 12.5: 589–603.

Thompson, S. J., A. Safyer, and D. E. Pollio. (2001). Differences and predictors of family reunification among subgroups of runaway youths using shelter services. *Social Work Research* 25.3: 163–72.

Tyler, K. A., D. R. Hoyt, L. B. Whitbeck, and A. M. Cauce. (2001). The impact of childhood sexual abuse on later sexual victimization. *Journal of Research on Adolescents* 11.2: 151–76.

Tyler, K. A., L. B. Whitbeck, D. R. Hoyt, and K. D. Johnson. (2003). Self-mutilation and homeless youth: The role of family abuse, street experiences, and mental disorders. *Journal of Research on Adolescence* 13.4: 457–74.

Unger, J. B., M. D. Kipke, T. R. Simon, J. B. Montgomery, and C. J. Johnson. (1997). Homeless youths and young adults in Los Angeles: Prevalence of mental health problems and the relationship between mental health and substance abuse disorders. *American Journal of Community Psychology* 25: 371–94.

Whitbeck, L. B. and D. R. Hoyt. (1999). *Nowhere to grow: Homeless and runaway adolescents and their families*. New York: Aldine de Gruyter.

Whitbeck, L. B., D. R. Hoyt, and K. A. Ackley. (1997). Families of homeless and runaway adolescents: A comparison of parent/caretaker and adolescent perspectives on parenting, family violence, and adolescent conduct. *Child Abuse and Neglect* 21.6: 517–28.

Whitbeck, L. B., D. R. Hoyt, and K. A. Yoder. (1999). A risk-amplification model of victimization and depressive symptoms among runaway and homeless adolescents. *American Journal of Community Psychology* 27.2: 273–96.

Wright, J. D. (1991). Health and homeless teenagers: Evidence from the National Health Care for the Homeless Program. *Journal of Health and Social Policy* 2.4: 15–35.

Yates, G. L., R. G. MacKenzie, J. Pennbridge, and A. Swofford. (1991). A risk profile comparison of homeless youth involved in prostitution and homeless youth not involved. *Journal of Adolescent Health* 12.7: 545–48.

Yoder, K. A., D. R. Hoyt, and L. B. Whitbeck. (1998). Suicidal behavior among homeless and runaway adolescents. *Journal of Youth and Adolescence* 27.6: 753–71.

Yoder, K. A., L. B. Whitbeck, and D. R. Hoyt. (2003). Gang involvement and membership among homeless and runaway youth. *Youth and Society* 34.4: 441–67.

Zimet, G. D., E. J. Sobo, T. Zimmerman, J. Jackson, J. Mortimer, C. P. Yanda, and R. Lazebnik. (1995). Sexual behavior, drug use, and AIDS knowledge among Midwestern runaways. *Youth and Society* 26.4: 450–62.

Index

Abrams, Robert, 222n30, 223n32

acid rock (music), 73; drug use and, 80

adulthood: changing nature of, 18–20, 24; premature, 20–21

adventure: running away as, 30–33

age of majority, 18–20, 228n42–43, 229n47; PINS statute and, 130–31, 259n18, 265n20

alternative service agencies, 97–121; autonomy of clients, 105–106; as bridge between child and parent, 110–11; as bridge between hip and straight worlds, 98, 111–15; changing views of, 187–88; confidentiality and, 108–109, 167, 254n35; emergence of, 97–99; family services of, 253n24; funding of, xvi, 120, 185, 219n2; government

recognition of, 153; guidance counselors in, 106–108; history of, 252n4; interagency communication and, 165; legal vulnerability of, 111–12; legitimization of, 98–99, 120–21; long-term service needs and, 252n10; outcome evaluation of, 185–86; pedophile priests and, 224n44; as PINS placement options, 145–46; police relationships with, 161–62, 164; professional vs. volunteer roles in, 103–104; public/private sector relationships in, 104; religions community and, 101; right of clients to keep running, 109–111; under Runaway and Homeless Youth Act, 183–86; services provided by, 104–105, 253n24;